Case Studies in Contemporary Management

Case Studies in Contemporary Management

Editors:

Sanjeev Bansal

Director

Amity Business School

R.Sujatha

Associate Professor

Department of HR

Amity Business School

Ashok Sharma

Assistant Professor

Amity Business School Noida

TECHSAR™

NEW DELHI

Published and Printed by

Techsar Pvt. Ltd.
4435-36/7, Ansari Road, Daryaganj,
New Delhi 110 002 (India)
E-mail: tech_info@techsarworld.com
Website: www.techsarworld.com

ISBN 978-93-84588-75-5

Reprint 2026

Preface

Management - The quintessence of any business...

"I don't believe in taking right decisions,
I take decisions and then make them right" – *Ratan Naval Tata*

Today management has evolved from merely getting things done to empowering people to do the impossible, emphasizing that in the current competitive world, not even sky is the limit. It is time to 'think the unthinkable' and 'do the undoable'. The faculties of forecasting, planning, organizing, commanding, coordinating and controlling together form the concept of management. But at times the known, and many a times the 'unknown' yet 'inevitable' challenges demand that management constantly upgrades itself within each faculty to adapt itself with the changing environment and maintain equilibrium. If we analyze, every action of ours in our day to day lives, is unconsciously managed in its own way. Some term these actions as our 'karma' and for some these are simply the 'choices' that we make. But be it karma or choices, they do have some undeniable element of management involved.

In the business context, management is the very pillar of the existence of any business entity, organization or a business venture. It is by the virtue of this business management that the entire functioning happens effectively and efficiently. Management across various schools of thought has been interpreted variedly. While some interpret management as a science, for some it is an art. Few refer it to as an academic discipline and others as a process or an activity. Many people best understand management basically as a profession. But in any construal, management involves transforming some inputs into desired outputs using various 'factors of production'.

The Early Management thought pioneered by Adam Smith's concept that market and competition are the regulators of economic activity laid emphasis on *'division of labor'* for increased productivity. Robert Owens on the other hand criticized division of labor suggesting that each worker can perform various tasks and must switch from one to another. Charles Dupin stressed on the need of giving clear and crisp instructions to workers and laying down the most efficient way of doing any work with minimum energy of the worker being utilized. Thus factory system and its challenges dominated this time period.

This was then followed by the Scientific Management era. The most eminent pioneer of this period Frederick Taylor introduced incentives to be given by the piece-rate system based on disintegration of tasks into its basic movements. He emphasized on management finding *'one best way of doing a job'*. Henry Towne also proposed the *'gain sharing'* to enhance the productivity of workers. Henry Gantt contributed the *'Gantt Charts'* as a graphical tool for assisting management's planning and controlling functions. Frank & Lillian Gilbreth (the 1st lady of management) propounded the *'Time and Motion'* concept.

The management theory then encapsulated the Administrative aspect with Henri Fayol's contributions. He gave the '14 principles essential for management'. He believed that management could be taught and was indispensable as an individual was promoted in position. Max Weber introduced *'bureaucracy'* as the idyllic form of management. Another major contributor was Peter Drucker who proposed three managerial roles of managing a business, the mangers and the employees. Also he hinted that there could be non-economic repercussions of any managerial decision.

The Behavioral School of Thought was enriched by Elton Mayo and 'the Hawthorne study' highlighting *'the mental attitudes of social units'*. Chester Barnard gave the most widely accepted dichotomy of *'effective & efficient'*. He also proposed an interesting theory of *'acceptance of authority'* which stated that only if the subordinates accept the authority of the boss, he is the boss.

The Modern management has been greatly pioneered by W. Edward Demming who laid emphasis on 'quality improvement'. He summarized his teachings into the famous 14 points guidelines for quality management. Joseph Juran gave the 'Pareto principle of 80-20'. The System's approach to management has also been conceptualized in this period. William Ouchi's 'Theory Z', Tom Peters' 'Eight Attributes of Excellence' are few of the major contributions of this period. Also the ideologists of the modern school of management have laid great emphasis on the social responsibilities of any business.

However today there are various managerial challenges that need to be dealt with. The 'Make in India' campaign among the new generational entrepreneurs had created a demand for a paradigm shift in the rules of the business. The ecosystem of the country had promoted a wave of change and challenges among the top corporate houses. The market consolidation had become a routine strategic decision. Rapidly developing technology needs to be incorporated into management for existence of any business. Knowledge management, Information Overload and Data Storage are critical areas on which management needs to be focused. Data Mining can be used for Customer Relationship Management and Decision Support Systems can aid various managerial decisions. Six Sigma, TQM (Total Quality Management) and Quality Circles can ensure Operations and Supply Chain Management can be done with zero defects. For the survival of businesses in competitive an environment, there is more focus on attracting and retaining customers through marketing decisions that concentrate to the concept and Ideas to gain market share in short time. Red tape, dearth of finance and inadequate risk coverage had today become major reasons to hamper the growth of big as well small enterprises in India.

Another key challenge is the uncertainty that is prevalent in all economies globally. This compels the business management to concentrate more on short-term planning only. Strategy for any business needs to be constantly altered to adapt to changes. Also diversity is the key issue around which modern management revolves. Whether it is diversity in terms of market offerings, product portfolios or even the workforce, decisions regarding all are pivotal for organization's growth and existence.

But for a business, above all the challenges lies the core issue of finding the 'best fit' employee and then employees' retention. Individuals today are either highly skilled or under skilled creating a disparity and a dilemma for organizations to consider.

Thus at present, this evolving management has landed into an era of technology marked by innovation, uncertainties, competitiveness, and strategic decision making and risk taking. Various cases and experiential learning of diverse individuals who are directly or indirectly dealing with today's changing and dynamic environment can be one of the best ways of tackling the challenges. And this is just the very motive behind the entire effort behind this compilation of several management case studies highlighting some of the contemporary issues and problems of business management. The management cases are gathered under three major categories particularly to spur the interest of the students, faculties and managers while understanding the various management practices and functions in the Indian Organizations. The first section of this book opens up with ***"The Influencers: Pockets of Opportunities to taking a High Road"***.In this section, we have introduced cases related to new ideas and process practiced by organizations to increase their visibility in the market, creating uniqueness to the products and services offerings, accessing technology to meet the customer expectations and focusing on customer care, improving operational efficiencies and learning to co-create. In the last few years not much of optimism is shown towards India Growth Story. This major concern is covered in the second section of the cases and readings gathered as ***"Understanding the Business Propositions-Partnering to scale up"***. The authors are sure that this section will help readers to appreciate functional topics in the area of strategy, finance and financial products and services. It also introduces few imperatives for understanding the ecosystem of the Indian Business Environment.

The third section is compiled with cases in the area of Human Resources as ***"People Management Processes: Art as well as Science"***. The cases pertaining to this section focuses on a wide range of challenges faced by organizations in aligning internal stakeholder exceptions to the business objectives, new age talent Acquisition and retention policies that brings in new people to manage different functions and emphasizing to create organizational culture that promote a conducive work environment.

Sanjeev Bansal
R. Sujatha
Ashok Sharma

Contents

Part I

"The Influencers: Pockets of Opportunities to Taking a High Road"

1

Controlling Diesel Pilferage in Sites of Telecom Tower

Tarang Maheshwari • Rosy Kalra[1]

Abstract

Telecom industry in India is one of the fastest growing industry, with the subscriber base of over 892 million. This increase in the subscriber base has necessitated the network requirement and significant investment in telecom infrastructure to reduce the costs and to focus on core operations by Telecom Companies. For efficient functioning Telecom Tower Companies need to run BTS and other equipment's 24 × 7. At a typical site, continuous power supply is required for uninterrupted functioning of the BTS, but in the countries like India the power supply is not continuous and even. In some areas power cuts are even more than 12 hours. So for the continuous power supply to BTS companies have to rely heavily on diesel generators. Energy cost is the part operating cost incurred by the tower telecom companies on supplying power to run BTS and other telecom equipment. That's the reason **Indus Towers Private Ltd,** a telecom tower company operates withspecial attention towards reducing energy cost as it directly affect its ARPU (Average Revenue per Unit). Energy cost compromise approximately 40% of the operating cost incurred by the Telecom companies. This case concentrates on how the Telecom Tower companies are now focusing on adopting new methods and making diesel filling process standardized to minimize the diesel pilferage.

Keywords: Telecom tower, Power supply, Diesel pilferage, Operating cost.

INTRODUCTION TO THE TELECOM SECTOR

Telecom sector is pivotal to a country's socioeconomic growth. It has become the key ingredient for the growth and progress of the different sectors of the economy. Telecom increases the connectivity which helps in bringing more governance and improves the business communication and thus helps in overall strengthening of economy of a country. With

[1]Tarang Maheshwari is a student of MBA programme Class of 2015 and Rosy Kalra, Asst. Prof in the Area of Finance with Amity Business School. The authors have developed the case solely for class discussion for the programmes in management. The author does not intend to illustrate effective or ineffective handling of a managerial situation. The case study does not represent or endorse the views of the managements about the issues in the case. The case has been compiled with both primary and secondary information.

the subscriber base of over 892 million by the end of 2013 India is second biggest telecom market in the world and it is likely to contribute 400 billion US $ to country's gross domestic product. In the past decade India's telecom industry recorded the growth of 2600 percent in the subscribers currently it is the second largest telecom market in the world which is expected to overtake China by the year 2020. Tele density known as the number of telephone connection over thousand people has also increased in India from 18.3 in FY07 to 78.7 in FY12.

EMERGENCE OF TOWER TELECOM INDUSTRY

India's telecom boom has been well charted. Some 18 years after the mobile phone first appeared on the Indian consumer stage, there are more than 900 million mobile phone users in a country of 1.2 billion, more people than have access to a toilet, according to a statistic often touted by development agencies, and three times the entire population of the US. And the growth of the sector in the last decade has been explosive—in 2002, the number was just 6.68 million. India's telecom sector is now the second largest in the world, and the fastest growing. Providing network coverage to these hundreds of millions of users are around 500,000 telecom towers, covering more than 90% of the country's land area, and unnoticed for the most part by the people who rely on them. Most are made of iron girders painted red and white, with up to six long, bar-shaped antenna pointing skywards, linked with wires to a small shed at the base. A tower connects two callers to each other via switching centres or telephone exchanges, providing urban and rural India with access to mobile communication on a scale second only to China.

The robust increase in the subscriber base and penetration of telecom services in to the rural India over the year has necessitated the network requirement which covers a wider area and created a need of significant investment in telecom infrastructure and to reduce the costs and to focus on core operations, telecom companies diverting their tower projects to separate companies. Creating separate companies helps the telecom companies to reduce the operating cost and to improve capital structure as the separate companies can focus their full attention to the infrastructure. The growing need for telecom towers has led to the rise of independent telecom companies and telecom owned tower companies.

BIRTH OF INDUS TOWERS

Airtel & Vodafone came jointly & signed an MOU for tower sharing in 2008, decision was taken to create an independent tower company to which tower assets would be transferred & will be managed by it independently. JV's members agreed on point system based on weighted tower attributes to share investments. Further Vodafone and Airtel approached Idea too and joint venture got formed in 42-42-16 partnership. With this joint venture Indus Towers was born as the world's biggest startup. It is the classic example of 'Coopetition'. Coopetition is a neologism coined to describe cooperative competition.

In 2008 when Indus Towers started it had 63,400 towers, 73,800 tenancies and only 3 customers. Since then Indus towers is continuously growing in tower numbers and tenancies. Now Indus towers is the world's largest tower telecom company with the holding of more than 113,490 towers and have 11 customers. Indus towers is operating in 15 circles in India and have the widest coverage in India. Among various tower telecom companies Indus Towers pvt. Ltd is market leader with the total 32.2% market share followed by the BSNL and Reliance Infratel ltd. With market share of 15.2% each. In India **Three out of every five calls are made through Indus site.**

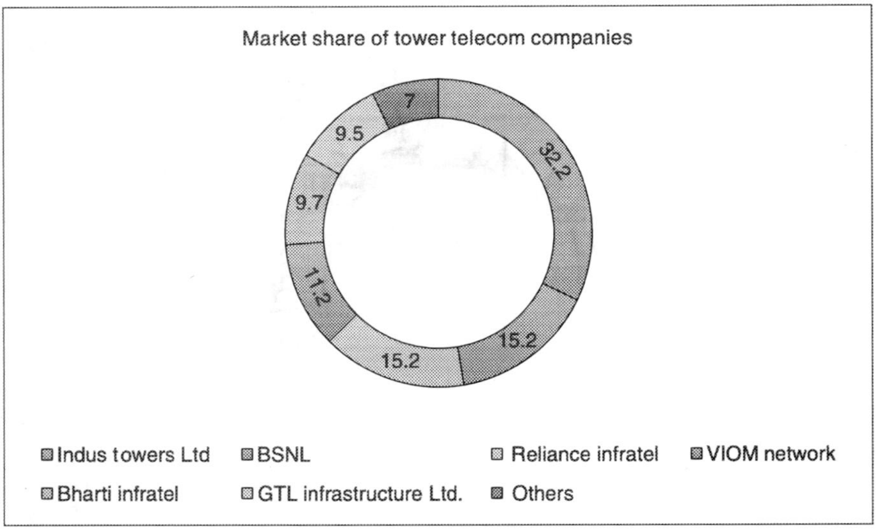

Figure 1.1 Market share of tower telecom companies.

Since its inception Indus Towers is paying special attention towards the tower industry's biggest challenge of minimizing energy cost and diesel pilferage. Indus Towers has taken several steps to control mounting energy cost and to minimize the diesel pilferage up to a significant level and have been successful in achieving their goals till now. Because of the number of tower holdings even small numbers leaves very big effect on the profitability.

ENERGY COST

At a tower site, continuous power supply is required for uninterrupted functioning of BTS. Energy cost is the part operating cost incurred by the tower telecom companies on supplying power to run BTS and other telecom equipment. At a tower site power demand ranges from 1 KW to 8 KW but most of the sites requires less than 4.5 KW. To power the BTS primarily electricity grid supply is used with the battery bank and diesel generators as the secondary source to back up the electricity grid failure which is very common in our country.

Energy cost comprises of the cost incurred on the electricity bills for using electricity grids and cost incurred on purchasing diesel for running diesel generator for bridging the gap between the energy requirement the electricity supply. Energy cost incurred per site is different and depends upon the load and sharing of the tower sites. Energy cost also differs with the circles as the per unit grid rate and per litre diesel rates are different in circles.

There is a very strong correlation between the energy cost and the operating cost. That's the reason Indus towers pays special attention towards energy cost as it directly affect its ARPU (Average Revenue per Unit). Energy cost compromise approximately 40% of the operating cost incurred by the company. Irregular grid supply and increasing use of diesel to compensate the gap and the increase in price of diesel over the time are increasing the energy cost. Increased energy cost increases the operating cost and affect the profitability. To reduce the energy cost incurred by the company Indus Towers is using various strategies like transferring the maximum tower sites in green sites by increasing the capacity of the battery bank, installing using solar energy. These technology helps to reduce the OPEX cost but increases the CAPEX cost burden on the company. So the company have to maintain a balance between the two. Due to increasing pressure from TRAI and mounting energy cost which reduces the profit margin, companies now are looking and trying new alternative energy options like solar energy, heavy battery bank etc.

According to the analysis done on the tower sites of Karnataka Circle average energy cost per normal site is 55,328 Rs. per month on the other hand the energy cost incurred on the green sites is 50,170 Rs. per month. A green site basically runs on electricity supply and the additional battery bank. to convert a normal site into green site electricity supply in that particular area should be very good. Some sites fully depends upon the Diesel Generators and consume lots of diesel due to various reasons like disputed property, non-availability of EB at the site. Energy cost incurred at these non eb sites are generally higher as the diesel is the costly substitute of the electricity. These sites 24 × 7 works on DG. Energy cost of the no EB sites comes around Rs. 1,80,000 . Because of the continuous working of DG the maintenance and repairing cost of the DG also increases which also adds to the Operating cost. In starting Indus Towers had several non EB sites, which it is devastating strategically.

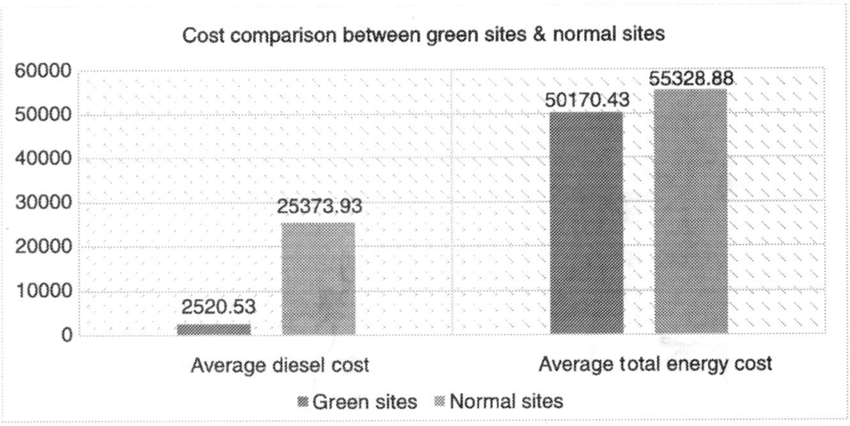

Figure 1.2 Cost comparison between green sites & normal sites.

Indus Towers is taking initiatives to convert all the sites into the green sites in the area where the grid supply is at least more than 20 hours. Indus have started a campaign to convert all the sites into green sites by 2015 in Chennai region as the electricity conditions are very good. Company incurs one time CAPEX cost of around 2-2.5 lacks on installing additional battery bank, which helps Indus to save around 5,000 Rs. per month. Converting all the tower sites into the green sites will help to increase the revenue by many folds.

Improper maintenance and repairing also increases the cost. In an analysis done on the sites of Karnataka circle it was found that various maintenance issues like higher C.P.H (consumption per Hour) of the DG, Poor battery bank back up increases the energy cost incurred per site.

DIESEL PILFERAGE: AN ADDITIONAL COST

Because of unreliable grid supply at many tower sites diesel generators has become the part of the sites, a good amount of diesel is used to run these DG's to supply uninterrupted power to BTS. Telecom industry is second biggest consumer of the diesel after Indian Railways. The whole process of diesel filling in DG sets is a very long and during this whole process diesel changes many hands and completes the journey of several kilometres. During this whole process a very big amount of diesel gets spilled, wasted and robbed. This very high pilferage ads to the mounting cost of energy incurred by the company.

DIESEL FILLING PROCESS

Diesel filling is a very lengthy and complex process which is generally outsourced to the OME (Outside Management Experts). In different clusters different OMEs take care of the diesel filling process.

This diesel filling process starts with the request of technician for the diesel requirement at his sites, supervisor forwards his request to Cluster manager. Then the cluster manager transfer money to the fleet cards. Supervisor then reaches to the Indian Oil corporation's Oil bunk who is the Indus Towers excusive diesel supplier, where the supervisor purchases the diesel by the fleet card and get it loaded into the vehicles (generally the three wheeler or the cargo truck) and the tells the diesel filler about the filling schedule for the day. Some sites are even several kms away from the oil bunk. After reaching at sites diesel filler checks the opening stock and take various reading like HMR readings, EB reading and then fills the diesel. Diesel pilferage during this process starts after when the vehicle left from IOC bunk for the sites. Sometimes even the diesel fillers steals the diesel in between the transit and does not fill the whole quantity in the tanks as per the schedule, this is the biggest reason of the diesel pilferage in telecom sector as there is no measure to check upon them. Even after the filling diesel into the tank diesel is robbed by the thieves. In some areas the diesel theft is very normal thing. They rob the diesel by breaking the locks and doors of the generators. Red area in the above Figure 1.3 shows the steps of the process where the diesel pilferage is highest.

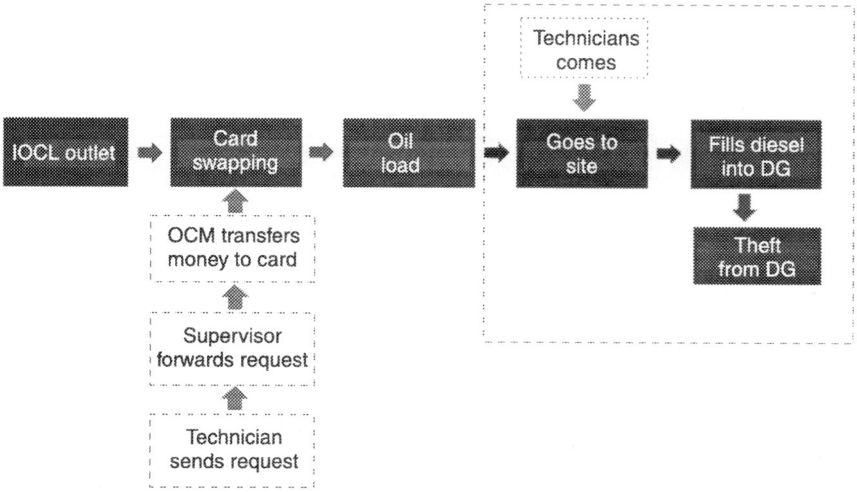

Figure 1.3

When the Indus Towers was formed and acquired the towers from Bharti Infratel, diesel pilferage was in very poor condition. There were no supervision and no check on the whole diesel filling process. Diesel fillers used to make the transactions and the containers and the cans used by them were very poor and the condition of diesel theft was very acute. Since then Indus Towers has done tremendous job and has taken several measures to control and minimize the diesel pilferage and to improve its diesel filling process. Some of them are as follow.

All payments for diesel purchase is through IOC fleet card: All the payments for the diesel purchase is made by the IOC fleet card only and these cards are held by the supervisors. Even in the case emergency filling payment is made by the fleet card after taking the permission from the cluster manager of that district/cluster. This system also help to keep an eye on the overall diesel consumption.

Compulsory presence of supervisor and technicians at diesel bunk and tower site: Indus has made it mandatory for the supervisor to be present at the diesel bunk at the time of diesel purchase and diesel loading. It has also made it compulsory for all the technicians to be present at the tower sites at the time of diesel filling. This step helped a lot to increase the supervision at the ground level and to control the diesel pilferage and theft.

Filling SMS System: All the diesel fillers have to send a message to Indus towers from the site where the filling has been done. They have to send filling information like opening stock, Filling, MHR reading and EB meter readings.

Setting up SMT (Security management team): Indus also created security management team to take a rapid action against the theft incidents and can reduce these kinds of incidents by analysing the condition of the security at the site and by regularly visiting sites. These SMT generally consist of one to three retired army or police officer and are in charge of the whole cluster.

CURRENT SCENARIO

All the measures taken by Indus over the time have helped them to minimize the theft incidents and diesel pilferage to a significant level. According to one supervisor who is working with Indus since inception the diesel pilferage in his area in the starting when the Indus towers started was at very high level of around 60%. In 2008 they use to purchase on an average 2,000 to 2,500 litres of diesel daily for the whole area under him and now the numbers of the tower holding is doubled but they use on average 750-850 litres of the diesel daily.

In some areas the diesel pilferage and theft is still very high. As the diesel filling process is very unstandardized, there is lack of supervision at the ground level as all these activities are controlled by the offices Kms away from the sites. Some of the measures are not followed by the supervisors and the diesel fillers like due to inconvenience many a time the supervisors and technicians do not come to the Indian oil bunk and tower sites. Diesel fillers don't use any standardized equipment and tools, they take the reading of opening stock of diesel on approximation basis.

The process of diesel allocation among the various sites is very poor, this process lacks proper planning, at many places the diesel allocation is not according to the requirements but according to the convenience of calculations, which result in frequent site failures and emergency filling which also affects the whole schedule. Technicians generally make the diesel filling plan based on their rough estimations which results in site failures and frequent emergency filling. Diesel allocation can be better particularly considering the distance a vehicle has to travel, due to power shortages diesel requirements in summer increase thereby increasing the frequency of filling, vehicles had to travel more than 300 km in a day to complete filling, there was no area wise zoning to make filling quicker and efficient. Stock keeping was also not very good at sites, based on power cut history minimum levels of diesel stock are not being followed, sites are being run on batteries close to drop voltages. Technician request were at fault at some places while at others allocation is not as per need and power cuts.

According the study done in the many districts of the Karnataka and Andhra circles, 40% and 55% of the diesel fillers in Karnataka and Andhra circles respectively are not even using the proper equipment (like funnels, Scales etc.) And tools for the diesel filling which causes the diesel pilferage.

The cans and drums used by the diesel fillers are in such bad conditions that causes the leakages and the wastage of the diesel. Even after giving the instruction almost all the diesel fillers don't use proper funnels many of them they just suck diesel by the long pipe to fill the diesel into the DG sets which not only increases the diesel pilferages but also very injurious to the health of the diesel fillers. Many of the diesel fillers do not maintain proper energy log which is mandatory to maintain by all the diesel fillers. Energy log book contains all the records like diesel quantity filled, opening stock, filling date etc. Maintaining proper energy log book help in making proper energy plan and to know the requirement of the diesel at different sites and also leaves the very small room for fillers and technicians to window dressing of diesel.

After loading Diesel from their assigned Indian Oil corporation's outlets diesel filling vehicles move according to the schedule planned by their supervisors. Average area covered by the vehicle is different in different areas. Ideally it should be between 150-200kms. Less area covered increases the cost of logistics and wide area covered increases the chance of Diesel pilferage and site failure. In Andhra circle where 27% covers 150-200kms daily only 15% vehicles in Karnataka circles covers ideal average area. In Andhra 43% of vehicles covers more than 200 kms and in Karnataka 55% of vehicles covers more than 200kms. Which increases the cost of the diesel filling process.

Security management experts team is also not very active, they generally play a very retroactive, many supervisors and technicians complained that the SMT have only 2-3 people which is insufficient to look after a whole cluster which is generally 200-250 km long and they don't perform proactive role. They take actions only after any theft incidents take place.

Drums and cans gets obsolete after some time but OMEs do not change the containers. After some time these drums and containers gets obsolete because of tiny holes and loose caps. Poor conditions cans and drums causes the spillage and wastage of diesel. While auditing it was found that about 34% and 45% of the diesel fillers in Andhra and Karnataka respectively were using cans and drums which were in poor condition and was old. These drums were having tiny holes which causes diesel leakage in some cans even caps were loose or even missing.

After adopting these measures Indus towers was able to minimize the diesel pilferage to a significant level. But still the diesel pilferage and wastage is a very big issue in unstandardized filling process, bad road condition, lack of proper supervision or reasons are wastage and theft. According to an estimate around 20-25% of the diesel remains unaccounted. In some areas, pilferage is expected to be as high as 50-60% questionable mark. This diesel pilferage makes huge loss for the operators. It increases the OPEX cost and works as an additional cost which affects their profitability.

Questions for Discussions

"The main problem is the difficulty to measure and monitor the exact amount of fuel used as it is impossible to predict it by any logical measuring system"- Design a Mechanism to reduce the losses caused to Tower Operators. Is it possible to improve the Supervision and Security management in remote sites to avoid the fuel pilferage?

References

- www.industowers.com
- www.asa.in/pdfs/surveys-reports/telecom-sector-in-india.pdf
- http://businesstoday.intoday.in/story/2014-year-roundup-telecom-sector-growth-2g-spectrum-auction/1/213823.html
- www.trai.gov.in

2

First Page Priorities of Print Media

Kavita Dugar • Namita Kapoor[2]

Abstract

A discriminating classification of the first page reporting necessities of the four heading newspapers 0û The Hindustan Times, The Indian Express, The Times of Indiaand The Hindu reveals a number of interesting shifts in the paradigms of news reporting and news values. The analysis, which involves the first page news coverage (including headlines, type of content, photos and advertisements), offered an insight into the departures from the traditional news values. The study has witnessed a growing trend for first reporting and investigative reporting increased use of large photos (especially photos of the main players in each story), and the use of long titles and large fonts for even short reports. These findings suggest an increasing tabloidization and trivialization of news. This study applies the strong market and weak market orientation theories of Randal Beam to the Indian media, and attempts to correlate developments in India's newsrooms with broader changes in Indian life styles and values within a society experiencing increased incidences of crime, corruption and litigation.

Keywords: News values, Globalization, Market orientation, Tabloidization and Trivializationt.

INTRODUCTION

The Indian media is blasting on all the fronts—print, electronic and web news coverage. This owes its credit to globalization and monetary changes introduced amid 1991-96. The push and stimulus the monetary changes and globalization got, both before 1991-96 and after, brought about the reformatting of the newspapers, particularly print media, which expanded its number of pages as well as started to issue exceptional supplements every day, for the sake of distinctive classifications sex insightful (ladies' page), subject savvy (Education, Employment or Opportunities, Finance/ speculation, Health, Youth page Matrimonial, Classifieds, and so forth.)

---

[2]Kavita Dugar is a student of MBA programme Class of 2015 and Namita Kapoor, Asst. Prof in the Area of Economics with Amity Business School. The authors have developed the case solely for class discussion for the programmes in Management. The author does not intend to illustrate effective or ineffective handling of a managerial situation. The case study does not represent or endorse the views of the managements about the issues in the case.

keeping in mind the end goal to extend its readership and to pander to the immense publicizing prerequisites of business stations, extensive programming and equipment multinational and national companies, engine and vehicle commercial ventures, other than banks and framework (telecom and versatile) association.

Further, to conquer the opposition emerging from the Magazine sorts, for example, India Today and Chitralekha, which by then as of now went into shade print in general, most of the high contrast English national newspapers (The Indian Express, The Times of India, The Hindustan Times, and so on) newspapers transformed into colour, emulated by hued uncommon Sunday versions and supplements. Consequently a remarkable rivalry had resulted among the national and local newspapers to pull in the per users both by method for slicing the costs and expanding the quantity of pages as extraordinary every day supplements.

Very nearly all supplements and increments reserved a considerable measure space for classifieds and substantial ads. These structural progressions emulated by substantial mechanical alterations in the creation forms intelligently prompted overwhelming dissemination figures therefore earning overwhelming commercials from enormous business houses and expanding the terrible incomes of print media. This denoted the start of the business driven or business turned news-casting in India; however it initially started in the US in 1980s yet grabbed energy in late 1990s and spread to the creating countries like India, China, and so on.

It ought to be noted that the greater part of the print media promoting is progressively losing its ground to the electronic media particularly TV and it has been watched that in spite of business sector driven reporting of the solid business sector turned media, the last held the responsibility to people in general and its antagonistic part.

It tries to analyse the materialness of substance contrasts, responsibility and ill-disposed part. The Times gathering alone which is a 15 billion rupees behemoth produces anyplace between 25-30 percent income in terrible edges. The Hindustan Times produces a horrible benefit around 800-900 million consistently. The print media involves around 43% aggregate publicizing as against 46% of promoting completed by TV and Cable stations. The Hindu and The Indian Express gatherings do produce terrible incomes between 3.5-4billion a year.

OVERVIEW OF THE INDUSTRY- COMPETITOR ANALYSIS

Daily paper organizations in India came to be anticipated as open administration foundations after freedom. Not with standing, in the late 1980s, they got to be only one more quick moving buyer item. The organizations began forceful promoting and special methods to build course and readership. The business saw intense rivalry both territorially and broadly. In 1999, the main 10 daily papers represented around 90% of the readership and the main two made 90% of the benefits. There was wild rivalry for the publicizing rupee By late 1990 s, electronic media like TV had made an imprint into the print media incomes. Print media was confronting a press because of the expanding notoriety of TV at first color TV and afterward satellite TV. The advertisement market worth about Rs. 90 billion eased off and daily papers saw an enduring decrease in publicizing offer - from around 75% in 1995 to very nearly half in 2000.

- **The Times of India**

India's most generally flowed English every day and the bunch's head super brand. The Times of India is appraised amongst the world's six best daily papers and draws in a day by day dissemination level of more than a million duplicates. The Times of India is distributed from Mumbai, Delhi, Bangalore, Ahmadabad, Lucknow and Patna.

"The Times of India", Newspaper does not require any extraordinary presentation. The Times of India is simply not a paper it's a brand. The Times of India is the most obvious English day by day in India further more has the most noteworthy flow on the planet in English every day.

- **The Hindustan Times**

The Hindustan Times is a heading daily paper in India. It has its establishes in the autonomy development of the first a large portion of the twentieth century. It was altered now and again by numerous critical individuals in India, including Devdas Gandhi (the child of Mahatma Gandhi) and Khushwant Singh.

Hindustan Times (secured in 1924) is the leader distribution of HT Media Ltd. It is has an across the nation arrive at in India (not with standing Southern India), with concurrent versions from New Delhi, Lucknow, Patna and Kolkata. It is likewise printed from Bhopal, Chandigarh, Jaipur and Ranchi. HT has additionally dispatched India's first youth every day HT Next in 2004. The Mumbai version was propelled on 14th July 2005. Different distributions of Hindustan Times are Hindustan (Hindi Daily), Nandan (Monthly kids' magazine) and Kadambani (Monthly scholarly magazine).

Hindustan Times has noteworthy online vicinity:

- http://Hindustantimes.com (Online version of Hindustan Times),
- http://Hindustandainik.com

HT Media as a feature of its forceful development plans, tried for an IPO, made its raid into Mumbai, propelled its radio channel and chose to commence another business daily paper. HT Media has likewise propelled a national business daily paper, Mint, with a select concurrence with Wall

Street Journal to distribute Journal marked news and data in India. It is the fourth biggest read every day newspaper.

- **The Indian Express**

During an era when India was battling for her flexibility, persecution was overflowing and the press practically choked and it was courageous and genuine.

From a solitary release paper in Madras in 1932, The Indian Express developed into a different version paper impacting thought and strategy the nation over. Stuffed with a reasonable blend of news, information and data, The Indian Express hits the heart of the issue without any alarm or support and is related to sound and wildly free reporting in India called 'News-casting of Courage'.

In excess of 75 years, The Indian Express has been perused by the individuals who have their own particular novel perspective of taking a gander at thing.

The Sunday paper reveals the pursuer in news and perspectives on individuals, innovation, diversion, business and books by means of The Sunday Express. The Sunday Express positively fortifies the clever pursuer consistently. The Financial Express (FE) is a business paper that is closest to the individuals who are in the matter of business. From business approaches to market patterns to new advancements, The Financial Express comes pressed with sharp news on every applicable issue. In doing in this way, it enables the pursuer with instructive perusing that makes for heading edge fiscal choices. The Financial Express conveys various unique pages each day of the week. These pages convey reports and examination on far reaching subjects, for example, vehicles, framework, the matter of excitement, capital markets, little and medium undertakings, exchange and keeping money.

- **The Hindu**

The Hindu, English-dialect day by day daily paper distributed in Chennai (Madras), by and large viewed as one of India's most powerful dailies.

Made in 1878 as a week by week, The Hindu turned into an everyday in 1889. While India was under British tenet, the paper stood up for autonomy however in a moderate vein. After India accomplished autonomy in 1947, The Hindu assembled a system of outside agencies while broadening its scope of India.

The Hindu is recognized for its extensive scope of national and universal political news and for its stress on correctness and adjusted scope. Despite the fact that it is distributed in a common capital, The Hindu's reportage and articles are perused deliberately and considered important in the national capital. At the start of the 21st century, its every day dissemination surpassed 900,000. The daily paper's guardian organization, Hindu Group Publications, likewise distributes The Hindu Business Line, an everyday business paper, and prevalent magazines, for example, Frontline and sport star.

KEY FOCUS - FIRST PAGES OF ENGLISH NEWSPAPERS

The detailed analysis of these Indian Newspapers reveals that the first pages of four heading English newspapers—Times of India, Hindustan Times, The Indian Express and The Hindu each one involving numerous issues. The decision is made to draw proper examinations with respect to scope, photographs and commercials between national level newspapers. Further the study is confined to first page alone as first page assumes an extremely imperative part in the connection of passing on news features of the day as fast as the TV features pass on to the viewers. First and foremost pages expect gigantic essentialness as far as pulling in the per users at look and all things considered its promoting effect has horrendous potential.

In appreciation of scope, the dissection bargains how distinctive daily papers treated the news under the heading basic reporting versus assorted reporting prioritized reporting under diverse perspectives, for example, open issues, commercial concerns, wrongdoing, lawful, and social. The second part of dissection additionally harps on diverse business sector driven procedures the print media news rooms resort to as space filling systems in lieu of the news by making up the first page with long features for shorter news things, expansive textual styles for shorter titles, other than utilizing photographs for immeasurably essential characters of news and permitting the valuable first page space with Advertisement.

The pattern of publication necessities has started to increase force transcending the customary reporting and news values in standard news-casting. The present case study thus tries to build how this move need to come to stay and settle as a branch of business arranged or business sector driven news coverage, other than investigating a portion of the results of such a deviation.

PRIORITY FOR REPORTING-UNFOLDING THE STYLES FOR EXISTENCE

The Indian newspapers cover the news processed from the newsroom in the order of their importance and priority. The order followed is:

Political> Crime>Legal>Social>Economic>Investigative

Political reporting: As an arrangement, just about all the daily papers have embraced political reporting as essential order of first page scope. However the political scope over years expected more new measurements with the expanding legislative issues. Case in point the late Indian Premiere League (IPL League) cricket matches and ICL framing started to fall in broad daylight issues area where The Hindu had most noteworthy scope of Political News, The Indian Express remained next with emulated by The Hindustan Times and The Times of India .However in appreciation of common issues and social and games, it was The Times of India which had reported greatest things took after by The Indian Express, The Hindustan Times and The Hindu. Truth be told The Indian Express had run extraordinary stories for the sake of 'Missing Muslim' versus Rajendra Sachar Committee's Report amid this period and accordingly its own particular reporting scope in this respect would consequently be high while different papers did not take to the extent that as The Indian Express had demonstrated aside from blanket the announcements of the Ministers including the Prime Minister on this issue.

Crime reporting: The primary page reporting today is implanted with extraordinary wrongdoing reporting, the majority of which is again commanded by the political wrongdoing and roughness. Though The Hindu had reported the most noteworthy, the staying emulated the request: The Indian Express > The Hindustan Times> The Times of India. Then again, non-political wrongdoing scope was high in The Times of India emulated by The Hindu, The Hindustan Times and Indian Express. Along these lines Crime Reporting constituted next most imperative favoured reporting, alongside political reporting, in the first page necessities. A large portion of the wrongdoing reported in the front page relates to the wrongdoings, (for example, assault or homicide) submitted against the ladies of world class society.

Legal reporting: Next to crime, it is the legal stories, which involved most elevated imperativeness in the first page reporting. Particularly the verdicts of the lower courts, tribunals, disciplinary transactions of different discussions including court military request of Military, High Court and Supreme Court decisions or judgments, and processes of the Election Commission secured this real segment. The Hindustan Times emulated by The Times of India had given most astounding scope for the lawful stories contrasted with The Indian Express and The Hindu.

Social reporting: The Times of India has given more significance to the stories radiating from the social subjects scenery. While The Hindustan Times and The Indian Express had done some giving an account of the social topics, The Hindu had done the slightest. The Times of India had reported all the more on Infrastructure and improvement took after by Welfare. Whereas Times of India's scope of social issues incorporated a confusing assortment social topics including Abhishek Bachan and Aishwarya Rai's proposed marriage, Abhishek getting the Uttar Pradesh

State Film Award, the Indian Express had sort of diverse approach and offered various articles or gives an account of untamed life to space science.

Economic reporting: It is one critical territory of reporting in the post globalization and monetary changes. Yet it finds most reduced necessity among the others of the first page necessities. As far as scope likewise, The Indian Express had given the most noteworthy scope contrasted with least of The Times of India. Truth be told the value rice, spiraling swelling, the predicament of ranchers because of absence of help value and advertising from the Government side and expanding stories of agriculturists' suicides ought to have taken more priority over different classes and sub-classifications. Anyhow, actually opposite happens with no clarification rising up out of the media sources.

Investigative reporting: The study uncovered that aside from The Indian Express and The Hindustan Times no other paper under the study has demonstrated profound duty to the Investigative reporting. However to the degree both the papers, The Indian Express and The Hindustan Times, had done investigative reporting. It doesn't imply that The Times of India does not do investigative news-casting. It does yet infrequently contrast with The Indian Express and The Hindustan Times. Investigative news-casting turned into a strong point of the paper be it The Indian Express or The Hindustan Times.

NUTSHELL

The study of the first page necessities of the four heading English Newspapers uncovers that the Indian print media excessively had gained the shapes of business driven news-casting initially radiated in the US as an after effect of globalization and privatization. Whereas the Times of India with its solid business introduction reflected all the imperative attributes of business sector driven news coverage, The Hindustan Times, The Indian Express and The Hindu stayed experiencing significant change stage. In any case, the vast majority of these papers still held their responsibility and capacity to request from the Government clarifications for expanding defilement, wrongdoing, falling flat administration, and so on.

The characteristics for the page layout are driven by the market drivers where it is found that the Indian print media reflected the same qualities basic features to long features and extensive size textual styles, an excess of photographs and ads - that were preferably found in the papers, which took to the way of business driven news-casting. The surrounding of features suggested more than scholastic and abstract contemplations for the pursuer. Indeed a feature of a front page of a daily paper should be much the same as that of the screen of the news features of the Television.

It is characteristic to try for shorter news titles with more clear and straight forward English. Though The Times of India, The Hindustan Times and The Hindu emulated the pattern tuned in to the above rationale, the titles of The Indian Express are discovered to be excessively protracted with a ton of content spot upon the feature and beneath the features. It is also to consider and measure or vitally audit photograph insertion in the front page however advertisers contemplate direct utilization of more shade photographs. Generally instructive establishments and banks were the noticeable promoters in the first page.

Questions for Discussions

Suggest new ideas as to how the respective newspapers can make more effective use of first pages in regard to prioritize the photos, advertisements and news. Analyse and understand the strategies being used by the different newspapers.

References

- C.S.H.N. Murthy et al. (2010), Trends in first page priorities of Indian print media reporting - A content analysis of four English Language newspapers, Journal Media and Communication Studies Vol. 2(2) pp. 039-053.
- https://www.**politicshome**.com/**front-pages**
- www.newseum.org/todays**frontpages**
- Jeffrey R. (2000). Indian Language Newspaper—a series essays published in 'Economic and Political Weekly'. Special Reference to Telugu: Ingredients of Growth and Failure".
- Vanita K., (2003). The Indian Media Business (Response Books, Sage Publications New Delhi pp. 13-20.
- Clausen L. (2004). Localizing the Global: "domestication' processes in international news production. Media, Culture and Society 26(1): 2544.
- http://timesofindia.indiatimes.com/
- www.thehindu.com
- www.hindustantimes.com
- www.indianexpress.com

3

Cartels in the Indian Cement Industry – Pinching the Real Estate

Ashutosh Pant • Pooja Sehgal Tabeck[3]

Abstract

In the recent decade the Indian Real Estate Industry has seen a boom. The boom has additionally brought on a sudden and sharp increase in cost of cement. The increase in cement costs has been as high as 17% per month. The ascent in cost could be because of 2 reasons: either because of high manufacturing cost or because of high demand/low supply. However there are situations when despite having high supply, at the end of the day the costs of cement is high, i.e. it is because of Cartel establishment. Cartel refers to the unlawful conduct of firms inside an industry to expressly or implicitly control their business sector in order to confine competition. Cartel members agree on fixing prices, total industry output, market shares, rigging bids, setting common sale agencies, allocating territories, or a combination of these measures to gain supernormal profits. In times of high demand, with capacity limitations, greater firms join the cartel. This case study is about the arrangement of such cartels and their impact on the builders who use the cement from such companies.

Keywords: Real estate, Cement, Cartel, increased price, Competition.

CEMENT INDUSTRY IN INDIA

Cement is a substance that sets and hardens and can bind other materials together. Cement is used widely in construction and a basic building block. The most common use for cement is in the production of concrete. Given the seasonality of the construction business (with peaks in the summer months and a reduced activity in the winter months) cement demand is not even throughout the year.

Today, the Indian cement industry is very large, second just to China in terms of installed capacity, and has developed at a quick pace lately. The rate of development in the course of recent years has been incredible.

---

[3]Ashutosh Pant is a student of MBA programme Class of 2015 and Pooja Sehgal Tabeck, Asst. Prof in the Area of Marketing & Retail Management with Amity Business School. The authors have developed the case solely for class discussion for the programmes in management. The author does not intend to illustrate effective or ineffective handling of a managerial and administrative situation. The case study does not represent or endorse the views of the managements about the issues in the case.

Since 1992 India's cement production has more than quadrupled from around 50 million tonnes/yr to 220 million tonnes /yr in 2011.

Although the Indian cement industry has some multinational cement giants, like Holcim and Lafarge, which have interests such as ACC, Ambuja Cement and Lafarge Birla Cement, the Indian cement industry is broadly home-grown. Ultratech Cement, the country's largest firm in terms of cement capacity, holds around 22% of the domestic market, with ACC (50%-owned by Holcim) and Ambuja (50%-owned by Holcim) having 15% and 13% shares respectively.

Many of the remaining dozen top players are Indian and are (in order of diminishing market share); Jaiprakash Associates (10%), The India Cements Ltd (7%), Shree Cements (6%), Century Textiles and Industries (5%), Madras Cements (5%), Lafarge (5%), Birla Cement (4%) and Binani Cement (4%).

Between them the main 12 cement firms have around 70% of the household market. Around 100 little players deliver cement on an extensive variety of scales yet are frequently limited to little regions.

Porters Five Forces Model of Cement Industry

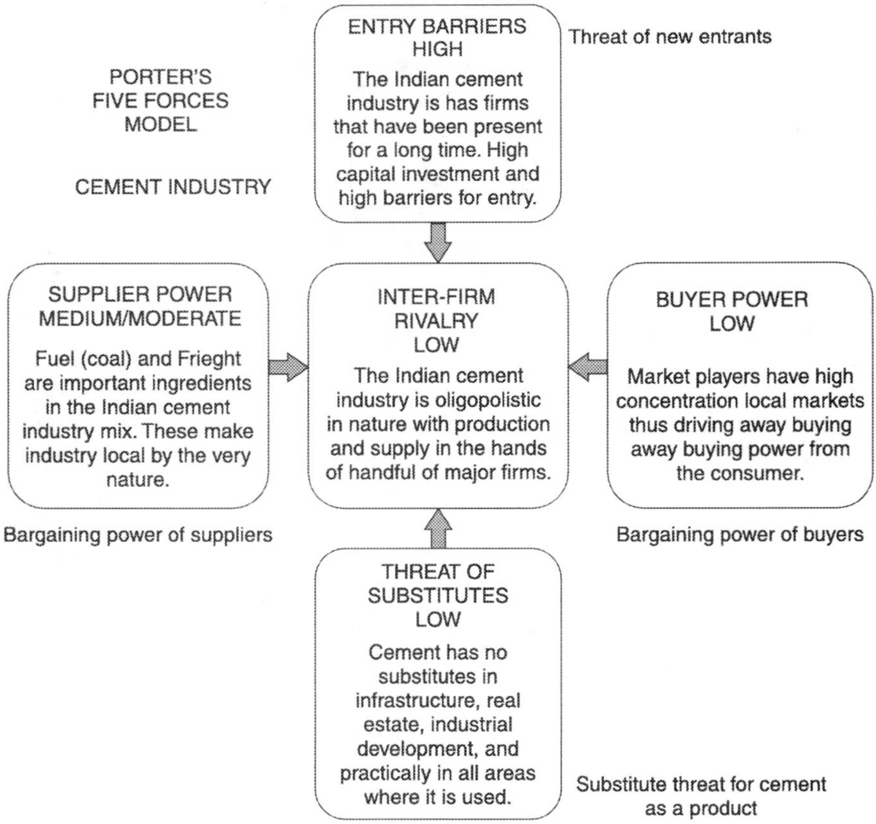

PROPERTY PRICE DETERMINANTS

During the old times the sole price determinant of a property used to be just location. However with time more functions have come up which significantly determine property prices. There are two types of prices: implicit and explicit. According to studies there are three main determinants which model price variation. Chau et al., (2001) and So. et al., (1995) said that the determinants can be categorized into structural, locational and neighbourhood attributes.

Apart from all this the cost of the construction also affects the price of the property. Cement is the biggest construction material used in construction and hence it is a major factor.

DEMAND DRIVERS FOR CEMENT IN INDIA

The Figure 3.1 below illustrates that residential real estate sector contributed towards 63% of the total domestic cement demand in the country during FY 06-10.

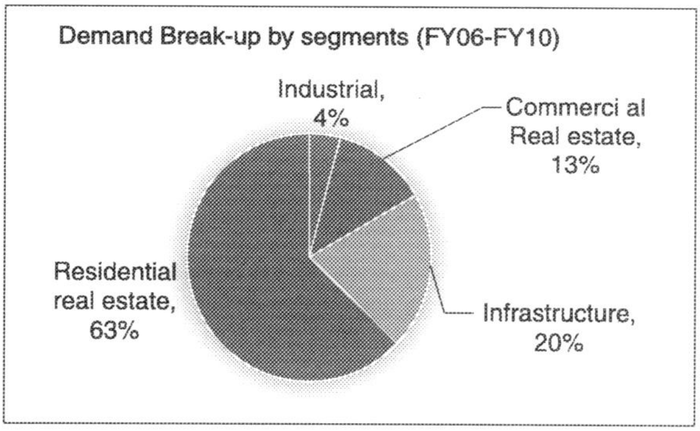

Figure 3.1 Demand break-up by segments.

The major players are ACC Ltd., Ambuja Cements Ltd., Ultratech Cement Ltd., India Cements Ltd., Century Textiles & Inds. Ltd., Jaiprakash Associates Ltd., Birla Corporation Ltd., Lafarge India Pvt. Ltd., Madras Cements Ltd., Shree Cement Ltd., Binani Cement Ltd., and Kesoram Industries Ltd.

What is a Cartel?

A Cartel is essentially a gathering of seller or buyers who rally and attempt to wipe out rivalry. Cartels are similar to cancer on the open business sector economy. Cartels devastate competition and cement cartelization has created genuine damage to numerous developing economies and consumers.

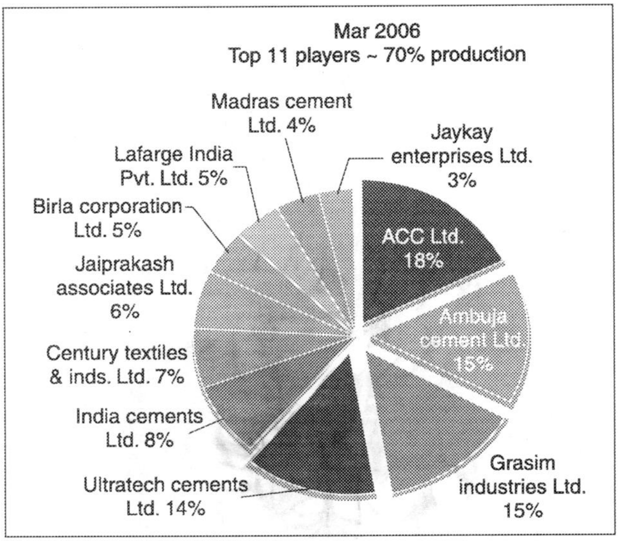

Figure 3.2

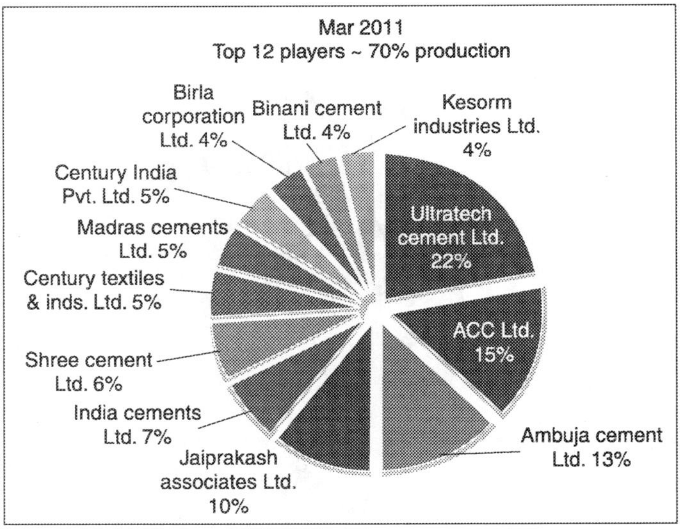

Figure 3.3

Categories of Cartels

(1) Customer Cartels: Customer cartels assign clients or suppliers to specific producers.

(2) Specialization Cartels: Specialization cartels partition the market differentially.

(3) Territorial Cartels: Territorial cartels partition market share by distributing the area geographically.

(4) Quota Cartels: Quota Cartels constrain the production output of members and therefore falsely making supply constraint. This leads to increase in price of the product. However in these cartels the monitoring is very difficult.

(5) Price Cartels: In Price Cartels, cost is discussed among the members and generally a free organization is made to monitor the compliance of members and hold them accountable.

Strong reasons supporting cartel formation

- Few players in market
- Similar production cost
- High dependence of consumers on product (no substitute)

Cartel Profitability (Sector Wise)

Industry	Price and profitability trends.
Beer	Possibly above the monopoly level, due to political pressure to keep price high.
Bromine	Close to joint profit maximizing level in some periods; other collusive periods barely above cournot price level.
Cement	10% above world price.
Diamonds	Prices nearly doubled after initial formation of cartel.
Mercury	Prices higher in first incarnation than in second.
Ocean shipping	Close to joint profit maximizing level.
Potash	Prices rose following agreements; in 1910, prices were double average cost.
Steel	Less than joint maximizing price but one third higher than world price.
Sugar	Prices rose after cartel formation.
Tea	Prices rose 80 percent in 1993 after cartel was re-established.

CEMENT CARTEL - THE CASE

Investigating a complaint filed by the Builders' Association of India, the Competition Commission of India last June discovered 11 cement organizations, including ACC, Ambuja Cement and Grasim Industries (now blended with Ultratech Cement), indulging in a cartel. The Commission slapped a fine of Rs. 6,698 crore on these organizations.

The main four bond organizations — ACC, Ambuja Cements, Ultratech Cement and Jaiprakash Associates — were fined in overabundance of Rs. 1,000 crore each. Others that were fined incorporate Grasim, JK Cement, India Cements, Madras Cement, Century Cement, Binani Cement and Lafarge India.

These companies were fined 50 per cent of their average profit for fiscal years 2009-10 and 2010-11, the period for which they were investigated.

Quantum of payment

ACTS AND LAWS FOR CARTELS IN INDIA

In India, before enacting M.R.T.P. (The Monopolies and Restrictive Trade Practices Act, 1969), the only legislation worth mentioning to curb the evil effects of monopolies and restrictive trade practices was the Indian Contract Act, 1872.

In 2002, The Competition Act was enacted by the Parliament of India and governs Indian competition law. It replaced the Monopoly and Restrictive Trade Practices Act, 1969. Under this legislation, the Competition Commission of India was established to prevent activities that have an adverse effect on competition in India.

The Competition Act, 2002 under Chapter II prohibits certain agreements, abuse of dominant.

Position and regulates combinations with the power to lay charges and impose considerable.

Fines on individual(s) and enterprise(s).

How can Competition Commission of India (CCI) detect a Cartel?

Proving cartelization is tough. Most cartels leave no paper trail of an arrangement that could be utilized against them and are quiet in nature. Getting proper data and enough confirmation to build a case against the cartel members is tough. Information gathered by government organizations in typical course would be lacking.

In the cement case, the CCI utilized information on output, limit, price hike, economic growth, construction activity and profit margins of 11 cement companies to demonstrate there was a cartel. It didn't have any confirmation in the form of communication between the cement organizations to demonstrate that they were lowering output or increasing cost again and again. This has brought up issues about the sustainability of the CCI. "The proof was exceptionally solid," says the CCI member Geeta Gouri. "Unless we can get exact confirmation, the commission won't intercede," she includes.

In the past investigations concerning the onion cartel fell because there was not enough confirmation, despite the fact that it was clear to everybody that there were connections working all through the chain beginning from the farmers to the stockists and wholesalers. The Commission might relook at the situation when it gets enough proof to establish the presence of a cartel.

Questions for Discussion

- What is a cartel and what are the types of cartel?
- What steps can be taken to stop cartelization? Mention some ways adopted by the government to stop cartelization?

References

****

4

Project – 'Raheja Revanta' and Its Strategic Scheme for Survival

Kushal Malik • S.S. Pal[4]

Abstract

The Indian real estate sector has traditionally been an unorganized sector but it is slowly evolving into a more organized sector. Raheja Developers Limited, a Real Estate Company was founded in the year 1990 by Mr. Navin M. Raheja, who is amongst the first generation entrepreneurs. Raheja Developers in achieving their vision to lead the Industry has come up with a project named - ***"Raheja Revanta"***. The project with its unique attributes and pay options is facing challenges in selling its single BHK units. The case describes how revealing disadvantage have been overcome by the developers with a strategic solution- '*Subvention Scheme*'.

Keywords: Real estate, Project, Subvention scheme.

INTRODUCTION

Raheja Developers Limited was founded in the year 1990 by Mr. Navin M. Raheja, who is amongst the first generation entrepreneurs. At present, the company have a strong market in the region of Delhi NCR and is one of the largest companies in the Real Estate Industry. Company is expanding its business at a rapid rate in constructing entities in the real estate sector with added customer benefits such as luxurious properties at reasonable costs, excellent customer relationship management.

The Company have expanded and grown at a steady pace which is evident from the increasing turnover and profits year after year. Existing business models have been strengthened and new processes were too added to it. The total revenue and matching profits is above INR 5 billion for the current financial year. With the considerable amount of revenue and a solid land bank of approx. 58 million sq. ft. developable area at

---

[4]Kushal Malik is a student of MBA programme Class of 2015 and S.S. Pal, is in the Area of Operations Management with Amity Business School. The authors have developed the case solely for class discussion for the programmes in management. The author does not intend to illustrate effective or ineffective handling of a managerial and administrative situation. The case study does not represent or endorse the views of the managements about the issues in the case.

prime locations, Raheja Developers aims at becoming the front runners in Indian realty sector.

The company's workforce includes highly qualified professionals who are fully dedicated to the company and ensure the high standards in quality construction, timely delivery and customer satisfaction are followed. The company have always aimed to keep its commitments and thus it is awarded with an extremely resonant reputation in the Indian construction industry.

THE REAL ESTATE SECTOR AND ITS CHALLENGES- A COMPETITIVE LANDSCAPE

The Indian real estate sector has traditionally been an unorganized sector but it is slowly evolving into a more organized one. The sector is embracing professional standards and transparency with open arms. The major established domestic players in the sector are DLF, Unitech, Hiranandani Constructions, Tata Housing, Godrej Properties, Omaxe, Parsvanath, Raheja Developers, Ansal Properties and Infrastructure and Mahindra Lifespace Developers Ltd. to name a few. International players who have made a name for themselves in India include Hines, Tishman Speyer, Emaar Properties, Ascendas, Capitaland, Portman Holdings and Homex. Real estate industry grown in different fields. Real estate can divided into 3 categories - Commercial, Residential and Agricultural.

The key challenges that the Indian real estate industry is facing today are:

- Lack of clear land titles.
- Absence of title insurance.
- Absence of industry status.
- Lack of adequate sources of finance (Dependability towards the Banking Sector and SEBI guidelines on lending).
- Shortage of labour.
- Rising manpower and material costs.
- Approvals and procedural difficulties.
- Development rate.

FUTURE PROSPECTS FOR REAL ESTATE

India has huge potential to attract large foreign investments into real estate. With real estate reaching a point of saturation in developed countries and the demand and prices falling, global real estate players are looking at emerging economies such as India for tapping opportunities in real estate. Indian real estate will stay attractive due to its strong economic fundamentals and demographic factors. Moreover, there is a high level of global uncertainty looming over the developed and developing nations of the world. Investments in Indian real estate will fetch higher returns for investors as compared to other global markets. In the coming years, the opportunities in the real estate sector will attract more global players to India and hence will help the industry to mature, become more transparent, improve management and adopt advanced construction techniques.

DREAM OF THE DEVELOPERS- "*RAHEJA REVANTA*"

Raheja Developers in achieving their vision to lead the Industry has come up with a project named - ***"Raheja Revanta"***. The project details as under-

- **Location Advantage**

The location of the project has its own advantage. The project is situated at sector 78, Gurgaon just on NH8 near the intersection of Northern Periphery Road, Southern Periphery Road and NH8. also the project vests in the domain of proposed Metro line neighbouring a hub of planned 5 star hotels, office developments, golf courses, shopping malls.

- **Development of the Area**

Raheja Developers found it beneficial to invest at such a growing stage so that it would be able to reap profits in the long run. They thought of purchasing the land at subsidized rates as they knew that in the near future after the development process is completed the company would earn huge profits from this investment.

- **The Features of Project**
    - Revanta is a mix of high rises and independent floors. There are three towers joined together. SURYA TOWER would be more than 56 stories. There is a provision of helipad* too over the top of the building. The company is awaiting approvals. With a luxurious double height entrance lobby, high speed capsule lifts, with bourgeois architecture and a clean glass facade, Surya tower is iconic. Available in options of 1, 2, 3, 4, 5 and 6 bedroom condominiums and luxurious penthouses. Revanta would change the skyline of Gurgaon.
    - The independent floors are Ground+3 and are named TAPAS TOWNHOUSES. It is available in 3, 4 bedrooms and penthouse options. They have lawns at the ground. They too come with elevators and double height lobby. Revanta would be a landmark project of India as it brings to you facilities that were never provided by any other developer so far in the country. It's a marvel of sophisticated technology and truly an achievement of modern day engineering.

- Revanta would have the tallest and highest sky bridge with infinity pool, viewing gallery, fine dining restaurant at the 46th floor. The residents would have the facilities of Laundromat for a quick wash of clothes, a mini theater to watch movies on the big screen, automated car wash and Valet parking. The other amenities in the complex would include world class swimming pools, sports facilities like tennis, squash, table tennis, basketball & billiards, a club house, dedicated retail centre and a business centre.

RAHEJA REVANTA PROJECT- COMPETITIVE STRATEGIES

(a) Built by Largest Construction Company in UAE – Arabtec, the makers of Burj Khalifa, tallest building in the World.

(b) Safety Assurance by Thornton Tomasetti of USA. The structural engineers of Kingdom Tower, Saudi Arabia 1 km high, tallest building in the world under construction, the Petronas Towers, Malaysia and Taipei 101, Taiwan.

(c) Club house managed by one of the Best Spa in India with full menu of Spa Massages, Jacuzzi, Sauna, Steam, Wellness treatments.

(d) One of the Tallest Buildings in India.

(e) Sky Bridge with India's Highest Infinity Swimming Pool.

(f) Choose your game with Golf, Tennis, Billiards, Squash, Table Tennis, Basketball facilities.

(g) Amenities like Laundromat, Mini theatre, automated car wash, Valet parking, Complete 3 tier security, Earthquake safe building, Power back up, Advanced firefighting/fire alarm/smoke detection systems.

UNIQUE PAYMENT PLAN OFFERED

Down Payment Plan

In this payment plan, the investor had to pay 10% of the total amount at the time of booking the unit within 60 days/2 months from the booking date, the investor have to pay 85% of the total amount to Raheja Developers. Remaining 10% of the total amount is paid when OC i.e. Occupancy Certificate is given by Raheja Developers to its customer.

Deferred Payment Plan

Raheja Developers have a Deferred Payment Plan for Revanta project. Deferred payment plan is as follows:

- Deferred payment plan = Construction Linked payment plan + Time bound payment plan.

In this type of payment plan, Raheja Developer receives payment from its customers on the basis of construction done as well as over a specific time period. 10% of the total amount is paid by the customer to the builder at the time of booking. 20% of the total amount is paid within 120 days /4 months by the customer from the time of booking the unit. After 12 months from the booking date, 10% of the total amount is paid by the customer to Raheja developers. So within one year the Raheja Developer is able to get 40% of the total amount for a particular unit from its customers. Next payment is made by the customer after 18 months from the booking time and again 10% of the total amount is paid to Raheja Developers. After 24 months from the booking date, 10% of the total amount is paid to Raheja Developers by the customer. Within two year period Raheja developers is able to accumulate 60% of the total amount from its customers. Next 30% is paid on completion of structure. For example: If Revanta project is 46 floors project then 30% of the total amount is only received once the structure of 46 floors is completed. Final 10% of the total amount is received when Occupancy Certificate is issued to the customer by Raheja Developers.

Deferred payment gives benefits to both investors as well as builder. Through this payment plan Raheja Developers were able to sell its 2, 3, 4, 5, 6 BHK units.

Key Problems Faced by Revanta Project

- Most of the 1 bhk units remained unsold.
- Lack of demand for 1 bhk.
- Overall dampening of the real estate market.
- Prices for 1 bhk were too high to attract the small investors.

COMBATING THE KEY PROBLEMS – NEW SCHEME LAUNCHED

In order to overcome the problems mentioned above the strategic group of the Raheja Developers came with a new scheme- *'Subvention Scheme'.*

- **Subvention Scheme:** This scheme was launched due to the unsold 1bhk units. Main purpose was to attract many investors for this type of particular unit. Under this scheme, the investor had an option to either opt for subvention without or with buyback option.
- **Subvention Scheme without Buyback Option:** In this scheme only 25% of the total amount is paid by the investor and rest 75% is paid by the bank. This scheme allows Raheja Developers to attract more investors as EMI on the 75% amount is paid by Raheja themselves to the bank.

  In this BSP i.e., Base Selling Price is increased from Rs. 7675/sqft to Rs. 8075/sqft.

  10% of total amount at the time of booking by the investor.

5% of total amount within 60 days by the investor.

35% of total amount is paid by the BANK to the Raheja Developers at the time of Agreement.

10% of the total amount is paid by the investor within 12 months from booking date.

Remaining 40% is paid by the bank to the Raheja developers within 36 months from booking date.

- **Subvention Scheme with Buyback Option:** In this scheme, Raheja Developers gives investors an option to sell the purchased unit back to the builder at higher Base Selling Price after the 36 month period. It offers customer BSP of Rs. 9475 per sqft which customer previously got at Rs. 8075 per sqft. In this Memorandum of Understanding is signed between investor and Raheja Developers.

Benefits of this scheme

- Loan Eligibility- As the price for 1 bhk is less as compared to the other units the loan can be easily drawn on it.
- This scheme attracted many investors as it increase walk-in at the site office.
- Increase in BSP up to Rs. 400 per sqft gives investor a profit of 66%.
- Due to this scheme all the units of 1197.82 per sqft were sold out. So this scheme can be called as successful step taken by Raheja developers.
- Due to this scheme small investors were able to buy the units.

Questions for Discussions

'The real estate sector in India is facing challenges in the entire value chain of the real estate development. Do you think that subvention scheme of the Raheja Developers will be in a position to attract more buyers?'

References

- www.ficci.com/sector/59/Project_docs/real-eastate-profile.pdf
- www.cci.in/pdfs/surveys-reports/Real-Estate-Sector-in-India.pdf
- Vandna Singh and Komal (2009). Prospects & Problems of Real Estate In India, International Research Journal of Finance and Economics, Issue 24.
- Sahu. R. Sandeep, and Shreekumar Menon (2011). Recessionary Challenges in Real Estate Business, APJRBM, Volume 2, Issue 1.
- Taipale Kaarin (2012). "From light green to sustainable buildings." Chapter 14, State of the World Report 2012, Worldwatch Institute, Washington.

5

Reinventing the Newspaper Industry With ICT Tools

Diksha Singhal • R.R. Ghatak[5]

Abstract

Among the few countries that have a business newspaper India is one which not only mirrors the vibrancy and vitality of the media, but also the new vitality of our economy. The vast readership for these business daily papers transcends from the quickly developing corporate segment, it likewise shows the developing premium that the overall population now manifests in monetary matters which reflect the developing criticalness of business and economy in our national discourse. Business daily papers focuses basically on business news, smart perspectives on critical issues and far reaching scope of money markets. They can convey the message in more prominent detail and clarity, all the more in-profundity data and examination, which helps organizations and their business. There is a gigantic extent of development for Business daily papers in impending years as just a negligible 0.1% of the populace is perusing business daily papers at present. Newspapers reach only 35% of our grown-up populace despite the fact that the grown-up writing proficiency is something like 65%. To manufacture this hole in the middle of readership and reading proficiency furthermore to stay focused the distributions have kept their costs low and depended totally on sponsors to sponsor the pursuer and to expand the deals. They are using different strategies to attract the customers of different sectors.

ICT (Information and Communication Technology) has changed the whole arrangement of creation and showcasing within the print media. Each industry is influenced in restricted or the other by the data insurgency. The present paper manages a hereto untouched territory of exploration, i.e., effect of ICT on daily paper industry and potential outcomes of embracing the profits of e-administration in the domain of daily paper industry. The paper is designed and takes a glance at the effect of use of ICT on the item plan, quality, generation procedure, cost, showcasing and innovative work and breaks down the apparent upgrades in the courses of action. Towards the end a reasonable model is created where four measurements of individuals strengthening are recognized and clarified through the cooperative connection between daily paper industry and e-government.

---

[5]Diksha Singhal is a student of MBA programme Class of 2015 and R.R. Ghatak, is in the Area of Operations Management with Amity Business School. The authors have developed the case solely for class discussion for the programmes in management. The author does not intend to illustrate effective or ineffective handling of a managerial and administrative situation. The case study does not represent or endorse the views of the managements about the issues in the case.

Keywords: Newspaper industry, Express group, E-paper, Information and Communication technology.

INTRODUCTION

The Indian Express Group

There is more or less 1,907 daily papers distributed in India of which daily papers in the vernacular dialect contain 49.0% of the aggregate daily papers, followed by Hindi (42.1%) and English (8.9%). (sitsc: office of RNI).

The vast majority of the vernacular and Hindi daily papers has a territorial catering. Verifiably the English daily paper industry in India has been divided with every daily paper having a provincial centre, for example, the Deccan Chronicle in Hyderabad , Indian express in Mumbai, Hindustan times in Delhi, Hindu in Chennai, broadcast and statesmen in Kolkata, Deccan proclaim in Bangalore, Gujarat samachar in Ahemdabad. Lately however the bigger English dialect daily papers has been growing their geological, and it accept the English dialect fragment Is moving towards combination.

The Indian Express Group is one of the country's biggest media combinations with a wide choice of distributions and a system of business locales spread over the length and width of the nation. Developing in quality from a solitary version to 29 national versions and 3 dialect dailies that arrive at in excess of 5 million the nation over. The Indian Express gathering productions incorporate the Indian Express, The Financial Express, Loksatta and the exceptionally regarded Bollywood week by week - Screen among others. Today, the Indian Express Group gloats a broad newsgathering and advertising framework and additionally a state-of-the-craft interchanges arrange inside the Indian distributed industry.

The Group is likewise the pioneer in propelling specialty business and exchange productions only oversaw by its key specialty unit: Business Publications Division (BPD). The Division is the biggest and quickest developing specialty distributed house in the sub-landmass coating all significant parts - Hi-Tech, Hospitality, Travel & Tourism, Pharmaceuticals, and Business Trade.

As the print due date approaches, there is a feeling of desperation circulating everywhere. It is late night-time at the business areas of the Indian Express and in a couple of more hours the first evidences of the paper need to be ready. The daily paper has a week after week course of more than four thousand duplicates, however its work places are unassuming. Notices are the backbone of this daily paper and its pages are loaded with characterized postings for employments and administrations.

Income from these is developing, and keeps the paper working. More daily papers are connecting with spots where they haven't some time recently

THE GLOBAL SCENARIO-REALTY Vs MYTH

The news media are in emergency over the created world. News-casting as we know it is continuously depicted, clearly with some misrepresentation, as 'collapsing',' disintegrating', in 'meltdown'. In this computerized age, there is melancholy in most created nation, or 'developed', media advertises over the eventual fate of daily papers further more telecast TV. Two decades after a call issued from a gathering in Windhoek, Namibia for the station of World Press Freedom Day, 'the landing of the computerized unrest – the advancement of the Internet, the rise of new manifestations of media, and the ascent of online informal communities – has reshaped the media scene and made "the press" of 2011 something that those assembled in Windhoek in 1991 couldn't have envisioned' (UNESCO 2011). There is a solid sense that 'the news business is no more in control of its own future' and that it is innovation organizations like Google and the social media that lead the way. The worldwide budgetary emergency and financial stoppage of 2008-2009 sent several western media associations into a spiral. Publicizing incomes, the help of the daily paper industry, took a body blow amid this period. A lot of people enormous daily papers, whose qualities had been sapped and whose situational focal points had been undermined throughout the years, went into liquidation or insurance against chapter 11. The New York Times was rescued by a crisis credit of US $250 million from Mexican tycoon Carlos Slim: 'to help the daily paper organization back its organizations' (NYT 2009). A huge number of columnists lost their employments in the United States, where newsrooms are 30 for every penny more diminutive than in 2000 and crosswise over Europe.

There has been some recuperation, or to be more exact, a log jam in the decrease starting mid-2010. Yet printed daily paper flow and readership are in irreversible decay over the created world; they have been in relentless, long-term, mainstream decrease much before the late subsidence hit these nations and their news media. 'Dissemination is similar to the sun. It keeps on ring in the East and decrease in the West', Christoph Riess, CEO of the World Association of Newspapers and News Publishers (WAN-IFRA), told those amassed at the World Newspaper Congress and World Editors Forum in Vienna in October 2011 (Riess 2011). His presentation concentrated on 'six key territories': the media utilization shift; monetary improvements; daily paper course and number of titles; promoting Consumption by media; daily paper income; and web versus versatile (Ibid. 2011). The worldwide daily paper industry is withstanding the risk from the web with flows for paid-for titles climbing by 2.75% in 2007, however add up to disseminations in the UK were down 3.46%. As indicated by figures distributed by the World Association of Newspapers (WAN), even in nations where paid-for flows are on the decrease, the free sheet business sector is augmenting the scope of daily papers. At the point when free dailies are added to the paid-for daily paper dissemination, worldwide course climbed by 3.65% in 2007, and by 154.3% for as far back as five years. The picture for UK daily paper distributers was not all that blushing then again, with the WAN figures demonstrating that there was a 3.46% decrease altogether flows in 2007. Over the EU, paid for dailies were around 2.37%. The UK's Metro is the second biggest free day by day on the planet, behind Italian title Leggo, which conveys a normal of 1.95 m duplicates a day contrasted and 1.37 m duplicates of the Metro. Print remains the greatest promoting medium on the planet, with a 40% offer of the whole plan used by advertisers.

ISSUES

This brings us to an oddity, which appears to be integral to this transformational age. Amidst this old media emergency, more individuals are perusing daily papers digitally and it is a worldwide gathering of people for the best distributions. Around the world, printed daily papers, with a reported course of 519 million, achieve an expected 2.3 billion individuals consistently, 20% more than the web (Riess 2011). Anyway the 'terms of exchange' are moving callously for the web, versatile, and more up to date intelligent computerized stages. Numerous daily papers have astounding sites offering rich, diverse, multi-media substance, including long-structure characteristics, investigative articles, and insightful dissection. A few reporting schools round the world now consider advanced news-casting important. In any case it is generally allowed to-air however some significant western daily papers have started to value their advanced substance and some new income streams have opened up. Versatile stages and tablets headed by the iPad hold guarantee, with a few daily papers and TV slots thinking of inventive and alluring applications. Anyhow this does not make any sense to a feasible income and plan of action for advanced news coverage. The web publicizing model is doing exceedingly well yet it is the web search tools, most importantly Google, that take the lion's offer of the income; the paid-substance model is additionally settled on the portable stage, what with a huge number of clients tolerating 'month to month contracts, prepaid telephones, and paid-for applications', however here as well, the new children on the piece, Apple and the versatile administrators, take the majority of the income (Riess 2011). The daily paper industry confronts a twofold press: the print business proceeds with vigorously to finance computerized news-casting, which can't pay for itself by drawing in enough publicizing or memberships or a mixture of the two; and the new advanced players put expanding weight on daily paper course, readership, and the business itself.

This conspicuous difference to that of numerous nearby daily papers in the US and the UK, which have been compelled to close down or scale back due to lessening promoting wage. The story in India is very distinctive on the grounds that nearby organizations are developing due to globalization and opening up of the businesses. Internet factor- Web has yet to completely enter the rustic and less created parts of India.

While numerous daily paper markets have been hit by the development of online news-casting the standpoint for Indian print media stays light. The figures on the quantities of daily papers in India shift extraordinarily, however its accepted there are thousands as opposed to many in the the nation, with a lot of people more releases being included constantly. One of the key reasons is the low entrance of web outside substantial urban focuses. "India is considered among those creating nations that will last see the fury of advanced entrance in light of the fact that Internet infiltration is still beginning and shopper relocation has not yet happened," says KPMG.

In the West, the ascent of the web has been a driving variable in the end of numerous print versions. Web entrance is still moderately low yet that will soon change. Each daily paper understands there's a parcel more rivalry than there was before. Information is the essential include and additionally the last yield of Newspaper industry. It gathers crude data and believers it into classified, characterized and valuable bits of data. In this way it won't be an embellishment to say that the radical progressions acquired the domain of data through Information and Communication Technology (ICT) insurgency are sure to influence Newspaper more than another industry. The selection and retention of Information and Communication Technology are continuously done in daily paper industry by accumulating efficiencies all the useful wings including generation , publication and showcasing to addition focused advantage. Information and Communication engineering is currently utilized by press as well as progressively by news people and editors likewise. Its profits are continuously perceived at each purpose of the whole inventory network of daily paper.

This paper studies the effect of Information and Communication innovation on every part of Newspaper, on the item, the generation process, showcasing and appropriation of the item and examination & advancement. It additionally endeavors to discover how engineering has reinforced (debilitated) Newspaper Industry and what opportunities (dangers) it makes for the business. The scientists expect the part of government as that of facilitator all the while and attempt to investigate the potential outcomes of use of e-government in the connection of daily paper industry.

By 1990s, machine and its auxiliary devices had gotten to be part and bundle of each business operations. Daily paper industry excessively took stride towards the computerization of different exercises and turned into one of the first businesses to perceive the guts of magnetic ascertaining machines like Apple Macintosh (or Mac). Innovation advancement and ingestion in Newspaper industry enhanced the printing process and diminished the working time of publication work areas. The lavish utilization of online substance and offices has prompted predominance of a lot of people to-numerous model in excess of one-to numerous model of data gathering. The extensive variety of altering, page making, database, photograph imaging, and blending programming gave bleeding edge offices to daily paper business which could now streamline and incorporate intra-wings works inside a daily paper. The utilization of telefax, sites, online database, electronic data locales, and online per users and newsmakers, made the lumbering employment of data gathering and reporting simpler than any other time in the recent past. The offices of messages, individual sites, and online exchange gatherings further have broadened the canvas of data as the news of remotest ranges could be held inside the due dates.

WHY SHOULD COMPANIES ADOPT ICT?

Taking after segments bargain with an investigation of effect of ICT on different angles, for example, the item (daily paper), the creation process (accumulation of news, altering and printing), advertising and conveyance. Part of innovation in innovative work is settled, subsequently a concise note is introduced on ICT and innovative work in daily paper. The feathered creature eye's perspective of innovation retention and ICT usage in daily paper industry provides for us an understanding in the quantum of mission and request of the business for overhauling its useful operations through nonstop redesigning of man and hardware both.

ICT AND PRODUCT INNOVATION

Data Technology made its vicinity felt in all quarters of news quarters. It not just affected the working of daily papers and different offices yet even conceived new symbol, the e-paper. Constraint of print forms, range and availability, expense of newsprint abetted by unbelievable vista of Internet swayed Newspapers organizations to dispatch electronic rendition of versions. Therefore, ICT made the daily paper accessible truly with a click of mouse anyplace at whatever time. However the e-paper is not a substitute to the print form rather a supplement to the same. The quantity of daily paper on-line locales developed 13.77 percent in 2007 and 50.77 percent over the five years from 2003 to 2008.

The extent of web adaptation is extending with the ascent in web integration in India. In 2007, 60,000,000 clients were enlisted in India (www.internetworldstats.com/asia/in.htm) which could be ascribed to expand in Ad income of the daily paper. Indian Express daily paper gathering recorded Rs 100 million through web form in its first year of propelling.

ICT AND NEWSPAPER PRODUCTION

The real measurements of generation methodology incorporate effectiveness, viability, expense and quality.

Ease of production: The presentation of internet recording of reports and online supply of pages to either head article work area or to generation units, have significantly decreased the creation time prompting auspicious production of last printed duplicates. The news which was created on line machines are currently gotten through online system of organizations, accordingly decreasing the reliance on tying faculty of generation. Computerized printing minimizes the use of movies and chemicals utilized as a part of the ordinary printing procedure. It further lessens the part of checking staff and faculty as machines guided by machines could now enlist and streamline printing employments set by the creation unit work force.

Low cost: Web renditions have cleared route for expense cutting measures in daily paper industry. The variable cost (the expense of newsprint) which constitutes 50 to 60 percent of aggregate expense could respectably be brought down by dispatching e-paper which generally requires just a machine and web association for its dispatch, as numerous entries are accessible on productive web system offering gigantic web spaces for facilitating locales and e-papers. In light of the way that News Print involves 50-60% of aggregate expenses for a daily paper, the web page has developed as an option against climbing expense of distribution.

Quality: The utilization of cutting edge business printing hardware has likewise empowered daily paper industry to print duplicates with overall characterized properties. Equipped for delivering high accuracy realistic prints alongside other post office based mail printing administrations, the cutting edge computerized printing machines are printing 30 thousand or more duplicates for every hour as against 3000 to 4000 duplicates for every hour distributed by old printing press.

ICT AND NEWSPAPER MARKETING

The web form of daily paper has without a doubt extended the range of daily paper, the daily paper version of Allahabad city could now be perused through web by an individual sitting in London. This demonstrates a slow slant of daily papers towards reception of B2c model as now daily paper could connect straightforwardly with pursuers. With the development of data and correspondence innovation, sound and visual media are in the field with moment and wide scope. Conflicting to what prior was assumed that the appearance of data engineering would hurt the print media, detail demonstrates that no innovation can beat the print media, which dependably thinks that its own particular level. The print media has reacted to the new changes and difficulties with its modernization. They have acknowledged the data engineering, which brought about better scope with incredible velocity and reasonable cost (https://rni.nic.in/pii.asp).

Questions for Discussions

According to a report of World Association of Newspapers conducted in US year 2008, 81 percent of online daily paper users additionally read a printed daily paper at any rate once a week and 50 percent of them invested the same time as they did a while ago with daily paper substance, while 35 percent invest more of a chance general with daily paper content. How has digitization and web influenced the intensity and the quality system in the publishing sector?

References

****

6

Marketing Strategies for Kara Wipes in Punjab

N. Karthi • R.R. Ghatak[2]

Abstract

There has been a key change in the market shares of the wet wipes all over the country and it is of great importance to improvise the wipes into the market especially during summer season. The influence of the Chinese wipe products into the country, thereby affecting other wipe prices. The present case tries to unveil the Distribution Logistics of Kara wipes in and around the district of Ludhiana to capture the challenges in the market. The case aims to explore new markets for Kara wipes within the market and develop marketing strategies to increase the sales. The case study was conducted in 3 cities Moga, Phagwara and Jalandhar, India. The findings revealed that the selection of the potential and capable distributor for an area resulted a better scope of increasing the market shares and value of KARA wipes in that region.

Keywords: Distribution channel, Logistics, Marketing strategies.

INTRODUCTION

Birla Cellulose is the Aditya Birla Group's umbrella brand for its range of cellulosic fibers. It comprises versatile sub-brands; Birla Viscose, Birla Viscose Plus, Birla Modal, and Birla Excel. These brands offer a wide range of functional benefits such as soft feel, high moisture absorbency, bio degradability and comfort to the wearer. These fibers have multiple applications including apparel, home textiles, dress material, knitwear, non-woven etc.

Fiber is one of the oldest businesses of the Aditya Birla Group that commenced in 1954. Birla Cellulose is a world leader in viscose staple fiber (VSF). Its production is spread across six countries, viz. Canada, Thailand, India, Indonesia, China and Laos. The Group independently fulfils India's entire VSF requirements.

---

[6] N. Karthi is a student of MBA programme Class of 2015 and R.R. Ghatak, Asst. Prof in the Area of Operation management with Amity Business School. The authors have developed the case solely for class discussion for the programmes in management. The author does not intend to illustrate effective or ineffective handling of a managerial situation. The case study does not represent or endorse the views of the managements about the issues in the case. The case has been compiled with both primary and secondary information.

With a strong focus on Research and Development (R&D), the Group's R&D initiatives span the entire value chain Viz:

- Grasim Forest Research Institute pulp to plantation research.
- Birla Research Institute for Applied Sciences pulp to fiber research.
- Textile Research & Application Development Centre (TRADC) value chain from fiber to garments/made ups.

"Nature is the genesis of all that surrounds us; therefore, what other than nature could be the origin of Birla Cellulose. Nature is the source of Birla Cellulose and herein lays the inspiration of our logo.

'Fibers from Nature' is our theme and our message: Leaves fall and grow all over again; they are a renewable resource of nature. Birla Cellulose is much like these leaves and is made from the same trees. The floating leaves symbolize the key characteristics of Birla Cellulose which are "comfort and lightness". The vibrant green indicates that Birla Cellulose can take on vibrant colours. The circle signifies the cycle of nature and sustainability.

The company has certain issues regarding the sale of KARA wipes in some of the key parts of Punjab. Then it had the idea of appointing new trainees in some of the key cities and making them the headquarters of the distribution channel analysis. There had been a serious discussion going on in the company higher authority levels, regarding the reasons for the drastic decrease in the sales of the wet wipes during that quarterly.

BACKGROUND

Concept of disposable wipes have evolved into a global business generating more than $ 6 billion sales. Achieving strong growth year after year, the category now has a major role in the personal care market. Having a large number of variants from make-up removal and deodorant wipes in personal care to floor and furniture cleaning products in household care, disposable wipes have gradually grown to offer a wide range of new applications, replacing the traditional combination of cloth, cotton and cleaning solution. Changing trends in the wipes industry have also been driven by new product developments and the positive reception of new product applications by the consumer. Wet wipes continues to grow in the international market, still it is important to be cognizant with the difficulties to promote it in many other markets. The companies that combine cutting edge technology with the development of new and innovative ideas will be able to survive in the long run. In India wipes are generally made of Viscose and Spun lace.

PRODUCT PROFILE

Birla Cellulose manufactures 98% of the Viscose Staple Fiber in India, so it is positioned to do well against other local players as they would have to purchase VSF from Birla's. In last 3 years there has been a tremendous increase in the number and types of wipes available to the consumer. From baby wipes and facial wipes to disinfecting wipes, giving a much better substitute to conventional cloth and liquids. These wipes are mainly designed for convenience in this fast moving world, whether that is for own personal use or to deal with the unhygienic conditions for your family. The disposable facial wet wipes market is estimated at Rs 8 crores. Kara holds a dominant position in market with turnover of Rs. 4.5 crores thus capturing 56% of the market. However this sector in India is currently fragmented and unorganized. Ginni filaments (Noida) also hold a strong position in wet wipes market, though their product can't be matched in terms of quality to Kara.

People of US and Europe spend 6 to 10 per cent of their income on disposable products, whereas in India, it is only 0.0001 per cent. Wet wipes have a business of about $6-billion worldwide but in India, it's in a nascent category. It is assumed to be lifestyle product and not an essential one, so it will take a while before full potential is explored. Due to increasing advertising Consumer awareness about hygienic products have increased, price reductions and the launch of cheaper variants by other manufacturers over the latter half of the year have also resulted in increased awareness about the product. Skin Care wipes have also benefited because of the fast pace of life in cities and the rise in the number of working women, who tend to rely more on disposable products when working in the kitchen or travelling outside of the home for convenience. Leading market research agency KSA TECHNOPAK conducted a market survey and discovered that there is a huge untapped potential for wipes in India. The disposable wipes market in India face stiff competition from cheaper Chinese companies. These Chinese wipes are not of good quality and can have adverse effects on skin. However they are able to succeed in the Indian market because of the price factor as people in India are very price sensitive. But with increasing awareness about quality, gradually people will shift to a better product like Kara.

DISTRIBUTION LOGISTICS OF KARA WIPES-CONCERNS

Different strategy was always in demand for the requirement of the distribution channel expansion in new places for Kara.

How doKara wipes merchandise transfer from the manufacturer to the end user?

Intermediaries in the channel are called middlemen. Those who actually take title to the merchandise and resell the goods are merchant middlemen. Those who act as Broker but do not take title are agent middlemen. Merchant middlemen include wholesalers and retailers.

Agent middlemen include Manufacturers Representatives, brokers, and sales agents. Whether these exchange processes occur between manufacturers and their suppliers, retailers and consumers, or in some other buyer-seller relationship, marketing channels offer an important way to build competitive advantages in today's global marketplace.

This is so for two major reasons:

- Distribution strategy lies at the core of all successful market entry and expansion strategies. The globalization of manufacturing and marketing requires the development of exchange relationships to govern the movement of goods and services. New technologies are creating real-time (parallel) information exchange and reducing cycle times and inventories. Take as an example Dell Computer, which produces on-command, customised computers to satisfy individual customer preferences. At the same time, Dell is able to align its need for material inputs (such as chips) with customer demand for its computers. Dell uses just-in-time production capabilities. Internet-based organizations now compete vigorously with traditional suppliers, manufacturers, wholesalers, and retailers. Marketing channels always emerge from the demands of a marketplace. However, markets and their needs are always changing. Its true, then, that marketing channels operate in a state of continuous evolution and transformation. Channels of distribution must constantly adapt in response to changes in the global marketplace. This new selling orientation inspired the development of new intermediaries as manufacturers sought new ways to expand market coverage to an increasingly mobile population. The selling orientation required that more intimate access be established to a now more diversified marketplace. In response, wholesale and retail intermediaries evolved to reach consumers living in rural areas, newly emerging suburbs and densely populated urban centers. Relationship marketing is driven by two principles having particular relevance to marketing channel strategy:
- Long-term, ongoing relationships between channel members are cost- effective.

FUTURE PROPOSITION - MARKETING STRATEGIES TO INCREASE THE SALES

- **Launching kara wipes in canister packaging:** Though Canister packaging is not as durable as wipes packet. It offers more convenience when someone uses Kara while sitting on his office table or keeping it in car. This type of packing is quite common in foreign countries. Some of the companies which sell wet wipes in Canister packing are:

(a) Kleen Test Products, Ohio, America.
(b) American Hygienic Corporation, China.
(c) Shanghai Shine Plastic Co. Ltd., China is contract manufacturer for canister packaging.

- **Placing kara in cash and carry stores:** Cash and carry stores are a prime location for wholesalers and institutional buyer's. All the variants of Kara can be placed for bulk purchases.

- **Moisturizing and sunscreen wipes for gynaecologist:** Pharmaceutical companies can be Approached with moisturizing, sunscreen and other variants that do gifting for gynecologist.

- **Revising discount schemes:** Most of the companies were not convinced with Discount Slab as they assumed offered rate as Wholesaler rates and not corporate rates for Kara.

- **Approaching event management companies:** Event management companies can be targeted and corporate tie-ups can be done for High-end fashion shows, Polo matches, International conferences etc.

- **Blogging about kara:** A blog can be created on internet which can educate people about skin care and benefits of using Kara wipes. The blog can be made interactive by putting surveys on it. The link of the blog can be bulk mailed to various people falling within the target market.

- **Displaying customized stickers:** While explaining customization options to corporate Clients ,it is better to show them few customized stickers of our current client thus giving them affair idea of how we can customize their brand on sticker. Since, Handy are also a premium product from Grasim Industries; few suggestions for HANDY'S are given as below.

- **Using handy in high-end restaurants:** Handy is a very good substitute of conventional finger bowls which are used in restaurants. Expensive restaurants in 5 star hotels which offer Indian food to its guests, give finger bowls to them for cleaning their hands. It could be replaced by Handy which offers better sanitation properties and can help restaurants for environmental audit.

- **Advertisement for handy:** Handy has a vast potential in field of Hand sanitizing wipes. Advertisements on television can be aired to make people aware of it. One such concept is: 'Two house wives are sitting. One is disturbed because her son is not well and often misses his school. She says that she takes all the precautions to ensure hygiene of hiss on buts till he becomes sick. The second wife says that keeping an eye on child is difficult when he is in school. They may not know if he washes his hands before eating his Lunch. It is best if she keeps a sachet of Handy in his Tiffin box, so before eating his lunch, he can sanitize his hand. 'This advertisement can targeted for Housewives who can use this product for both her Husband and Children.

Questions for Discussion

Design an efficient Distribution system for Kara Wipes to reach its distributors, retailers and/or end users. Is KARA a substitute for Handkerchief? Promotional activity is highly needed for the company to make strong market position. How much important is this issue? Do you think Company should work on free sample; scheme to attract the retailer and consumer. Will it be of worth?

References

****

7

Effective Embedding of Implant in FMCG Supply Chain at GSKCH

Rishu Mittal • Ruchika Nayyar[7]

Abstract

The modern trade sales team of GlaxoSmithKline Consumer Healthcare is currently facing the problem in the back-end sales operations which leads to loss in sales opportunities for both the company (GSKCH) and their key modern trade accounts (Big Bazaar, Apollo pharmacy, etc.). The company realised that the role of supply chain is of utmost importance and is not just restricted to mapping the supply and demand at optimal cost and service output level, rather much more which includes competitive advantage too. Keeping the importance of effective and efficient supply chain in mind, this company is trying to maximize the utilization of the implant resource for the modern trade channel by understanding what are the service gaps the client or the modern trade account is facing and how the implant as a coordinator can be enabled with a robust process to support efforts to minimize these losses, where an implant can be defined as a secondment, i.e. a person who is detached from their regular organization (GSKCH in this case) for temporary assignment at the delivery centre of the modern trade account.

The company wants the clear picture of the expectations from the implant in modern trade retail and pharmacy outlets, standard job description of the implant and also wants to support implant's role with key reporting and monitoring formats using IT-based solutions.

Keywords: Modern trade, GSKCH, Sales, Supply chain, Implant, IT.

INTRODUCTION

Indian retail industry is witnessing an unprecedented growth and is amongst the top 10 retail markets globally. In 2013, it was estimated at US$ 520 billion. However, it is expected to grow at a CAGR of 13% to reach US$ 950 billion by 2018. The major contributor to this growth is the

---

[7]Rishu Mittalis a student of MBA (M&S) programme Class of 2015 and Ruchika Nayyar, Asst. Prof in the Area of Marketing and Sales with Amity Business School. The authors have developed the case solely for class discussion for the programmes in Management. The author does not intend to illustrate effective or ineffective handling of a managerial situation. The case study does not represent or endorse the views of the managements about the issues in the case.

growth in modern trade industry which is expected to increase from 7.5% in 2013 to 10% in 2018 at a robust CAGR of 19-20% in the same period.

By 2020, it is expected to reach US$ 1.3 trillion and modern trade will increase almost by six times from current 27 billion USD to 220 billion USD in 2020. The factors behind this growth are:

- **Regulatory factors** such as liberalization of FDI policies in retail coupled with the expected roll-out of the goods and service tax.
- **Demand-side factors** such as rising disposable income , increasing urbanization, highly aware and affluent young population, growing number of working women and change in consumer preferences.
- **Supply-side factors** such as rapid real estate and infrastructural development, easy credit availability, innovative physical and online channels and increased service orientation.

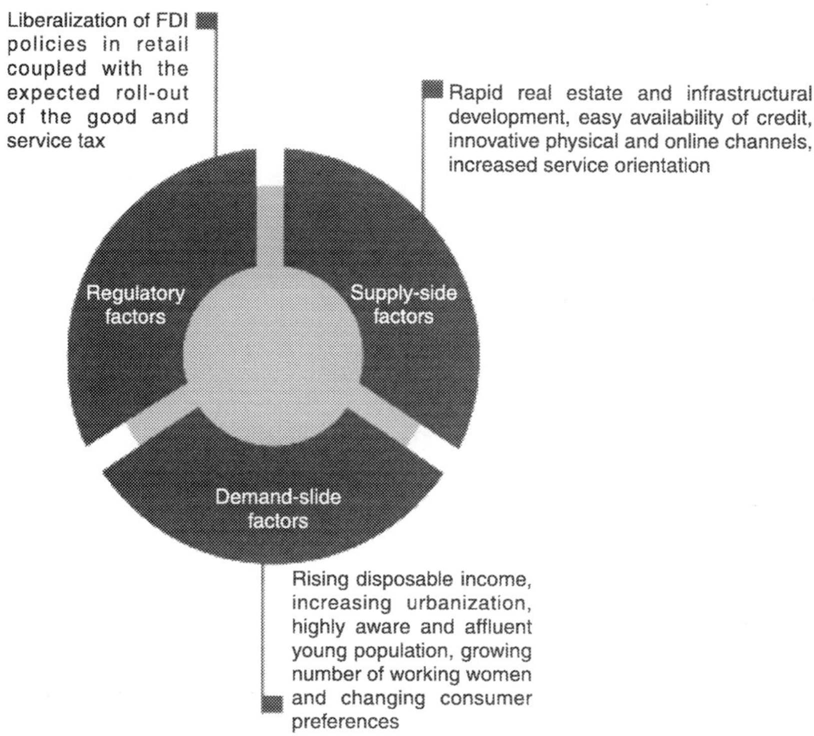

The role of supply chain is of utmost importance in almost every industry and is not just restricted to mapping the supply and demand at optimal cost and service output level, rather business leaders are demanding much more from supply chain which includes competitive advantage too because the companies in India are operating in dynamic environment and faces challenges from three dimensions namely, changing business context, evolving policies and regulations and ecosystem limitations. Also, India being the dispersed country requires excellent distribution and logistics management to reach widely spread Indian consumers. Although, the supply chain of FMCG industry is the most innovative and act as a role model for other industries but despite of this, FMCG supply chains faces distinctive challenges and issues such as bullwhip effect, higher transit losses and higher return goods. The productivity of any company can be greatly enhanced by efficient supply chain management. It is because of the fact that the supply chain activities directly or indirectly have a great impact on operating cost, revenue growth and asset management which effects company's financial performance.

This is an era of information technology and the use of IT tools are indispensable for any industry to survive in this techno-savvy world. There is a widespread use of IT tools to evaluate the efficiency and profitablity of supply chain in FMCG sector. The challenge posed by supply chain is in the form of significant wastages in the delivery centres and operations of the existing FMCG chains in India. The size of the country and varied taste and preferences of the Indian consumer across the country leads to complexities in inventory management for the FMCG chains. Since food products are perishable in nature, therefore, there is a strong need to develop a strong back-end sales operation support for the success in the modern trade industry in case of FMCG. The investment in specialised SCM IT solutions can help to manage not only the stores but also the delivery centres of the accounts. Although the use of IT tools and management information systems in FMCG supply chain is vital but still manual workforce is very much required to manage the back-end sales operations effectively.

Glaxo Smith Kline Consumer Healthcare (GSKCH) is a leading FMCG company. It deals with range of consumer healthcare products under following broad categories:

- **Health Food Drinks (HFD):** Horlicks, Boost.
- **Wellness or OTC:** Eno, Iodex, Crocin and Ostocalciun.
- **Oral Healthcare:** Sensodyne and Paradontax.
- **Foods:** Horlicks Biscuits, Foodles and Oats.

The Modern Trade sales team of GSKCH caters to the needs of modern trade retail as well as pharmacy outlets. The modern trade team follows the following sales organization structure:

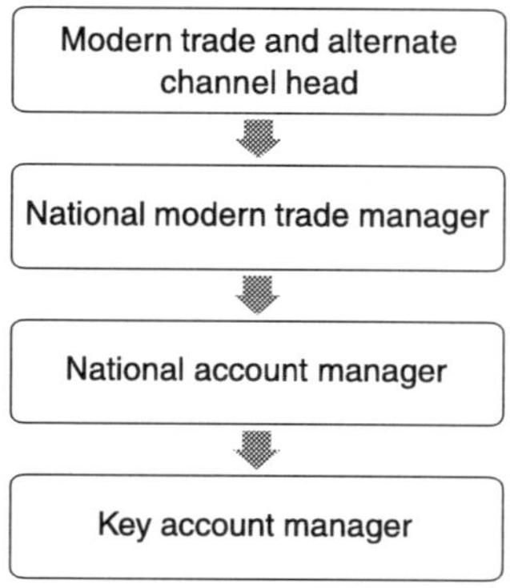

The supply chain process for modern trade at GSKCH is as shown:

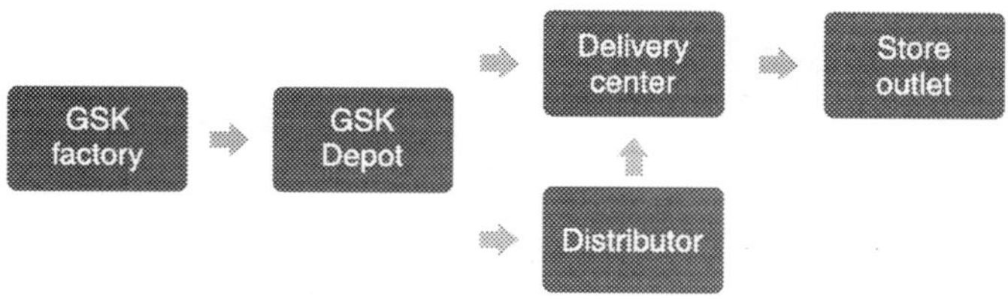

The modern trade sales team of the company is currently facing the problem in the back-end sales operations which leads to loss in sales opportunities for both the company (GSKCH) and their key modern trade accounts (Big Bazaar, Apollo pharmacy, etc.). The company is in the process of devising ways so as to minimize these losses.

OVERVIEW AND ANALYSIS

Currently, modern trade sales team of GSKCH is facing the problem of loss in sales opportunity due to inefficiencies in the back-end supply chain. To come with the solution to this problem, the managers at GSKCH decided to backtrack the supply chain so as to understand the problem at each level in the supply chain process. The managers then decided to observe the following at each level of the supply chain. The entire process of transferring the stock from the depot to the DC and then to the store outlets is monitored by an implant. An implant can be defined as a secondment, i.e. a person who is detached from their regular organization (GSKCH) for temporary assignment elsewhere (account's delivery centre in this case). The implant is a full time employee of GSKCH but is placed and works at the delivery centre of the account. The managers realised that to minimize these sales losses, the role and responsibilities performed by the implant must be accessed. The following are the key observations:

1. **Store outlet:** Market visit to the store outlets (both retail and pharmacy) for gathering data about the stock status and problems faced. Some of the findings are:

(i) Ostocalcium which is in huge demand has not been in supply pipeline from many days.

(ii) Some of the SKU are not at all mapped to some stores.

(iii) MRP is not updated.

(iv) The stock with old PROMO scheme is still available in the stores although the company has discontinued the PROMO scheme on the particular SKU.

2. **Delivery centre:** Personal observation at the delivery centres (DC) of the key accounts so as to track the movement in and out of DC and to devise the mechanism for increasing efficiency at DC. Some of the findings are:

(i) Delivery centres of the account not only cater to GSKCH but also to other companies. The arrangement of the stock in the shelf at the DC follows the dictionary rule regardless of the brand of the product. Thus, it is not an easy task for the implant to manage the stock health at DC.

(ii) Some of the accounts do not entertain implant in their DC which hinders the implant to perform their functions well.

(iii) Implant is most of the time idle at the DC when there is no delivery.

3. **GSK depot:** Personal observation at the depot so as to understand the reasons behind goods return and other problems which causes inefficiency in the depot operations. Some of the findings are:

(i) The major reasons for goods return are:

- EAN mismatch.
- Wrong SKU supplied.
- Number of PROMO items received is less than the number of SKU.
- Goods damaged during transportation (especially in case of biscuits, foodles and oats).
- The stock is not fresh as per account norms.
- Purchase Order (PO) has already expired.

(ii) The timely unload of the stock at the DC of the account is critical for efficiency in depot operations. In some cases, the transport vehicle is made to wait for long hours at the account's DC before the stock is unloaded which causes inefficiency in the entire supply chain process.

(iii) In some of the cases, the stock gets damaged during unloading which is the fault of account. Still, it is returned stating that the stock was damaged during transportation.

The implant usually maintain a master file and fill rate of key accounts. The managers asked for all the data of Q1, 2014 from the implants. (For the type of data, see appendix).

STATUS REPORT

According to the sales managers of the modern trade team of GSKCH, the following supply side gaps are leading to inefficiency in the supply chain operation:

(i) **PO-order Mismatch:** It signifies that the order could not be completed because of issues pertaining either in purchase order or in invoice.

(ii) **MRP Mismatch:** It signifies that the order could not be completed because there is a difference between PO per unit cost and invoice per unit cost.

(iii) **Discontinued SKU:** It signifies that the order could not be completed because order is for that SKU which no longer exist in GSK master.

(iv) **Incorrect Caselot:** It signifies that the order could not be completed because of errors during item creation.

(v) **Promo/Non Promo Order Mismatch:** It signifies that the order could not be completed because order is for Promo but only the Non promo stock is available or vice versa.

(vi) **Freshness Issue:** The agreement with modern trade account states that the stock supplied to these accounts must be at least 75% fresh. The freshness issue problem signifies that the order could not be completed because depot is not carrying fresh stock as per account norms.

(vii) **Block for Procurement:** It signifies that the order could not be completed because a particular SKU is blocked by the company for some changes such as change in packaging.

(viii) **Capped Quantity:** It signifies that the order could not be completed because depot cannot supply more than agreed (agreed with general trade) quantity to the account.

Also, the managers comes up with the following shortcomings in the current system of GSKCH:

(i) Currently, the role and responsibilities of the implant resource are not well defined. Every implant is operating in their own best way which leads to unaccountability on the part of the implant for the operations not performed.

(ii) The implant is not properly updated about the changes in MRP, discontinued SKU, block for procurement SKU and obsolete promotion schemes.

(iii) All the implants are currently using different formats on the basis of the format provided by their respective modern trade accounts.

(iv) With the current data available with the implant, the expectations of the supply chain team members cannot be met.

CASE PROBLEM

The sales team is concerned that these inefficiencies in the supply chain process will lead to poor results in the forthcoming quarter and will impact the sales from modern trade channel of the company. If the team will not take any action now, the chances are they will get stuck with the collapsed system. The modern trade sales team calls management trainees to help them by assessing the situation and come up with a reaistic and effective solution to minimize these losses. The team has asked the management trainees to define the role and responsibilities of the Modern Trade implant with standardized formats to measure implant performance and effectiveness and has asked for the following deliverables:

1. Expectations from the implant in Modern Trade retail and pharmacy outlets.
2. JD (Job description) of the implant and core KPI's.
3. Key reporting and monitoring formats to support implant performance.

Questions for Discussions

- Considering yourself as a management trainee, think over the situation and come up with the appropriate solution for the same.
- Suggest certain IT solution that can help in devising these standardized formats which can track performance of the supply chain against core KPI's.
- Comment on the statement that the role of sales team in any organization is not just restricted to ensuring sales but beyond.

References

****

APPENDIX

The following data has been collected by the managers from the implants:

1. **Master of key accounts:** It refers to the excel sheet used by existing implants. It contains the following information:

   (i) **GSK SKU Code:** It can be defined as a unique identifier for each distinct product that can be purchased from GSK.

(ii) **Customer Item Code:** It is a code used by accounts to identify different products available at their outlet.

(iii) **SKU Description:** It is short text which complements the SKU code for complete identification of a particular SKU.

(iv) **Depot Name:** Name of the GSK depots.

(v) **Depot Location:** It refers to the place where a particular GSK Depot is located.

2. **Fill rate of key accounts:** Fill rate is used to calculate the service level between GSK and the key accounts. This Excel table contains the following information:

(i) **Purchase Order (PO) Number**: It is a numeric code (e.g. 470265432) which identifies the particular commercial document issued by modern trade account to GSK.

(ii) **PO Date:** It is the date on which PO was generated by the account.

(iii) **PO Cancel Date:** It is the date on which PO will stand cancelled if the order is not supplied till date.

(iv) **PO Extension Date:** Occasionally mentioned, it refers to the agreement between GSK and Modern trade account to extend expiration period of a purchase order.

(v) **Delivery Date:** It refers to the date on which the order is supplied to the DC of the account.

(vi) **Order Quantity:** It refers to the quantity of items in number ordered by the account.

(vii) **Supply Quantity:** It refers to the quantity of items in number supplied by the GSK depot.

(viii) **Order Value:** It refers to the total amount (in INR) of the order placed.

(ix) **Supply Value:** It refers to the total amount (in INR) of the order supplied.

8

It's Time to Taste Eggless

Dheeraj Mugrai • Namita Kapoor[8]

Abstract

Bakery industry in India is the largest of the food industries, in which cake is an item preferred most for celebrations and deserts. People like to celebrate with their loved ones on any occasions making it special. In today's time people have become more specific about their choices. Their eating habits have changed about bakery products and resulted in a rapid growth in popularity among masses. This case study is about a famous bakery "Amar Bakery", located in Shahdara, which always gave their efforts to be the best in their market and always trying to meet the changing taste of their customers to woo them. Taking this changing eating habits and taste into consideration, they are deciding to make their all products egg free and be the first 100% eggless bakery in their area. Thus case study details about the situations, problems and parameters about this major decision of ending the use of eggs in their products.

Keywords: Bakery industry, Consumer behaviour, Customer satisfaction, Key retail, Product innovation, Expansion, Logistics management.

INTRODUCTION

Started in 1962, Amar Bakery takes great pride in the fact that they are known for their great taste, remarkable decoration and high quality standards of all their products. Producing quality bakery foods at a good value for customers is one their mission, and is a major reason for the company's near consistent year-over-year growth. Critical to the quality of the company's bakery foods is ensuring that their products are always served fresh.

Keeping the traditional taste for more than four decades, they were making fresh cream cakes which were made using the egg ingredients. But now there is a change in Indian culture, more people have changed

---

[8]Dheeraj Mugraiis a student of MBA programme Class of 2015 and Namita Kapoor, Asst. Prof in the Area of Economics with Amity Business School. The authors have developed the case solely for class discussion for the programmes in management. The author does not intend to illustrate effective or ineffective handling of a managerial situation. The case study does not represent or endorse the views of the managements about the issues in the case.

their preference to egg free cakes. They buy cakes not only for celebrating their occasions but also serve to god in temple. Some people also distribute cakes in temple; this has a very high cultural value. So taking this into consideration, Amar Bakery thought to make their products completely egg free. Before implementing this decision, they have to face numerous problems:

First is, they have to make the trust of 100% eggless guaranteed in customers mind that they were having earlier for egg products.

Second is, they have to change their complete labour so as to get the same perfection in production of egg free cakes also.

Third is, this change was all about for boosting their sales, but they are not sure about the effects of this change on their sales, whether it will be positive or negative.

Despite all these problems there was certain limitation also that there were still customers who always ask for fresh cream cakes only. So after implementation of their change of making egg free bakery, they will not be able to take orders for fresh cream cakes or any other egg product.

THE SITUATION

Producing quality bakery foods at a good value for customers is one part of Amar bakery's mission, and is a major reason for the company's near consistent year-over-year growth. Critical to the quality of the company's packaged bakery foods is ensuring that the baking environment and equipment is always clean and the products are served fresh. They always think to do something new to boost their sales.

The decisions of this firm are made keeping into account a number of factors like cost, quality, and presentation. But the most important factor is to enhance customer satisfaction. This can be realized by two recent changes made to the store.

There were renovations made to the ground floor of the bakery to improve the appeal of the room. Four new counters to showcase their products have also been added. These counters were selected among numerous other options because of how they made the products stand out. These were unlike the others that had remarkable designs because they provided more lighting and space for the products themselves.

A large flat screen monitor was also purchased and hung near the windows so that passers-by could look at the products on sale. This decision, too, was successful as the shop was located outside a main road.

Another thing that impacted the store was the improved packaging of the products. Earlier, all products below a certain amount were wrapped in plastic bags. However, in an attempt to enhance customer satisfaction, all goods are now packed in a large box with the Amar Bakery logo.

Now for the current decision, they have to find genuine egg free raw material supplier, which will be used for making egg free cakes. Also they have to ensure the standard quality of their products.

They have to make the trust of 100% eggless guaranteed in customers mind that they were having earlier for egg products.

They have to change their complete labour so as to get the same perfection in production of egg free cakes also.

This change was all about for boosting their sales, but they are not sure about the effects of this change on their sales, whether it will be positive or negative.

Right now, despite taking an extra effort in ensuring their products have the best quality chocolate and resources, their prices are relatively cheap. The reason, provided by them, is to accommodate the local customers of the region who stick to a particularly low budget. Therefore, it would be better that they set up a counter in a relatively more posh area, offering the same excellent quality but with increased prices. Since the brand of Amar Bakery is quite known in the area, since it would be a good reason to expand keeping the heart of the operations in Shahdara.

Amar Bakery has wide range of products; their main product being fresh cakes for all occasions. Amar Bakery also has chocolates, pastry and cake and chocolates combo in their product line. It also sells packaged cakes which are available at their stores. Amar Bakery also has different kind of breads and a variety of snacks for dine-in customers. It has also started home deliveries and online booking and gifting system.

Every area has a new hangout, a cake shop! The cake shops differ in variety, quality, price and more. The oldest known brand of cakes is Amar Bakery. Some of the flavors of Amar Bakery cakes include: Black Forest, Dutch truffle, Butterscotch and Pineapple are some of the popular choices. The range starts from Rs. 150 for half kilo cakes and so on. There are a variety of cakes one could choose from for their kid's special day. To mention a few cakes, of fancy shapes like alphabets, numerals and cartoons.

For kids, cartoon characters like Mr. Bean, Doremon, Ben 10 etc are charged somewhere in the same figures. They have the most delicious array of cream cakes, fresh fruit cakes and a variety of fancy cartoon-shaped cakes. At Rs.400 a kilo for the fancy cakes, it definitely is value for money. The new fantasies of personalised cakes are 'Photo Cakes'. An imprint of the image of your loved ones or your child on the cake is a hit amongst children. These could range of an approximate Rs. 500 a kilo.

A quote is apt especially in a corporate setting. Corporate gifting is an investment in relationships which are vital for future any organization. And, what other better article to strike a right chord than gifting "food consumables". Because, as the popular saying goes, "the way to man's heart is through the stomach".

A recent survey by American Express revealed that almost half of corporate gift selections are now food-related, replacing the flowers and gift cards that have dominated earlier.

Flexibility, choice and the near-universal appeal of indulgent foods allow businesses to easily find a custom solution that invokes a positive feeling and a sense of bonding in recipients. Cakes are strongly associated with celebrations and happy moments; If organization is targeting birthdays/anniversaries for gifting, then there cannot be a better gift than the Cake to create an everlasting impression; For festive occasions like X'mas/New Year, cake is the most appropriate gift. Last but not the least; it stands out in a clutter of gifts one receives on popular occasions.

Pricing is the only mix which makes an income for the company. The staying 3p's are the varying price for the company. It is to generate and design a product; it costs to spread a product and charges to advertise it. Cost must support these components of the mix. Expenses is difficult and must indicate provide and requirement relationship.

The customer's understanding of value is an essential aspect of the price billed. Customers attract their own psychological picture of what a product is worth. A product is more than a physical item; it also has psychological definitions for the customer. The risk of using low price as a promotion is that the customer may feel that quality is being affected. It is essential when determining in price to be fully aware of the brand and its benefits. A further impact of decrease is that opponents coordinate costs leading to no extra requirement. This means the profit edge has been reduced without increasing product sales.

Price of Amar Bakery cakes are reasonable as compared to its competitors. The prices of cakes vary on their size. On an average a half kg cake would cost something around 200 and it goes up to a 1000 depending on the size and the flavour.

Bakery shop is also the retail industry that has been widespread this time where the bakery shop is not only limited to offering only products, but service is one more point which will be owned by every bakery shop when the bakery shop provides a good service to every customer that exist. Service industries that are labour intensive, the need for manpower to do much because most of the activities of companies that cannot be replaced by machines. Based, the growth and expansion of industry in the present must be accompanied by an earnest effort to prepare staff and skilful leadership in the organizational structure capable of providing the best service to the purchaser.

Amar Bakery has used media such as TV, print, web, hoardings, etc. to advertise its products. It regularly comes out with offers on festive occasions.

Recently to promote its cakes and chocolates it came out with a range of a special cakes and chocolates for all those SSC (X^{th} Standard) students who passed out this year. It has also planned for chocolate baskets for the boys and girls. The successful boys can be gifted with a blue coloured basket filled with assorted chocolates and decorated with a Doll (Boy). And, similarly the girls can be gifted with a pink coloured basket filled with assorted chocolates and decorated with a Doll.

The backbone of any business is logistics. Amar Bakery receives orders from the retail shops in the night a day before and all the products are manufactured throughout the night and the shops are supplied through company vans by early morning. All the products need to be delivered within a span of 1 – 3 hours' time and they follow the rule ferociously. All their vans are insulated and even carry insulated shippers.

The backbone of any business is logistics. Amar Bakery receives orders from the retail shops in the night a day before and all the products are manufactured throughout the night and the shops are supplied through company vans by early morning. All the products need to be delivered within a span of 1 – 3 hours' time and they follow the rule ferociously. All their vans are insulated and even carry insulated shippers.

Some of the vans are refrigerated, which ply on the long routes. A single van generally covers 3 to 4 shops orders so that they can deliver the orders on time without any delays.

As mentioned in the earlier topic of logistics about when the retail shops place their orders for the next day it is equally important to know how their ordering system functions.

Initially they had to follow the telephonic ordering system. In this method they were provided a telephone help line number. The head of the retail shop have a checklist of items which contained all the items which Amar Bakery prepares. The person has to place orders in different categories of cakes, pastries, savories, and namkeens etc. as per their requirements for the next day.

This required manual efforts and was very time consuming method of order placing as the person has to name each and every item he requires. Also there were chances of mistakes being committed because of certain communication barriers which could lead to losses both to the bakery and the retail shop. To replace this method they came up with the fax system for placing orders. The fax system of placing order was practiced for a long period when the need for more innovation was required now with increasing use of technology and innovation in every sector, Amar Bakery has also come with a modern method for placing orders called as

E-ordering, this method involves placing orders through net. It involves use of the most popular and appreciated way of communication that is internet. This method can be much relied upon for quick placements of orders and does not involve any tedious task.

Another situation was about their logistics management. They were having three factories each for bakery, sweets and warehousing at different locations. This was costing around seventy thousand rupees per month for rent and transporting all their products to their retail showroom. So they decided to shift their factories to the floors above their retail showroom.

This would not only save their rent and transporting costs but also increase their product life span, as soon as products are ready, they will be placed in counters in a couple of minutes.

LOGISTICS MANAGEMENT

Logistics is the management of the flow of goods, information and other resources between the point of origin and the point of consumption in order to meet the requirements of consumers (frequently, and originally, military organizations). Logistics involves the integration of information, transportation, inventory, warehousing, material handling, and packaging, and occasionally security. Logistics is a channel of the supply chain which adds the value of time and place utility.

Logistics management is that part of the supply chain which plans, implements and controls the efficient, effective forward and reverse flow and storage of goods, services and related information between the point of origin and the point of consumption in order to meet customer and legal requirements.

The backbone of any business is logistics. Amar Bakery receives orders from the retail shops in the night a day before and all the products are manufactured throughout the night and the shops are supplied through company vans by early morning. All the products need to be delivered within a span of 1 – 3 hours' time and they follow the rule ferociously. All their vans are insulated and even carry insulated shippers.

Some of the vans are refrigerated, which ply on the long routes. A single van generally covers 3 to 4 shops orders so that they can deliver the orders on time without any delays.

ORDERING SYSTEM

As mentioned in the earlier topic of logistics about when the retail shops place their orders for the next day it is equally important to know how their ordering system functions.

Initially they had to follow the telephonic ordering system. In this method they were provided a telephone help line number. The head of the retail shop have a checklist of items which contained all the items which Amar Bakery prepares. The person has to place orders in different categories of cakes, pastries, savories, and namkeens etc. as per their requirements for the next day.

This required manual efforts and was very time consuming method of order placing as the person has to name each and every item he requires. Also there were chances of mistakes being committed because of certain communication barriers which could lead to losses both to the bakery and the retail shop. To replace this method they came up with the fax system for placing orders. The fax system of placing order was practiced for a long period when the need for more innovation was required now with increasing use of technology and innovation in every sector, Amar Bakery has also come with a modern method for placing orders called as E-ordering, this method involves placing orders through net. It involves use of the most popular and appreciated way of communication that is internet. This method can be much relied upon for quick placements of orders and does not involve any tedious task.

Since their decision would change their core product characteristics, they decided to start with one separate eggless cake counter so as to try market and get the customer preferences.

Not only this , they also took feedback from their customers through face to face communication and you will be amazed about their responses, every 9 out of 10 customers said " It will be an excellent step"...

Questions for Discussions

- Analyze the case and identify the main issues faced by the organization.
- If you were the head of department, what would have been your initiative over the issue?
- Which things have to be remembered before launching a new product?
- Explain the process to be followed in order to end up with high sales of the organization.
- Suggest some strategies for their further expansion in other areas.

References

****

9

Dimensions of Service Quality in Banks: Learnings From a BOI Branch

Ambuj Kumar[9]

Abstract

Banking sector in India is flooded with great opportunities and challenges. This has resulted in high competition among the banks for retaining their customer and to establish a long term relation with them. Various longitudinal, meta-analysis and multicultural studies and techniques have been conducted in the Banking industry and it reveals a strong relationship between customer service and Market share. Today banks are searching for niche service quality offerings to increase and gain high level of customer satisfaction. The present case is constructed based on Bank of India with an objective to understand the dimensions to increase the service quality in banks. The SERVQUAL model of Parasuraman et al. (1988) a five-dimensional construct of perceived service quality: tangibles; reliability; responsiveness; assurance; and empathy was used.

Keywords: Banking industry, Competition, Service quality, Customer satisfaction.

INTRODUCTION

Bank of India was established by a group of eminent businessmen on 7th Sept 1969 with it's headquarter located in Mumbai. Government of India owned it since nationalization in July 1969 along with 13 banks. The Bank of India was the first bank to operate a fully computerized branch and ATM back in 1989. In 1946, among all Indian banks, BOI was the first bank to open a branch at London in 1946. In 1976, BOI also opened its first branch in Europe, Paris. Internationally, Bank has spread its network at key banking and financial centres viz. New york, Paris Singapore, Hong-Kong and London. The international business has a total contribution of about 30% in bank's overall business. Bank of India follows ISO 9001-2000 accreditation in term of quality service. Bank of India aims to become

---

[9]Ambuj Kumar is a student of B. Tech & MBA programme Class of 2015 with Amity Business School. The authors have developed the case solely for class discussion for the programmes in Management. The author does not intend to illustrate effective or ineffective handling of a managerial situation. The case study does not represent or endorse the views of the managements about the issues in the case.

Bank of choice with an attitude of care and concern for their customer through superior pro-active innovation, an art banking service.

SERVICE QUALITY CONCERNS IN BANKING SECTOR

As per a survey over 1000 bank customers, it was found that majority of the customers believes that there is no improvement in the service quality of the banks over past 4-5 years. Most of the customer also thinks that it has become worse .Various complaints regarding the service quality have risen up to 5% from previous year. So there are a large number of factors indicating to poor service quality among the banks. Service quality has impact on services experiences, decision making of customers, relationship to costs, customer loyalty, customers satisfaction, customer retention and purchase retention. In order to provide better product and services it is important for the banks to understand customer specific need, expectations and wants.

SERVICE QUALITY MODEL

In this competitive world, there is no difference between a marketing company and banks. It is quite essential for the service centre in general and financial institutions such as bank in particular to identify the demand, need and want of the customers and find ways to meet these requirements effectively and easily. Since the product and price difference are not clearly seen between the banks by an ordinary customer, the only factor left behind with the banking institutions is to retention of its customer and maintaining long-term relationship with them by providing good service quality. Ensuring high level of service quality help any organizations in this banks to differentiate itself, gain competitive advantage and increase its efficiency among competitors. A good service quality can help retain internal customers- employees for longer period, external customers and stakeholders.

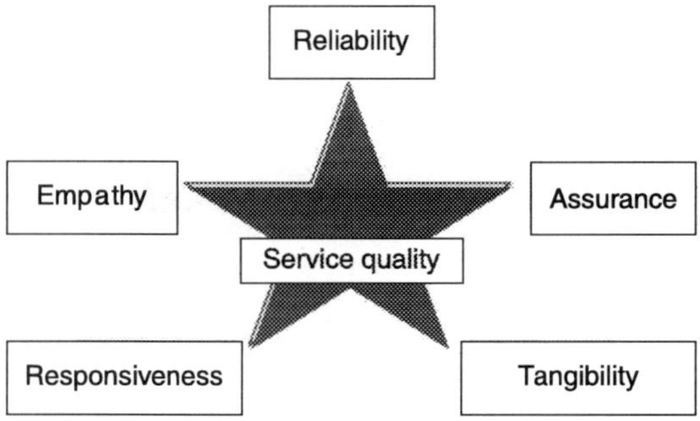

Figure 9.1 Service quality model.

FRAMEWORK FOR THE CASE BOI

Even though there are various tools developed to measure the level of service quality offered to customers the most acknowledged tool is the SERVQUAL, now called as RATER a quality management framework developed by the researchers Zeithaml, Parasuram et al., in the mid 80's in the service sector. In the present case to obtain primary data for understanding the service quality of the bank, the five dimensions of the RATER model is used to obtain information on the quality service of the Bank of India in relation customer perception.

Communication, courtesy, competence, reliability, security, understanding, responsiveness, tangibility, empathy etc. are some of the dimensions of a service quality as mentioned by Berry, Parasuraman ,and Zeithaml, (1985) . Out of these dimensions top 5 factors that represent a service quality are:

- Tangibles: Equipment's, appearance of personnel and Physical facilities of the bank.
- Reliability: Accurately and dependably performing the promised services.
- Responsiveness: Providing quick services and willingness of bank's personnel to help customers.
- Assurance: Ability of employee to build confidence and trust through knowledge and courtesy.
- Empathy: Providing individual attention and caring to the customers. (Include communication and understanding the customer).

In banking sector the interaction between customer and service provider is high. Customers are the direct observer or an active participant of the production process, so the execution of the process also influences the service quality. A small technical fault can provide a negative impression on the customer or can also provide positive impression on customer if personnel have worked very hard to overcome the fault and make the customer work done. These encounters between the service provider and the customer ensure the level of service quality and hence determine the level of customer satisfaction. The attitude, behaviour, knowledge and interest of the service provider can bring a great change in the perception of customer towards the service quality of bank.

Factor that ensures a good service quality is by intention, loyalty, and trust of the employee towards the company, whether bank performs its service at right time, whether the employee give the time duration of a process to be performed, whether bank fulfil its promises, Whether transactions made by bank is safe and error free and whether employs are interested in solving customer problem. In short, whether company is able to fulfil those promises that they made to the customers at the time of product sale. So, it is important to provide service at first at right time.

Accurately performing the services can ensure excellence of service quality. Performing the service inaccurately increases the cost to company in term of rework cost and cost of losing other customer due to negative viva voce spread by unsatisfied customer. Since services are intangible in nature hence criteria for perfect services are more subjective that criteria for imperfect goods. So, customer feedback is required after every service so as to ensure that the service provides is as per expectation or not. This gives the degree of reliability.

Tangible factor is one of the most important factors that ensure the service quality of the bank. These mainly consist of physical appearance of employ, physical facilities, materials that are visible to the customer as they enter the bank. These are the factors that a customer notice as soon he enters the bank forms initial impression about the bank. These tangible items if unmanageable can give a negative impact toward the quality service no matter how appealing the items may be. Using tangible items to improve quality require attention to small details that competitor may not give value .Visible details about the tangible product can provide a signal of caring and competence for the customer.

RATER TOOL FOR BOI

RATER is a useful quality assessment tool which can be used to measure and define various banking service quality.

The RATER can benefit Bank of India in following ways:

- Understanding the impact of customer values and belief with different quality dimensions.
- Exploring the Customer satisfaction and analysing it through multi-face tool.
- Customer's satisfaction and service encounter are linked through quality.
- At each level, different important information is obtained.
- Provide results that are useful to meet customer needs.

ANALYSIS OF CUSTOMER DATA IN A BOI BRANCH- LEARNINGS

There are four questions for each dimension in the questionnaire was asked to fifty customers by convenient sampling. Data of these questions were recorded and analysed to obtain the data for a particular dimension at the branch level (place of the branch not disclosed). The mean of the variables – tangibility, reliability, assurance, responsiveness and empathy for this particular sample comes out to be 3.8650, 3.6750, 3.9750, 2.4450 and 3.6450 respectively, with Test value = 3.

Table 9.1 One-sample statistics.

	Mean	*Std. deviation*	*Std. error mean*
Tangibility	3.8650	.46623	.06594
Reliability	3.6750	.68185	.09643
Responsiveness	2.4450	1.17401	.16603
Assurance	3.9750	.58739	.08307
Empathy	3.6450	.44633	.06312

One sample t-test statics for variables namely tangibility, reliability, assurance and empathy are 13.119, 7.000, 11.737 and 10.219 respectively with p value 0.000. The t-test static for variable comes to be -3.343 which is *negative* but significant.

Table 9.2 One-sample test.

	Test Value = 3					
	t	*df*	*Sig. (2-tailed)*	*Mean Difference*	*95% Confidence Interval of the Difference*	
					Lower	*Upper*
Tangibility	13.119	49	.000	.86500	.7325	.9975
Reliability	7.000	49	.000	.67500	.4812	.8688
Responsiveness	**- 3.343**	**49**	**.002**	**- .55500**	**- .8886**	**- .2214**
Assurance	11.737	49	.000	.97500	.8081	1.1419
Empathy	10.219	49	.000	.64500	.5182	.7718

Regression analysis was applied to link overall dependent variable i.e., service quality of the bank with the 5 dimension of service quality as independent variable. All the predictor variables (Tangibility, Reliability, Responsiveness, Assurance and Empathy). The value of y intercept for the given model comes to be – 0.944. The coefficient value for the independent value comes to be (Tangibility = 0.114, Reliability = 0.591, Responsiveness = 0.505, Assurance = 0.192 and Empathy = – 0.40).

The customers are satisfied with most of the dimensions of service quality offered by BOI. There is not much gap between all the dimensions, except one of the dimension as most of the customers are dissatisfied in responsiveness, Whereas other results shows that BOI is a better service provider in all other the dimensions. Therefore concentrations must be made to ensure that the employees give prompt services, be always are ready to answer the questions, be trustworthy and be willing to help the customers. So the present case highlights the area which require urgent attention of the management, employees and the policy makers of the industry is creating interventions to improve responsiveness of employees towards customers. To conclude, rationality and division of labour had definitely increased productivity but human responsiveness is mostly driven by emotions. Hence the question remains, will customers understand that bank employees can also break down like the servers in the computer network and will they accept that increase in response time is an error unavoidable!!!

Questions for Discussions

If you are the Branch Head, what would be your initiative to improve your branch score in the dimension 'Responsiveness'? Can BOI identify more competencies to add to its Service quality to customers?

References

- Zeithaml, V.A., Berry, L.L. & Parasuraman, A. (1996). The behavioral consequences of service quality. Journal of Marketing Research, 60(2), 31-46. http://dx.doi.org/10.2307/1251929.
- Zeithaml, V.A., Parasuraman, A. & Berry, L.L. (1990). Delivering Quality Service: Balancing Customer Perceptions and Expectations. New York: NY: Free Press.
- Malhotra, N. & Mukherjee, A. (2004). The relative influence of organisational commitment and job satisfaction on service quality of customer-contact employees in banking call centres. Journal of Services Marketing, 18 (3), 162-174.
- Kang, G.D. & James, J. (2004). Service quality dimensions: An examination of Gronroos's service quality model. Managing Service Quality, 14(4), 266-277.
- www.iibf.org.in/documents/reseach-report/Report-26.pdf

Part II

"Understanding the Business Propositions: Partnering to Scale up"

10

Supply Chain Finance for Petroleum Dealers in Meerut

Manu Jain[10]

Abstract

Today, the competition is so intense that every organization irrespective of its size wants to maximize their working capital to increase investment opportunities thereby increase the profitability chances. State Bank of India sees this as an opportunity, and to bridge this gap the bank is now offering a new facility to Indian Oil Corporation and Bharat Petroleum Corporation Limited's dealers with supply chain financing. This case is an attempt to understand the scope and opportunity of supply chain finance to petroleum dealers. It also focuses on money requirement needs of petroleum product vendors depending upon number of petroleum products they sell. It is evident from the case that more products require more working capital as the amount of transaction of very high value in petroleum business. The case reveals this facility is provided to the customer's online for their convenience it is also aimmense task to teach people to get friendly with internetusage especially in rural areas. It also draws a line between various facilities provided by various banks within the region and the factors which give a competitive advantage to bank.

Keywords: Supply chain finance, Dealership and online facility.

INTRODUCTION

Aberdeen Group defines Supply Chain Finance (SCF) as "a combination of Trade Financing provided by a financial institution, a third-party vendor, or a corporation itself, and a technology platform that unites trading partners and financial institutions electronically and provides the financing triggers based on the occurrence of one or several supply chain events."

Supply chain financing results speak to a mix of engineering and budgetary administrations that nearly interface, innovation in

---

[10]Manu Jain is a student of MBA programme Class of 2015 in Amity Business School. The author have developed the case solely for class discussion for the programmes in Management. The author does not intend to illustrate effective or ineffective handling of a managerial situation. The case study does not represent or endorse the views of the managements about the issues in the case.

administration of suppliers fiscal establishments. They are intended to increase the viability of money supply chains by avoiding hindering expense moving by enhancing the accessibility, preciseness, conveyance and expense of money for all members. They are centered around encouraging exchange led on an open record premise, which now makes up eighty for every penny of world trade market. Extensive and large varieties of commercial ventures were appropriate for (and have begun to embrace) supply chain finance results, including: substantial gear, retailing, automobiles, conveyance, gadgets, fabricating, nourishment and beverage, pharmaceuticals, and innovation. Supply Chain Financing is offered by banks to acknowledge lower costs for credits. This facility is offered to the suppliers on the premise of the financial soundness of the purchasers. Credits can hence been offered at a lower rate of interest, financing than the supplier would have the capability to arrange on its own. A series of exchange financing given by a money related establishment, or an organization itself, an outsider merchant and at an innovation stage that unites exchanging accomplices and monetary organizations electronically and gives the financing triggers focused around the event of one or a few supply chain occasions.

The main goals of supply chain financing are;

(a) To enhance a production network's working capital.

(b) To empower a purchaser to amplify the instalment terms of local and outside suppliers.

(c) To give suppliers access to reasonable liquidity by leveraging the purchaser's stronger FICO assessment.

Supply chain finance is an innovative plan to reduce the working capital of many organizations. Its underlying component is reverse banking making of the system purchaser as opposed to supplier-driven system. Executing supply chain finance is a troublesome and drawn out activity that requires top administration consideration. But it guarantees huge reserve funds. In their overview, results demonstrate that, on normal, organizations lessen their working capital by 13% and suppliers decrease their working capital by 14%. Three components separate effective executions of supply chain finance from less fruitful ones: picking the right keeping money, guaranteeing main sponsorship, and including no less than sixty percent of the supply-base.

Supply chain finance is more than simply a joint collaboration between the money offices of two or more organizations. Rather, supply chain finance is checked by the extreme focus on the use of monetary instruments or fiscal perspectives, which may apply to any branch of an association between organizations. Case in point, joint efforts between a modern organization and a budgetary administration supplier are dependably a monetary joint effort since the fiscal administration supplier offers money related backing or information. In this way, we can talk about supply chain finance if the relationship is centered on the supply chain items, courses of action, considering all streams, present and altered possessions, and in addition work force that are included in the production network of both the organizations.

Encountered with cumulative pressure to meet short term liquidity needs, companies are looking inward for ways to issue trapped cash from operations. Today's CFOs and bankers are taking a fresh look at how their corporeal supply chain is impacting their corporation's cash flow and working capital management. Worried about the rising risks in their supply chains restricting from the economic stress on suppliers, unpredictable energy and commodity prices, and broad based financial disorder, today's executives are actively looking at supply chain finance possibilities in terms of depressing their overall financial supply chain costs.

There is no interrogation that the philosophies of supply chain finance are robust and that the correspondent benefits are significant. The perception to get financed on the basis of the client's soundness should line up hordes of roaring companies demanding for such an attractive—and apparently low cost—facility. Yet, reality shows that supply chain finance programs are developing very slowly and are far from widespread implementation. Financial institutions have invested noteworthy resources in money, time, and staff to develop and market supply chain finance programs but have so far acquired relatively small returns compared to the preliminary opportunities. Non-finance companies represent a growing supply chain finance substitute to banks but their resources is a small fraction of what financial organizations may put in habitation.

A preliminary impression of the market and of its performers proposes likely lawful motives for such a slow uptake:

- The amount of actualities among companies about supply chain finance is still truncated.
- Banks are unenthusiastic to makeover antiquated credit-checking, threat and indemnity management processes and adapt them to the new offerings.
- Companies have already financing outlines in place and do not want to change.
- Some large conglomerates are already consecutively self-made supply chain finance programs.
- Corporations do not line up finance experts in supply chain finance program teams.
- Accounting and inspecting issues may recommend in contradiction of the introduction of supply chain finance programs.

- Corporation internal divides between treasury and procurement functions represent a thoughtful apprehension.

CASE PROBLEM

To support organizations in streamlining their payables process, fiscal fundamentals have made information technology as a mediating facility between buyer and supplier. These information technology results are by and large offered to the buyer permit free capacity. The monetary focal point for each one gathering will shift, contingent upon the terms of the transaction between supplier and the buyer.

Still after numerous attempts it is a big question mark on why people do not perceive online banking as a safer option. There is a prevailing gap that why people having limit in their account are not comfortable in availing supply chain financing services.

ANALYSIS

As per the analysis, 90.9% of the respondents are males and 9.1% are females. As per the analysis, 11.4% respondents belong to the age category from 20 years-30 years, 22.7% belong to the age category from 31 years-40 years and 65.9% respondents belong to 40 years and above. As per the analysis, 68.18% respondents possess Indian Oil Corporation Limited's dealership and 31.82% respondents possess Bharat Petroleum Corporation Limited's dealership. As per the analysis, 50% respondents offer 3 petroleum products, 47.73% respondents offers 2 petroleum products and 2.27% respondents offer only 1 petroleum products. As per the analysis, 45.45% respondent's petrol pump offers 16 hours facilities to people, 38.64% respondent's petrol pump offers 24 hours facilities to people and 15.91% respondent's petrol pump offers 12 hours facilities to people. As per the analysis, 97.7% respondents maintain stock and 2.3% respondents do not maintain stock.

As per the analysis, 36.36% respondents have their company's account in State bank of India, 11.36% respondents have their company's account in Punjab National Bank and Oriental Bank of Commerce, 9.09% respondents have their company's account in Syndicate bank, 6.82% respondents have their company's account in Union Bank of India, 4.55% each of respondents have their company's account in Axis bank, Industrial Credit and Investment Corporation of India (ICICI) and Allahabad bank and 2.27% each of respondents have their company's account in Housing Development Finance Corporation (HDFC), Industrial Development Bank of India (IDBI), Andhra bank, Central bank and Co-operative Bank.

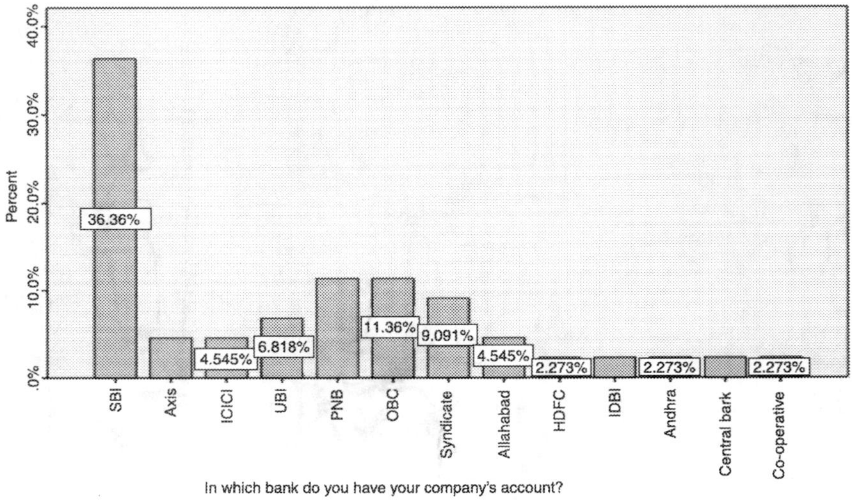

Figure 10.1

As per the analysis, 47.7% respondents have current account. As per the analysis, 10 respondents who have Limit account pay more than 12% rate of interest, 7 respondents who have Limit account pay 11.6%-12% rate of interest, 3 respondents who have Limit account pay 10.6%-11%

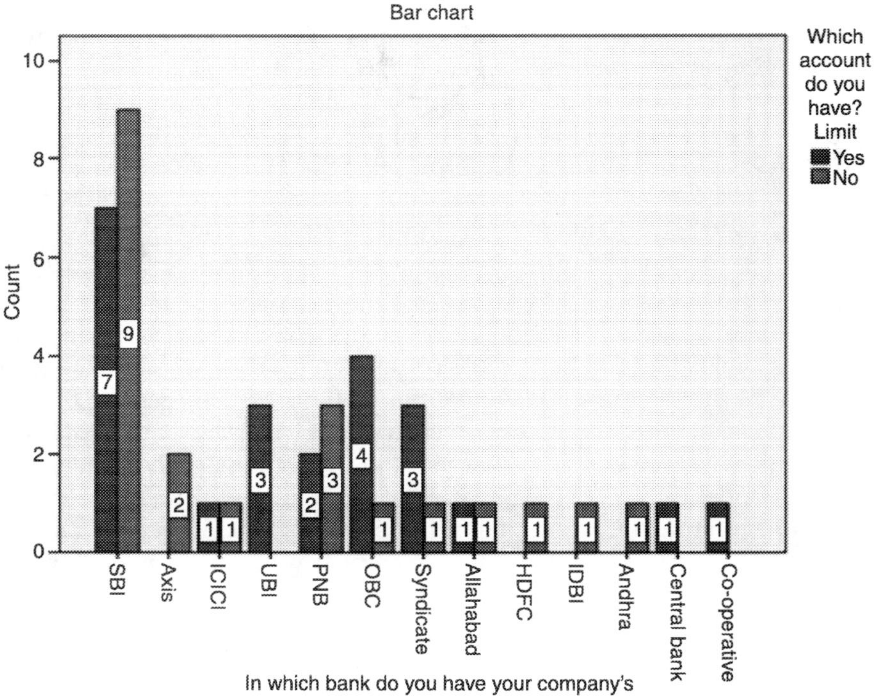

Figure 10.2

rate of interest, 2 respondents who have Limit account pay 11.1%-11.5% rate of interest and 1 respondent pays 10%-10.5% rate of interest. As per the analysis, 93.18% respondents do not have supply chain financing facility on their account and 6.82% have supply chain financing facility on their account. As per the analysis, 50% of the respondents have internet facility at their petrol pump and 50% of the respondents do not have internet facility at their petrol pump. As per the analysis, 86.36% respondents have not taken any loan and 13.64% respondents have taken loan. As per the analysis, 7 respondents have limit account in State Bank of India, 4 respondents have limit account in Oriental Bank of commerce, 3 respondents each have limit account in Syndicate Bank and Union Bank of India, 2 respondents each have limit account in Punjab National Bank, 1 respondent each have limit account in Central Bank, Co-operative Bank, Allahabad Bank and Industrial Credit and Investment Corporation of India (ICICI).

As per the analysis, 2 respondents have supply chain financing facility available in their State bank of India account and 1 respondent has supply chain financing facility available in their Industrial Credit and Investment Corporation of India (ICICI) account.

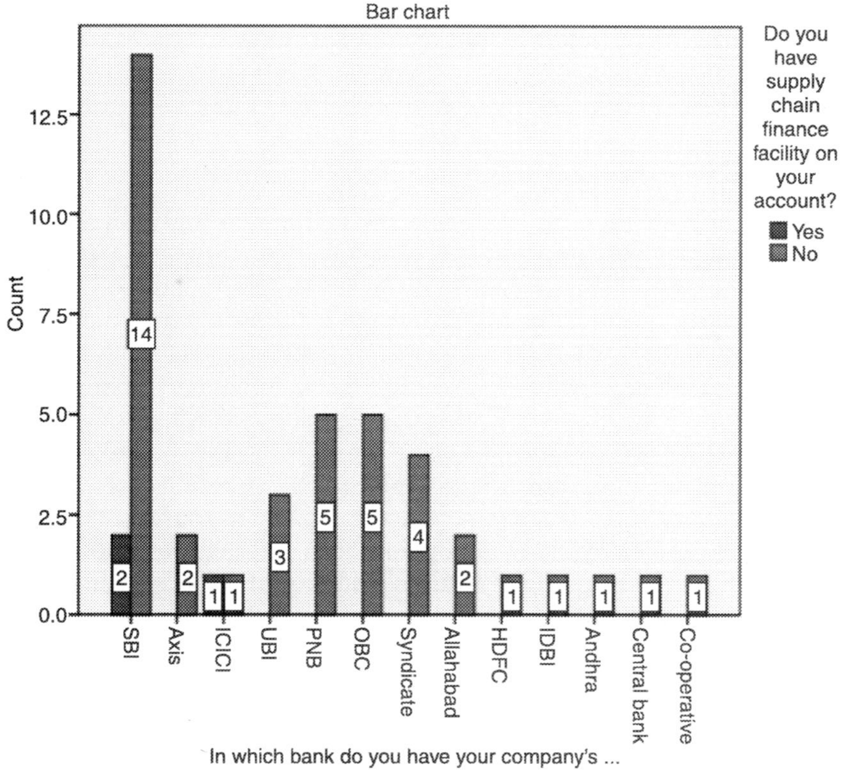

Figure 10.3

As per the analysis, the Pearson correlation between the respondents who have a limit account and they also have a supply chain financing facility available to them is .258 which is moderately positive. As per the analysis, the Pearson correlation between respondents who have an account in State Bank of India and have a limit account is –.129 which is moderately negative correlated and the Pearson correlation between respondents who have an account in State Bank of India and have supply chain finance facility available is .170 which is moderately positive correlated. As per the analysis, out of 7 respondents who have limit account in State Bank of India 2 respondents each pay more than 12%, 11.6%-12% and 10.6%-11% rate of interest and 1 respondent pays 11.1%-11.5% rate of interest. 1 respondent who has a limit account in ICICI pays rate of interest of more than 12%. Out of 3 respondents who have a limit account in UBI, 2 respondents pay rate of interest more than 12% and 1 respondent pays a rate of interest of 11.6%-12%. Out of 2 respondents who have limit accounts in Punjab National Bank, 1 respondent each pays a interest of 11.6%-12% and 10.6%-11%. Out of 4 respondents who have limit accounts in Oriental Bank of Commerce, 2 respondents pay more than 12%, 1 respondent each pays a interest of 11.6%-12% and 10%-10.5%. Out of 3 respondents who have limit accounts in Syndicate Bank, 1 respondent each pays more than 12%, 11.6%-12% and 11%-11.5%. 1 respondent who has a limit account in Allahabad Bank pays 11.6%-12% rate of interest and 1 respondent each who has a limit account in Central bank and Co-operative Bank pays a rate of interest of more than 12%.

REMARKS

The flexible policies that are made is more favourable to the Indian oil corporation's dealers as compared to Bharat petroleum corporation limited dealers as they are more in number. As customers having a limit account in state bank of India is quite high this points out to the stringent and regular demand of money to the petroleum dealers, so more advertisements and promotions are being done to reach out to the customers unaware of the services provided by state bank of India. As many petroleum vendors have access to internet they are also being reminded of the convenience of the service they can avail sitting at their place as a marketing cause. More number of branches are also being opened to reach out to the petroleum vendors in the remotest place so that their needs and requirements could be met which were not met due to unavailability of support from state bank of India.

Questions for Discussion

'Supply chain finance is an innovative plan to reduce the working capital of many organizations' Do you agree with the illustrating case.

How can banks strategize to capture more petroleum vendors through Supply Chain Finance?

References

Aberdeen Group, "Get Ahead with Supply Chain Finance: How to Leverage New Solutions for End-to-End Financial Improvement," July 21, 2006.

11

Loan Disbursement in Reliance Capital

Shoumik Goswami • Tavishi[11]

Abstract

Non-Banking Financial Companies (NBFC) are those financial institutions which offer financial support similar to a bank but they do not have a banking license. Reliance Capital, one of the prominent NBFCs of India, is a constituent of the CNX Nifty Junior and MSCI India. The company is India's one of the highly valued financial service company in the private sector. Reliance Capital has interests in asset management and mutual funds; life and general insurance; commercial finance; distribution of financial products; private equity; asset reconstruction and other activities in financial services. The operations of the company have been observed and studied. The credit mortgage department mainly has three different categories: Home Loan, Loan against property and Construction Finance. The study aims to describe the complete loan disbursement process and also find out the prime factors on the basis of which the company offer loans to the customers. Using Discriminant analysis, it is found that the company relies on the customer's income, property value and loan amount to grant loans. The study reveals that the company offers loans to an extent of 68.8% of the customer's eligible income and property value. Various other factors like education, property type, rate of interest and tenure also influence the decision making process of the company.

Keywords: NBFC, Loan disbursement, Discriminant analysis, Reliance capital, Credit, Mortgage.

INTRODUCTION

The NBFCs have proved themselves to be an important part of the Indian financial system. They behave as heterogeneous units and involve themselves in a variety of activities like making loans and advances, leasing, public fund offerings, and ultimately lend to the spenders directly or indirectly. They even work with the industries and self-employed professionals. Due to their involvement in the financial segment, they now

---

[11]Shoumik Goswami is a student of B.Tech + MBA programme Class of 2015 and Tavishi, Asst. Prof in the Area of Economics with Amity Business School. The authors have developed the case solely for class discussion for the programmes in management. The author does not intend to illustrate effective or ineffective handling of a managerial situation. The case study does not represent or endorse the views of the managements about the issues in the case.

act as complimentary to banks due to their attractive rates and flexibility. Reliance Capital Home Finance is a subsidiary of Reliance Capital which is one of India's leading and fastest growing private sector financial services companies. It is currently ranked among the top 3 private sector financial services and banking groups, in terms of net worth. It has interests in asset management and mutual funds, life and general insurance, private equity and proprietary investments, stock broking, depository services, distribution of financial products, consumer finance and other activities in financial services. Reliance Capital, a constituent of S&P CNX Nifty and MSCI India, is a part of the Reliance Anil Dhirubhai Ambani Group. The Home Finance division deals with vehicle loans, mortgages, loans for SMEs (Small Medium Enterprises) and Construction Finance and Construction Equipment. These are further divided in a number of segments and are handled by the respective departments of the company.

CASE POINT

Loan disbursement is a cumbersome process and customers are offered loans on the basis of some specific factors. The study tries to simplify the entire loan disbursement process and discover those factors which are primarily important for a customer to have in order to avail loan from the company. The study will help customers and the company to identify those prime factors on which the entire decision making process of loan disbursement depends. It will help the consumers to predict their chances of getting loans from the company.

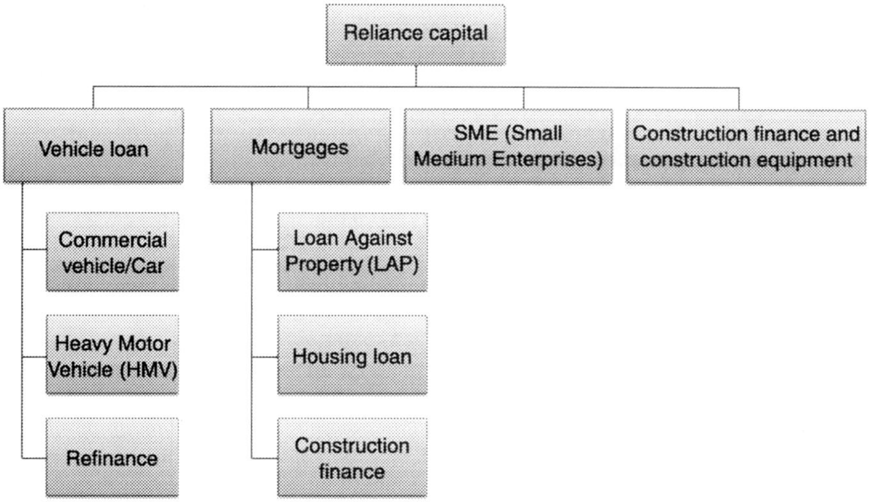

Figure 11.1 Product and services offered
Source: Compiled by author.

MEANING OF MORTGAGE

It is a debt instrument, which are used by the business firms and the individuals to buy a property/land without paying the entire value of that land. For many years, borrower pays interest every month and repays the loan in the specified period of time till he/she owns the property free from the bank. If the borrower will stop paying the interest on the loan, bank can claim on that property.

SEGMENTS OF MORTGAGE IN RELIANCE CAPITAL

There are 3 segments in Reliance Capital Housing loan (in housing loan there is Affordable housing also), Loan against property (LAP) and Construction Finance.

Housing loan: Loan given to the borrower by keeping that house (which borrower is supposed to buy) as a mortgage. In housing loan the borrower transfers the title to the lender company but on a condition that when the borrower repay its payment, the title would be transferred back to the real owner. In housing loan there is Affordable housing also which means the loan provided to the borrower is of the amount either of 25 lakhs and less than 25 lakhs.

Loan against property: Loan given to the borrower against his/her property i.e. the property which he/she already owes, by keeping that as mortgage to the lending company there is no compulsion like in the housing loan the money you are taking you can only use that money to buy the house, you cannot use that money for some other purpose but in the case of loan against property you can use the loan amount for other purposes also like for business purposes, for buying new property etc., but you have to give the reason for taking the loan before only to the lender company. In this, the nature of the property is determined by the value/ amount of loan and that property should not be mortgaged already.

Construction finance: This is financing the real estates by a mortgaged on the property which is being financed. The loan is given to cover the land cost i.e. for the development of the land and for construction of the building. The loan is disbursed- As and when needed, As the each stage is completed and according to a prearranged schedule. These loans are generally for long period like 20-30 years and it is repaid from the cash which is generated after the completion of the building.

Surrogate programmes: In case of self-employed individual, the documentation available such as income tax return profit and losses a/c may not reflect the actual income of the borrower. Accordingly the loan eligibility of the borrower is determined based on evaluation of alternate criteria to determine the borrower repayment capacity and the corresponding loan eligibility:

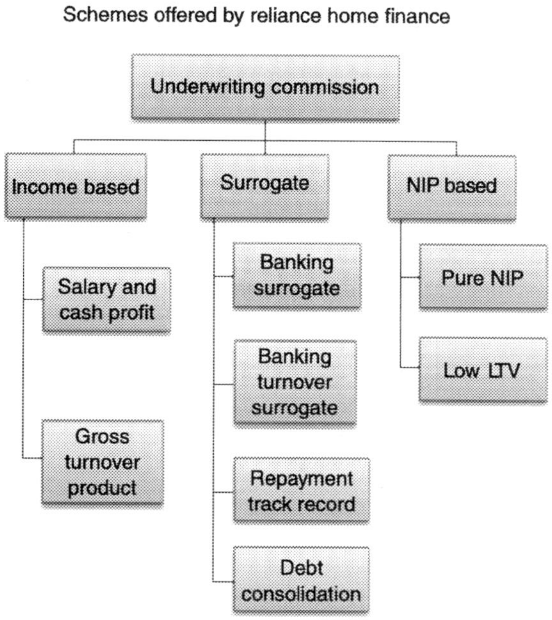

Figure 11.2 Schemes offered by reliance capital.
Source: Compiled by author.

- Banking surrogate.
- RTR surrogate.
- Debt. consolidation.
- Banking turn over surrogate.

Debt consolidation programs: In Debt consolidation the applicant having various loan of varying tenure and want to close these loans against a loan against property.

Multiplier of 1.25 times to be offered or POS for seasoning of 18 month. In case of 12- 18 month of seasoning of the loan, loan having seasoning of less than 12 month not to be consider for the purpose of consolidation.

Applicant should not have availed 30% of his total POS in last 12 month of his total borrowing. If the borrowing in last 2 months is exceed 30% upto 40% of the total borrowing then it need to be approved at 1.5% level. Beyond 40% the 40% case not to be consider for debt consolidation.

Loans in the name of directors and partner whose repayment is through company/firm's account can be considered for the purpose of the debt consolidation.

POS of loans availed in the last 2 months

Maximum loans are to be considered as:

- L1:3 loans.

- L3: 5 loans.
- L4: 7 loans.

The difference in the date of organization of 2 or more loans (with seasoning of 12 month or more) is less than 2 months, case need to be approved at L4 level.

LTV as defined in the policy of surrogate scheme.

Negative profiles are not to be funded under this scheme.

Applicant whose RTR is considered should be owner of the property and to be taken as main applicant. Age of applicant in such cases should not exceed 65 years at the time of loan maturity.

Track record of the loans consider for the purpose of should be clean, nil and bounces.

All other norms are applicant as per the basic mortgages policy.

RTR SURROGATE

Eligible - SEP & SENP

Period: Minimum 24 months repayment for fully disbursed loans pre EMI cases are not eligible. No deviation allowed in tenure norm.

RTR minimum loan: Personal loan (min of 2 lac), mortgages, car loan, medical equipment, office equipment (min of 5 lac) RTR accepted. In Non metros cases RTR criteria for car loan will be Rs. 3 lac.

Delayed payments: Maximum 2 cheque 12 months including EMI.

Obligation treatment: (i) POS of loans availed in last 12 months (from date of the application) to be deducted from eligibility. (ii) POS of loans with the vintage of 12-24 months have either to be taken over by RHF or have to be considered as obligation, if not closed by Reliance Home Finance.

Main applicant: Applicant whose RTR are considered should be the owner of the property and to be taken as main applicant. Age of applicant in such cases should not exceed 65 years at the time of loan maturity.

BANKING SURROGATE

Minimum 12 months bank statement only current account are allowed

Co-operative's banks accounts are not allowed a maximum of 2 cheque bounce allowed. This is including the EMI bounces in 12 months banking. For EMI bounces, cheque should be cleared with in period of 30 days from the date of bounces.

Eligibility computation: 12 months averages bank balance × 50% of averages of 12 months inflow = 5 times.

Product CAT: CAT A cities : INR 100 lac

CAT B & C cities: INR 75 Lacs.

BANKING TURNOVER SURROGATE

This program is applicable for SENP category only under this program, banking transaction of customer is to analyzed in order to calculate exposure amount

Additional Norms

Compute the credit summation for past 12 months in the OD/CC accounts of the client. Clubbing different bank account maximum of 2 accounts. If the credit summation for the past 12 months are to be arrived by clubbing 2 accounts then it is to be consider as 100% turnover.

Account should have average of at least 5 credit transaction per months for the 12 months.

Applications whose bank statements are considered as the owner of the property are to be taken as the main applicant.

Negative profile as not funded.

Pure NIP - In pure NIP (No Income Proof), in this case, client shows 40% or 50% of his/her income, in this case lending firm take into consideration other things than the income proof.

Low LTV - Low LTV (Loan To Value), in this case client gets only 10% or 20% of total value of the collateral property.

THE LOAN DISBURSEMENT PROCESS

The process of loan disbursement starts with credit appraisal when there is a client and clients are brought by the sales peoples or some agents working for the organization in Reliance Capital there are 3 channels/ sources through which clients come one is; DSA (Direct Source Agent) these are the companies which work for many organizations not only for the Reliance Capital and they get some share according to the loan amount, second one is; DST (Direct Source Team) these are the people who work Reliance Capital only but not as a part of the organization they are paid on fixed salary according to the decided slap/target and other than salary they get some incentive on the basis of the client's case, third one is; Direct it is through the employees working in the organization. Than process can only be started when there is some data about the client. Sales people search the client and talk to them and ask about their requirements and then tell what there company (Reliance Capital) provides, and collect the needed documents like;

- Sales people give application form to fill.
- KYC (Know Your Customer) documents.

The documents included in the KYC are Passport, PAN card, Voter's Identity Card, Driving license, Identity card (subject to the bank's satisfaction) and letter from a recognized public authority or public servant verifying the identity and residence of the customer to the satisfaction of bank. The collected data comes to Operation department of the organization and they generate a barcode for that individual client. The loan details are then entered into the LOS system and is checked for duplicity. The file then goes for underwriting by the Credit Processing Agents who check the CIBIL score and income eligibility. The average bank balance of the customer is checked by checking the bank statements of the clients mainly they focus on the 5th, 15th, 25th dates of the month because most of the banks draw their EMI's on these dates so CPA's track the record of the client, of those loans which are not shown under the CIBIL report. They check the RTR (Repayment Track Record), how the client is repaying his/her loan payment or the EMI's. Customers are required to go through a personal discussion session with the credit managers after which the Risk Containment Unit verifies all the documents. Finally the credit manager takes up the decision whether to sanction the loan or not and the loan gets disbursed.

LEARNINGS

NBFCs are now coming up with different services; they are not only managing their market share but also managing and protecting their profitability. In reliance capital the ratio of loan acceptance is not 100% and the reason it is lacking is that it has higher percentage of interest rate comparing others. Reliance Capital does it to minimize risk. The analysis provides an insight about the factors which determine whether the customer will be able to avail the loan or not. The primary factors which determine the outcome are income eligibility, property value and loan amount requested. The respective CIBIL scores and the requested rate of interest and tenure also plays an important role. Factors such as customer's education level, type of property and reason for loan are also considered by the company before coming up with a decision to offer the loan or reject it. The cases which were accepted only because of they had fulfilled the company's requirement and their eligibility was also coming out and they had given all the documents true and on time which out any questions from the credit managers, they revealed true information to the credit managers and credit managers also got positive response when they had went for the PD (Personal Discussion) and in Field Investigation was also positive.

Reliance Capital should try to increase their market share and involve customers from the mid-income segment as well to increase its sales. Also, a more competitive rate of interest will surely help to increase the number of customer turn overs. In order to sustain in the market, it is very necessary to offer something different to the customers to stand out in the crowd and Reliance Capital can surely do so.

Questions for Discussion

Analyze the case and identify the main factors on the basis of which the company offers loan to the customers. How can the decision making process get improved for efficient disbursement of loans?

References

- Jadhav, N. (2003). Loan Analysis: Understanding the Client and Business. *Reserve Bank of India Occasional Papers.*
- Kagan, M. (2012). *The Mortgage Game: The 5 Cs and How to Connect Them.* Advantage Media Group.
- Maysami, R.C. (2010). Understanding and controlling cash flow. *Financial management series. Retrieved November, 12.*
- Purohit, S.U., Mahadevan, V., Kulkarni, A.N. (2012). Credit evaluation model of loan proposals for Indian banks. *Internal journal of modeling and optimization.*
- Rajalakshmi, S., Pappeswari, C., Venkatesh, A. (2013). The study on housing loan borrowers of public and private sector banks in Thoothukudi area. *Researchjournali's journal of commerce.*
- Walia, B. (2014). The Home Mortgage Loan Crisis: A lesson in ignoring sunk costs. *Journal of Management.*

12

Market Strategies for SME Segment in Ludhiana and Chandigarh: A case of LeasePlan – Vehicle Leasing and Fleet Management Company

Harpreet Singh • Himani Sharma[12]

Abstract

LeasePlan is vehicle leasing and fleet management companyco-owned by Volkswagen Group and Fleet Investments. In western countries 40% of the total vehicle deals, companies are acquiring the vehicles on lease, in India it is only 5%. In India, many companies are not aware about the concept and ownership matters for them. This case study represents how Leaseplan conducted market research to make market strategies for SME segment in Ludhiana and Chandigarh. The market research was conducted to get the insights and information that how the companies acquire the vehicles in Ludhiana and Chandigarh. Interviews are conducted in mid and large size companies. CEO, MD, Finance heads etc are interviewed. Study reveals that it is mandatory for some companies to have own fleet to penetrate in such a huge market. Some companies hire the vehicles from local transport companies through bidding system. Companies are willing to pay a reasonable amount if drivers are also provided to company. All decisions regarding vehicles are taken at corporate offices. Companies prefer to finance their vehicles for different reasons.

Keywords: Operating lease, Penetration, Market strategies, Car leasing.

INTRODUCTION

LeasePlan is vehicle leasing and fleet management company. It is found by Anton Goudsmit and Huib van der Meulen in 1963. LeasePlan is co-owned by Volkswagen Group and Fleet Investments. The headquarters of LeasePlan is in the Netherlands. They make the life of their customers easier. They are continuously reinventing the leasing industry to save their customer's time and money. Started with open calculation system,

---

[12]Harpreet Singh is a student of MBA programme Class of 2015 and Himani Sharma, Asst. Prof in the Area of Marketing and Sales with Amity Business School. The authors have developed the case solely for class discussion for the programmes in Management. The author does not intend to illustrate effective or ineffective handling of a managerial situation. The case study does not represent or endorse the views of the managements about the issues in the case.

a revolutionary approach, a leasing company is created, which has now a global presence. With sustained growth and continue profit throughout the history, they are the world's leading provider fleet management services. They operate in 32 countries in across 5 continents bringing the many benefits of their approach to all their customers from multinationals to small businesses. Their innovativeness in tailored products and services, delivered real time saving solutions to fleet managers, so they have more time to manage the different kinds of fleet. From a single vehicle to a global fleet they keeps driver mobile and let them enjoy their ride. LeasePlan helps their customers to achieve their goal and improve efficiency. They are the value partner of business, large and small, around the world.

In 2013, LeasePlan has earned a profit of 326 million euro. LeasePlan has the assets of worth of 19.1 billion euro. LeasePlan is managing a fleet of 1.37 million vehicles. LeasePlan has 6571 employees working with them. LeasePlan is operating in Australia, Austria, Belgium, Brazil. Canada, Czech Republic, Denmark, Finland, France, Germany, Greece, Hungary, India, Ireland, Italy, Luxembourg, Mexico, Netherlands, New Zealand, Norway, Poland, Portugal, Romania, Russia, Slovakia, Spain, Sweden, Switzerland, Turkey, United Arab Emirates, United Kingdom, United States. The company has experience of 50 years and managing more than 1.3 million vehicles. Initially, LeasePlan provides products and services based on the model of American leasing practice, but company keeps on changing the products and services according to the customer's need. Lease Plan creates value along the automotive value chain. They do all things for their customers, except for manufacturing and distribution of vehicles. They do purchase, finance, insurance, maintenance management, accident management, rental, disposal and remarketing of vehicles. Lease Plan has different products for different customers. They customize the product according to the customer needs. Different vehicles are used by different companies for different purposes. Lease plan provide fleet for every need i.e. For Senior Managers, Field Staff, Tool for Trade, Business Applications. Company acquires cars to give it as a perk to their senior employees. For example: Audi, Mercedes, BMW. Company acquires for its field staff to travel from one place to another. For example: Swift, Toyota, Bolero, Polo. Company acquires vehicles for business purposes. For example: Tata Axe, Tata Magic, Tata Sumo, Tata 407.

In 1999, the company has started its operations in India. They have laid the foundation of corporate fleet management business in India. There are different products for different clients. LeasePlan has established its business in Mumbai, Delhi & NCR, Kolkata, Pune, Bangalore, Chennai and Hyderabad. LeasePlan has more than 1500 customers in India. Most of the customers are belong to Fortune 500 companies. Many people in India are not aware of Lease Plan. Lease Plan is doing B2B business. They want to make SMEs their customers. They have their operational reach in more than 250 cities. Lease Plan has products for big corporate houses. They don't know about the market potential in the identified cities, to sell their products and services in the same. They don't know what kind of product will be liked by SMEs. The main competitors of LeasePlan in India are ALD Automotive, BNP Arval (BNP Paribas), Oriks, Carzone. net etc.

LeasePlan wants to know how the SMEs are acquiring the vehicles in Ludhiana and Chandigarh. LeasePlan wants to know how much the concept of operating lease is popular in Ludhiana and Chandigarh, what financing options people prefer to acquire the vehicles. They want tosell their products and services in Ludhiana and Chandigarh.

SECTORAL OVERVIEW

In India, the infrastructure and lifestyle of people is improving day by day. In rural and semi urban area, the roads are improved. With the growth of education and service sector, the youth has more buying capacity and desire for luxury products like car. Today everyone needs a car. Companies also need different vehicles for different purposes. They are acquiring the vehicles in one or the other way. Company having sufficient fund with them prefer to purchase the vehicles. It is because they do not want to pay interest on it. Company having limited funds or want to expand their business with their personal funds, prefer to acquire the vehicles by taking loan from the banks. Company who do not want to own the vehicle for different reasons, prefer to hire the vehicles from local vendors and pay them rent for it. The vendors may have different agreements with different companies. Company who do not want to pay any down payment may go for finance lease. After paying all installments and residual value of the asset, the ownership of asset transfer to user or lesse. Company who wants to acquire the vehicle at low payment, want a simple solution for their fleet management, goes for operating lease. At the end of the term, the ownership is not transferred to the user and the vehicle is resold by lessor or owner. Lesse return the vehicle to leasing company who resale the vehicle in second hand car market.

Whenever we have a contract to pay rent more than eleven months, then we say we are paying lease. There are two types of lease i.e. Finance Lease and Operational Lease. It is very thin difference between loan and finance lease. In finance lease, lesse or user pay the value of asset in installments and after paying all the installments and residual value of asset, the ownership of asset transfer to lesse. In operating lease, the user of the vehicle has to pay fix lease rentals for the period, he uses the vehicle. These lease rentals are customized on the basis of the duration of using vehicles, distances to be travelled by the vehicle and other factors.

At the end of the term, the ownership is not transferred to the user and the vehicle is resold by lessor or owner. The leasing company also provides the services like maintenance, insurance, servicing, damage repairs, breakdown assistance etc.

Companies tell the leasing company about their requirements. What cars or vehicles they need. They also tell what services they are looking for. Lease rental amount is also depended upon the fact that which brand or model, companies want to acquire. If vehicle's value depreciates soon, then it has low resale value which means low amount will be subtracted from original asset value, resulting in higher lease rentals. Companies have to declare that how many kilometers they will drive a car. It helps the leasing company to predict that how much car will be depreciated over the contract period. If the companies drive a car more than the annual limit, then they have to pay certain amount per kilometer to leasing company. Companies have to give three months lease rentals in first month and they don't need to pay lease rent in second and third month. From fourth month onward, companies require to pay lease rentals till the end of the contract. If any company wants to terminate the contract before the agreed term, they have to pay additional charges for it.

Let us assume the original value of vehicle is Rs. 100. Company wants to acquire the car for 3 years. They drive the vehicle 20,000 kilometers annually. Leasing company will calculate the depreciation value of the vehicle during this period, for example Rs. 20 per annum. They will predict the residual value by subtracting the depreciation value from the original value of asset i.e. Rs. 100 – Rs. 60 = Rs. 40. Company does not need to pay the residual value. Residual value is recovered by leasing company by selling the vehicle in second hand car market. Company has to pay 60 rupees to leasing company. They don't need to pay 40 rupees. Company does not need to pay the residual value. Residual value is recovered by leasing company by selling the vehicle in second hand car market. Lease rentals will be made according to the vehicle company wants to acquire, residual value and the services they need from leasing company.

Companies have to take care of certain factors before going for lease. If the company wants more cash for different purposes, then leasing can be a good option. Due to low initial payment and small lease rentals, companies don't need to block their working capital. They can do many things with their personal funds. Companies should know that how much the use their vehicles. If they don't have an idea about the same, then it may become a costly affair for them due to decided annual limit of kilometers. Companies should also consider that how their employees drive the vehicles. If they are hard on vehicles, then companies have to pay heavy amount of wear and tear fees.

Acquiring vehicles under business name also help to save more taxes. If company acquires vehicle for few years and upgrade it with time, then leasing is a convenient option. But for long term, buying a vehicle is a good option. It is cheaper, if you buy the vehicle for long term. Buying is also good for the reason that, at the end, the company owns the vehicle. Of course, they have to pay bigger amount of EMIs rather than small lease rentals. Companies can also use and dispose the vehicle according to their needs. They are not bound to kilometers contract.

The decision to buy or lease the vehicle is depend upon the financial condition of the company. It also depends upon the company's policy. If company wants to own the vehicles and used them for long term, then they buy them. If they want to drive the vehicles in their best condition and minimize their expenses, then they go for leasing.

The research has revealed some facts about companies in Ludhiana and Chandigarh. In Ludhiana, Out of 53 interviewed companies, 30 companies have turn over more than 100 crores and 23 companies have turn over between 10 to 100 crores. All the companies prefer to purchase the vehicles under company's name. In order to claim depreciation and expenses and to get tax benefits 33 companies with percentage of 47.83%, buy vehicles under the company's name. 14 companies believe that the vehicle should remain with company as company's asset with percentage of 20.29%. In companies like Ludhiana Beverages Pvt. Ltd. (Franchise of Coca Cola), it is mandatory to have own fleet to penetrate in such a huge market. According to their logistic manager, they have sufficient funds and there is no need to pay interest too. It is not feasible for them to acquire vehicle on loan or lease, as they acquire vehicles for long term contribution. While in limited companies, shareholders are the real owners, so it is necessary to buy the asset in the name of company. The companies have to show the transactions. Another reason for buying the vehicle under company's name is that the vehicles are assets of the company. Asset should remain with company, so company can provide the vehicle to a new joinee.

Out of 53 companies, 36 companies use the vehicle for more than 4 years making a percentage of 67.93%. Analysis shows that 66.04% of the companies interviewed have LCVs for business purposes whereas remaining 33.96% of the companies do not have LCVs. Financing options, cost of maintenance and after sale support also play a useful role in purchase of the vehicle. Taking loan for the car is best option than purchasing the car in cash. Out of 53, 32 companies prefer taking loan over purchase for cars. Companies prefer loan because it is easy to pay in instalments and no need to pay huge amount at once with 31.57% of the companies opting for loan. Companies prefer loan because they can't afford to pay a huge amount at once and to get tax benefits. Companies can do many things with their own funds like investing in their own business and can earn good profits, keeping it as surplus funds for uncertain future needs, can expand their existing business etc they don't need to block their working capital. They have to pay small interest amount. Companies earn more than the interest amount, they have to pay. That's why, they prefer to acquire vehicle by taking loan.

Some Companies have some credit limits with their banks. According to Anish Bansal, GM, Garg Acrylics Limited, they have some credit limits with their bank. They use this limit for different purposes. Loan is easily available to them, less documentation and rate of intererst is low. Resale doesn't matter in luxury cars for them. They know they will get only 25% of the worth of car, when they resale it. Financing of vehicle contribute only 1% of my work. Rate of interest is important for them. When they finance the vehicles by bank, they have to pay, 13% interest on it. On the other hand, if they finance Mercedes by Daimler, they have to pay 5% interest.

16 companies, with 31.37%, prefer to take loan from HDFC Bank followed by 10 companies preferring ICICI bank and 9 companies preferring for SBI Bank.In most of the companies Driver/Employees are responsible for maintenance of the vehicle with 47.17% of the companies. Authorized dealer are responsible for maintaining vehicles in 9 companies. 15.09% of the companies prefer that the Transport/Administration departments should take care of the vehicles. At the time of breakdown of vehicle, driver can call on SOS no. and can also get the assistance from the vehicle manufacturing company. Car manufacturing companies take care of it; they provide services at the doorsteps. Eight companies have separate department for it, which maintain all records of vehicles and take care of everything regarding vehicles. Seven companies have In-house workshop. According to Kashmiri Lal Rana, Manager Accounts, Kitty Industries Pvt. Ltd., Private companies say many things but deliver only few things. They have their own workshop because they can't wait for the vehicles to be fixed by other party. It also saved their fuel expenditure.

Some companies prefer purchase over loan or lease because they believe if there are sufficient funds than there is no need to pay interest over loan. 41.5% of the Companies buy insurance from Direct Insurance Company rather than buying through dealer, which is opted by only 18.87% of the companies interviewed. After some years when the car is resold, the companies prefer to resale it to second hand car dealer than through friends and family. 34 companies making 52.31% resale their cars to second hand car dealers. 29.23% of the companies interviewed also prefer Exchange scheme by car dealer/manufacturer. In Ludhiana city, the awareness about operating lease is very minimal. Only 6 out of 53 companies know about operating lease. The most interesting thing that companies find about the operating lease concept is that the company needs to pay only for what they use. 41.07% of the companies liked this reason. Other interesting fact about operating lease concept is that the company takes care of all the things which mark percentage of 28.57% with 16 companies in favor. Big companies want drivers should be provided by leasing company. Leasing companies should have its direct presence in local market and lease the vehicles at low rate of interest. The interviewed companies did not know any other company in their industry segment, which acquire cars on lease.

In Chandigarh, Out of 54 interviewed companies, 27 companies have turn over more than 100 crores and 27 companies have turn over between 10 to 100 crores. Majority of the companies i.e. 47 companies prefer to purchase the vehicles under company's name, 34 companies use the vehicle for more than 4 years making 62.96%, 35 companies do not have LCVs for business purposes which make percentage of 64.81%. Features and specifications of the vehicle is the most important factor, which is considered by companies while purchase of a car, and agreed upon by 42 companies. Financing options, cost of maintenance and after sale support also play a useful role in purchase of the vehicle. Taking loan for the car is best option than purchasing the car in cash. Out of 54, 35 companies prefer taking loan over purchase for cars. Companies prefer loan because it is easy to pay in instalments and no need to pay huge amount at once with 55.7% of the companies opting for loan. 12 companies, i.e. 24.49%, prefer to take loan from ICICI Bank followed by 9 companies preferring HDFC bank and 6 companies preferring for SBI Bank. In most of the companies Driver is responsible for maintenance of the vehicle with 49.02% of the companies. 37.25% of the companies prefer that the Transport/Administration/HR/Commercial departments should take care of the vehicles. In Chandigarh/Baddi, the awareness about operating lease is very minimal. Only 6 out of 54 companies know about operating lease. The most interesting thing that 40% of the companies find about the operating lease concept is that the company needs to pay only for what they use. Other interesting fact about operating lease concept is that the company takes care of all the things which marking 20%.

CASE PROBLEMS

The research reveals that companies are hiring or owning the vehicles by different methods. These companies are not acquiring the vehicles on lease. The research finds two major problems with these companies. There are two different cases, (a) When companies own the fleet (b) When companies hired the vehicles.

(a) When companies own the fleet: For large companies, it becomes mandatory to have their own fleet to penetrate in a huge market. They take vehicles for long term contribution. Most of the companies have own workshop because they can't wait for the vehicles to be fix by other party. If the other party does not repair their vehicle on time, then they have to suffer a loss. Most of the companies are not able to bear the cost of owning the fleet due to high maintenance charges and drivers. The companies are not able to handle the drivers. Many drivers claim false expenses, are not productive and sincere. They also do theft of fuel and create a trouble for company. There are different cars owned by the company for their employees. It is also difficult for companies when they want to resale their vehicles. They are not able to sell their vehicle at reasonable rates. Employees also want to continue with their existing system to acquire the vehicles.

Most of the people are not aware about the leasing. They don't want to shift to other system of acquiring the vehicles. It is complicated for them to understand new innovative method to acquire the vehicle. Ownership also matters for them. They want to be owner of their car. They don't want taxi.

Most of the companies don't trust private companies. They believe that private companies will charge more and provide no services. According to them, Private companies never keep their words. They tell different things and do different things. Private companies say many things but deliver only few things. They earn money in one or other way from customer.

(b) When companies hired the vehicles: There are many companies which have the offices and plants across the nation. These companies need vehicles for different purposes. Most of the companies are hiring the vehicles from local vendors. Different cars are used by the employees of the company. High rank officer get the better car than other employees. Companies mainly hire the vehicles for the transportation of the employees.

Companies hire vehicles from vendors for different purposes. They evaluate different vendors on different parameters i.e. how big his company is? , has he enough number of vehicles and drivers? Can his drivers work for different shifts? They take quotations from different vendors. The contract can be revised if needed. When they are hiring vehicles, they don't have to manage manpower.

Positive thing in hiring system is that companies don't want to hire the vehicles. Hiring drivers will be costly to them and there are many legal obligations, they have to take care when they are hiring employees. Most companies avoid hiring the drivers due to same reason. Companies are also comfortable with 50 years old hiring system.

Negative thing in hiring system is that, the vehicles which are used by the top management have to pay entry tax while travelling from one state to other. Vendors do not supply the same vehicles to the company daily. Vendors are not maintaining the vehicles according to the guidelines. Companies have to deal with different vendors to fulfill their needs. Sometime the vendor charge high prices to companies for its services. The other problem with hired vehicle is that the company employee cannot keep the vehicle for the whole day and night.

Questions for Discussions

1. Is the Market research done sufficient to identify the scope? Then identify the scope of car leasing in India?
2. What is better to buy or lease the vehicles? Compare
3. What should be the market strategies for SME segment in Ludhiana and Chandigarh?

References

****

APPENDICES

Let us take an illustration

Car: BMW 320d

Ex-show room Chennai: 31.5 lahs, on road price: 38 lakhs

Option 1: Take a loan for 3 years, for 31 lakhs @10.8% interest

- One time down payment of 7 lakhs.
- Monthly EMI of 1.01 lakhs.
- Monthly expense on insurance: Rs. 11 k (1.26 lakhs per year).
- End of 3 years, you'd have spent 63 lakhs on your car (7 lakhs down payment + 31 lakhs loan amount + 5.5 lakhs interest + 2.5 lakhs on insurance + 1 lakh, approx on other maintenance + 14 lakhs in income tax (i.e. 30% income tax paid on your earning through salary, which was spent on EMI and other vehicle expenses) + 2 lakhs in lost interest on down payment.
- Resale value of your BMW 320d after 3 years will be around 17-20 lakhs, when in reality, you've spent **63 lakhs** on this car (**Total cost of ownership**). But you get to own the car and use it as you please.

Option 2: Take the 320d on financial lease

- One time down payment: 0.
- Monthly lease rental: 2.2 lakhs on first month, 1.1 lakh second month on wards till 35th month.
- End of 3 years, pay 3 lakhs to fully own the car or return the car to the company.
- Your employer will pay you less salary and pay the car company the lease amount. Say instead of taking a salary of 2 lakhs and then paying 30% of it as income tax, you take a salary of only 1 lakh,

thereby saving 30% right away, while company shows remaining 1 lakh as expense and pays to car company as lease amount.

- End of 3 years, you'd have spent 52 lakhs on your car (450000 lakhs in rental i.e. 1.25 lakhs monthly lease rental for 36 months and VAT & service tax) + 3.5 lakhs in residual value + 2.5 lakhs on insurance + 1 lakh, approx on other maintenance.
- Resale value of your BMW 320d after 3 years will be around 17-20 lakhs, when in reality, you've spent 52 lakhs on this car. As you've noticed, total cost of ownership in this model is less than option 1, main reason being savings of 30% income tax when company pays you less salary and uses the difference to pay the rental.

Option 3: Take the 320d on operating lease

In operating lease, BMW owns and operates the vehicle, takes care of maintenance and insurance. Operating lease comes with a km restriction. Below illustration is for a rental with 20000 kms annual usage. If usage is more rental will be slightly higher.

- One time down payment: 0.
- Monthly lease rental: 1.15 lakhs per month for 36 months. This includes insurance & maintenance.
- End of 3 years, company takes the car back, you get nothing.
- Your employer will pay you less salary and pay the car company the lease amount. Say instead of taking a salary of 2 lakhs and then paying 30% of it as income tax, you take a salary of only 1 lakh, thereby saving 30% right away, while company shows remaining 1 lakh as expense and pays to car company as lease amount.
- End of 3 years, you'd have spent 41.5 lakhs on your car (1.15 lakhs in rental+tax on rental * 36 months). No insurance expense, no maintenance expense, no money lost as income tax or tax on down payment.
- Resale value of your BMW 320d after 3 years will be around 17-20 lakhs. You've spent only 42 lakhs on this car but own nothing in the end. If you had paid 63 lakhs as in option 1, you would have paid 20 lakhs more to end up with a car that is worth close to 20 lakhs. So this option (option 3) still makes sense.
- Please note that there's a km restriction and any damage to the vehicle will have to be paid separately.

13

Emergence of GST in Indian Economy

Aman Jain[12]

Abstract

The Indian tax structure has been continuously evolving since independence and the government has tried its best to regulate every sector to the benefit of both the people and the government. Out of all sectors, the Infrastructure sector in the country has been through a purple patch in the recent decades and went on to be a major contributor to the GDP.

There are some problems or obstacles in the clear practice of the tax regulations in the country such as multiplicity of levy, lead-in time, the problem of implementation, major goods and services being exempted from the tax and every state having different grounds for the calculation of this tax. Keeping all this in mind the system of VAT came into effect although not adopted to the full potential. Since its adoption, it has made the system more transparent, rather than having multiple rates there are only three rates to be concerned with, also the Goods and Services Tax (GST) which is based on the system of VAT can prove to be a good tool to be implemented so as to achieve easy, transparent, less regressive and more hassle free tax regulatory body functioning and overcome the shortfall of the existing taxation system.

Keywords: GST, Tax, Economy, VAT.

INTRODUCTION

India has been seeing substantial improvements in Indirect taxes since two decades; it is on the verge of yet another main reform edge which will bring this practise to a peak. As an Advanced and welfare concerned Country, India should bring steadiness in the requirements of direct and indirect taxes in the right manner. Hence too much dependency on direct taxes will be brutal yet would simultaneously pass the hefty burden to the general public by technique of indirect taxes constituting hardships for a common man. Past experiences have shown that half-baked reforms

[13]Aman Jain is a student of MBA programme Class of 2015 in Amity Business School. The authors have developed the case solely for class discussion for the programmes in Management. The author does not intend to illustrate effective or ineffective handling of a managerial situation. The case study does not represent or endorse the views of the managements about the issues in the case.

in the name of VAT have done more harm than good in evolving a tax system required for a competitive environment. It is important to assess how this scenario changes from Sales tax to VAT and VAT to GST.

Indirect tax reforms have been an integral part of the liberalization process since 1991. In the first phase, India has been steadily attempting to move towards a tax structure that is simple, moderate, rational and easy to administer and comply with. At the central level, the move has been to bring down the tariffs - both excise and customs, reduce the number of rates, correct anomalies, get rid of the complexities in the system and on the whole reduce the interface with the government. In addition to indirect taxes levied by the centre, states are empowered to levy certain indirect taxes and sales tax forms major part of revenue for almost all states. There is wide variation in sales tax rates of the same commodity in different states. In the existing sales tax structure, there are problems of double taxation of commodities and multiplicity of taxes, resulting in a cascading tax burden. The viable solution found was to shift to estimations based VAT i.e. Value Added Tax. Value Added Tax is one of the most radical reforms that have been proposed for the Indian economy after years of political and economic debate. Revenue growth is the most important aspect by which to judge the success of VAT in India in general.

The importance of this study is to study the effects of VAT, Sales Tax and GST as during the past there has been the problem of double taxation, cascading effects and complexity in the structure of indirect taxation. The case is confined with the limitation of geographical boundaries of the states and also time and data confidentiality.

THE PROBLEM

According to the present Finance Minister bringing GST into the economy is one of the major issues the government is focusing on, therefore, the problem in the discussion lies to choose whether there is enough support for the implementation of the GST and abolition of the other prevailing taxes. Whether this choice would be profitable or not and if it is going to be in favour of all then how to implement the framework for it?

OVERVIEW

India has been developing under the present taxation system to an extent that might seem satisfactory to all but there are complexities also that are developing within the structure itself rendering cascading effects to the framework. For the removal of these negative effects the government of India has been in the process of developing the GST with the help of the existing framework of the VAT which had been developed to build well upon the sales tax that existed in the earlier times. The study of GST would enlighten if it may be beneficial after its implementation or not.

So to study the GST, VAT is an important proponent of knowledge one should have.

VALUE ADDED TAX

The Value Added Tax system is designed to address various problems associated with the conventional sales tax system. In sales tax, there is no provision for input tax credit, which means that the end consumer may pay tax on an input that has already been taxed previously. This is known as cascading and leads to increase in the consumer tax and price levels, which increases the rate of evasion and can be detrimental to economic growth. The value added tax system deals with these problems quite efficiently. As VAT is imposed on value addition – at every single stage – there is lesser incidence of cascading. The value added tax system allows for input tax credit, or ITC, on the amount of tax levied at the preceding stage of the value addition chain."

Features of VAT

- Discretion has been given to the states when it comes to finalizing the RNR along with the restrictions. The mentioned rate must not be lower than 10 percent.
- No Tax Concessions to new industries
- Adjustment of the tax paid on the goods purchased from the tax payable on the goods of sale. All the tax paid on the goods purchased within the state would be adjusted against the tax payable on the sale, whether the sale is within the state or from another state.
- Collection of tax by seller/dealer at each stage.
- VAT is not cascading or additive because the net effect would be- the tax, previously paid on the sale of goods, and would be finally adjusted.

Advantages of VAT

- It helps to ascertain the relevant period of the tax. This is vital as the CST Deed stipulates that the tax levies at the early period or the last period differ. Consequently, the question of that period of tax it falls below becomes one more reason for litigation. Under the VAT arrangement, tax should be levied at every single period of the goods of sale or purchase.
- Adjustment of tax paid on bought goods under the present arrangement, the tax paid on the manufactured goods is adjusted according to the tax paid on the previous levels of manufacturing.

- On inter-state sale on tax paid goods, no refunds would be admissible.
- Fair and Equitable VAT introduces the uniform tax rates across the state so that unfair gains cannot be seized as levying the tax.
- VAT system proposes to treat everybody equal and minimize the discretion. For example, there would be no discretion involved in the filing of the tax, penalties, late payment tax, non-filing etc.
- The computerization of the VAT system enables the management information system to form an integral part and thus making the department more efficient and responsive.

Disadvantages of VAT

- VAT is regressive: it is claimed that VAT is regressive as it tends to burden the poor disproportionately. Since they are going to spend more percentage of their income relative to the rich, VAT makes room for the basic necessities by applying lesser rates of progressivity on items such as clothes, medicine etc. But allows for steep taxation on luxury goods, this creates problem for the administration and may also be a cause of the evasion of taxes by way of deliberate misclassification.
- VAT gets too difficult to operate from the position of both the administration and the business: although, VAT is supposed to be a single replacement of many taxes combined but still there is a level of difficulty that is associated with the dealing of value added tax at the administrative level.At the business level, there is a lot of complexity for the business as there has to be a number of procedures to be followed while the filing of the tax, one such example is to maintain record of the deductions that have been done so as to justify them.
- VAT is inflationary: some businesses will not stop in seizing any opportunity to raise prices and the introduction of VAT offers one such opportunity. Although, this price rise would be temporary but yes the vat rates could easily facilitate this rise in prices.
- VAT favours the capital intensive firms: VAT places a heavy direct impact on the labour intensive firm as compared to the capital intensive firms; therefore, the ratio of value addition to selling price product is higher for the former.

GOODS AND SERVICES TAX (GST)

"The Kelkar Task Force on implementation of the FRBM Act, 2003 had pointed out that although the indirect tax policy in India has been steadily progressing in the direction of VAT principle since 1986, the existing system of taxation of goods and services still suffers from many problems and had suggested a comprehensive Goods and Services Tax (GST) based on VAT principle. GST system is targeted to be a simple, transparent and efficient system of indirect taxation as has been adopted by over 130 countries around the world. This involves taxation of goods and services in an integrated manner as the blurring of line of demarcation between goods and services has made separate taxation of goods and services untenable.

Introduction of an Goods and Services Tax (GST) to replace the existing multiple tax structures of Centre and State taxes is not only desirable but imperative in the emerging economic environment. Increasingly, services are used or consumed in production and distribution of goods and vice versa. Separate taxation of goods and services often requires splitting of transactions value into value of goods and services for taxation, which leads to greater complexities, administration and compliances costs. Integration of various Central and State taxes into a GST system would make it possible to give full credit for inputs taxes collected. GST, being a destination-based consumption tax based on VAT principle, would also greatly help in removing economic distortions caused by present complex tax structure and will help in development of a common national market.

A proposal to introduce a national level Goods and Services Tax (GST) by April 1, 2010 was first mooted in the Budget Speech for the financial year 2006-07. Since the proposal involved reform/restructuring of not only indirect taxes levied by the Centre but also the States, the responsibility of preparing a Design and Road Map for the implementation of GST was assigned to the Empowered Committee of State Finance Ministers (EC). In April, 2008, the EC a report to the titled "A Model and Roadmap for Goods and Services Tax (GST) in India" containing broad recommendations about the structure and design of GST. In response to the report, the Department of Revenue made some suggestions to be incorporated in the design and structure of proposed GST. Based on inputs from Government of India and States, The EC released its First Discussion Paper on Goods and Services Tax in India on the 10th of November, 2009 with the objective of generating a debate and obtaining inputs from all stakeholders.

A dual GST module for the country has been proposed by the EC. This dual GST model has been accepted by centre. Under this model GST have two components viz. the Central GST to be levied and collected by the Centre and the State GST to be levied and collected by the respective States. Central Excise duty, additional excise duty, Service Tax, and additional duty of customs (equivalent to excise), State VAT, entertainment tax, taxes on lotteries, betting and gambling and entry tax (not levied by local bodies) would be subsumed within GST.

In order to take the GST related work further, a Joint Working Group consisting of officers from Central as well as State Government was constituted. This was further trifurcated into three Sub-Working Groups to work separately on draft legislations required for GST, process/forms to be followed in GST regime and IT infrastructure development needed for smooth functioning of proposed GST. In addition, an Empowered Group for development of IT Systems required for Goods and Services Tax regime has been set up under the chairmanship of Dr. Nandan Nilekani.

The GST model has been proposed because of certain shortfalls of the system of VAT which account for a lot tax evasion and complexities resulting in ambiguities in the whole system. VAT has the following shortcomings:

- Cascading effect of taxation: According to VAT laws, the sales tax is payable on the aggregate vending worth that contain CENVAT. Here there is no set off benefits available. Likewise there are countless situations in the nature of cascading result for instance, State VAT on CST, Entry tax on VAT etc. Nowadays Govt. has selected to abolish tax on tax result by requesting GST.
- Shortfall of Existing VAT: Indirect taxes like luxury tax, entertainment tax, are yet to be encompassed in the VAT. These taxes are yet continuing and payable.
- Shortfall of Existing CENVAT: Several taxes like supplementary habits obligation, surcharges not encompassed below CENVAT. Input tax and ability tax set off is out of grasp to the producer and dealers. (GST- Overview, 2012).

The GST model that is proposed would work under a two way model taxation system of the CGST (Central Goods and Service Tax) and the SGST (State Goods and Service Tax).

Under these two subdivisions of the GST the taxes that would be subsumed are:

State Goods and Services Taxes

- VAT/Sales tax.
- Entertainment Tax (unless it is levied by local bodies).
- Luxury tax.
- Taxes on lottery, betting and gambling.
- State cesses and surcharges in so far as they relate to supply of goods and services.
- Entry tax not on in lieu of OCTROI.

Central Goods and Services Tax

- Central Excise Duty.
- Additional Excise Duty.

- The Excise Duty levied under the medical and Toiletries Preparation Act.
- Service Tax.
- Additional Customs Duty, commonly known as Countervailing Duty (CVD).
- Special Additional Duty of customs-4% (SAD).
- Surcharges.
- Cesses.

Benefits of GST

- GST furnishes comprehensive and wider coverage of input credit setoff; you can use service tax credit for the payment of tax on sale of goods etc.
- CST will be removed and need not be paid. At present there is no input tax credit available for CST.
- Many indirect taxes in state and central level subsumed by GST need to pay a single GST instead of all.
- Uniformity of tax rates across the states
- Ensure better compliance due to aggregate tax rate reduces.
- By cutting the tax burden the competitiveness of Indian products in global marketplace is anticipated to rise and there by progress of the nation.
- Price of goods are anticipated to cut in the long run as the benefits of less tax burden should be passed on to the consumer.
- Overall tax compliance cost will reduce for government and can ponder on GST.

THE GST MODEL IN INDIA

Many states are pursuing solitary GST. But it is counselled that dual GST is suitable for combined state like India. The end user, i.e. customer cannot recover taxes but a company can recover by asserting input tax setoff.

Dual GST: Dual GST way, the suggested ideal will have two constituents called as:

1. CGST - Central Goods and Service Tax for levied by central Govt.
2. SGST - State Goods and Service Tax levied by state Govt.

There should be several statute one CGST statute and SGST statute for every single state.

Taxable event:

- Supply of goods and supply of services will be believed as taxable event below GST.

- Any commercial attention that is not supply of goods is indulged a supply of service.

Tax payer identification number:

- Each tax payer will be allotted a pan based identification number having 13 or 15 digit number.

Payment of tax: The central GST should be paid to central government and state GST paid to state government in the prescribed account head.

Collection of GST: It is like VAT; Tax is amassed on the basis of worth supplement on every single period of sale. Both CGST and SGST should have to be charged in an every single service bill and sale bill and paid after adjusting input credit available on both.

Input tax credit setoff: The input tax trust of SGST can be utilized for the payment of SGST merely and input tax trust on CGST can be utilized for the payment of CGST only. This way that cross utilization of input tax credit will not be allowed. Making it clearer; input tax credit of CGST cannot be utilized for the payment of SGST and vice versa. Though there is an exemption for the above in the case of interstate deal .For interstate deal IGST is counselled and should be requested alongside CGST and SGST.

Constitution amendment for levying service tax by the states: The manipulation of levying service tax is rest alongside central Power and a legitimate correction is vital for inspiring states for levying service tax.

APPLICABILITY OF CGST AND SGST

The applicability of taxes is as usual there should be a counselled check of annual turnover, additionally little goods and services are exempted below GST. The dealer whose turnover is below check limit need not pay tax. Threshold for annual turnover for goods and services should be 10 lakh for SGST and threshold of CGST for goods could be 1.5 crores and service should have a distinct threshold that too will be appropriately high.

VAT has been adopted instead of sales tax in India from 2002 by Central Government of India, but only seven states has implemented VAT and other shown their inability to impalement that. Subsequently from 2005 all state in India has adopted VAT and rate of tax was uniformly accepted which was 1%, 4%, 12.5% & for other products like petroleum etc. discretion was given to state for rate of tax. Initially for few years states found it very inconvenient and difficult to implement VAT as no proper administrative machinery was available & large Scale Computerisation was not done, even the manufacturer, trader and retailers were not computer competent. So they were also finding very difficult to cope up with VAT so there was resistant from business community, but in due course Government machinery has been improved to cope up with VAT. At the same time last few years large scale computerisation was done in all sectors and liberal National Policies to import computers has reduced the computer prices and increase the computer literacy which also help business community and Government to cope up with VAT. All above factors are giving better result and total indirect tax revenue has been increased in last few years even after reducing tax rates. Tax evasion in India has been reduced to the great extent after successful implementation of VAT now Central Government of India has decided to implement GST from 2011 which is a step ahead of VAT where excise duty, service tax, octroi will be covered under GST."

Questions for Discussion

1. Being a developing economy, how will introduction of GST impact India vis-à-vis the previous taxation system?
2. The GST system is introduced to abolish the pitfalls of the VAT system in evading tax. How will the change impact? Comment.

References

- Rao, R.K. (2008): Goods and Services Tax for India' Working Paper, NIPFP
- Bird, M.R. and Pierre-Pascal Gendron (October 2005): 'VAT Revisited: A New Look at the Value Added Tax in Developing and Transitional Countries'
- Garg G. (2014), Basic Concepts and Features of Good and Service Tax In India, IJSRM, Vol. 2 Issue 2.
- http://www.gstindia.com
- http://www.ey.com/IN/en/Services/Tax/EY-goods-and-services-tax-gst

14

Trends in Working Capital Management: An Analysis of Accounting Ratios

Aman Singhal • L.K. Dhillon[14]

Abstract

In this ever-changing world of Finances, it has become very important for maintaining check and balances and ratio analysis is one apt tool for this very purpose. BHEL (Bharat Heavy Electricals Ltd.), the company that produces a wide range of advanced power generation equipment and systems, as well as the state of the industrial, transportation, defence, telecommunications, petroleum business systems is studied. The Standard Current Ratio for BHEL is good and satisfactory and the same performance should be maintained this in the future period. The Standard Acid Test ratio of BHEL is not very high which signifies lack of excessive liquidity. Debtors of the company are fluctuating every year which shows that the recovery is slow as most funds are blocked but the Inventory turnover ratio shows there is no consistency which shows overstocking in the company it should be worked for reduction in the ahead. Working capital turnover ratio is going down which means capital is not utilized effectively in the company. Production capacity is also not utilized or effectively used to the full extent in the company part.

Keywords: Working capital, Liquidity ratio, Turnover.

INTRODUCTION

For a successful business enterprise two types of assets are very important i.e. fixedassets and current assets. Fixed assets viz., land & building, plant & machinery, furniture etc., Current assets viz., stock, debtors, bills receivable, cash andBank balance etc. are purchased for the production of goods and sales of those goods through the process of working capital cycle i.e. conversion of raw material into work-in-progress, work-in-progress into finished goods, finished goods into debtors and debtors are converted into cash or bills receivable. The fixed assets are used in order

[14]Aman Singhal is a student of MBA programme Class of 2015 and L.K. Dhillon, Asst. Prof in the Area of Finance with Amity Business School. The authors have developed the case solely for class discussion for the programmes in Management. The author does not intend to illustrate effective or ineffective handling of a managerial situation. The case study does not represent or endorse the views of the managements about the issues in the case.

to increase the production of an Organization and the current assets use the more fixed assets in day to day working. The management of this working capital is known as working capital management (Pandey & Jaisal, 2011). Working capital plays an important role in firm's growth and profitability and is tightly interlinked with the concept of liquidity. This liquidity-profitability relationship is associated with the maintenance of the proper level of working capital. Liquidity and Profitability are the two important and vital aspects of corporate business life. No firm can survive without liquidity. Without making any profit a firm may be considered as sick but one having no liquidity may soon meet its downfall and ultimately die. As a matter of fact, liquidity is a pre-requisite for the survival of a business firm. Thus, the liquidity management has become a basic and broad aspect of judging the performance of a corporate entity (Bardia, 2001).

The term 'Liquidity' refers to the ability of a firm to meet its short-term maturing obligations within one year.This is an attempt to assess the working capital management with focus on the profitability and the liquidity of the firm.

CASE PROBLEM

The company's liquidity and profitability position is weak in comparison to its competitors and also with the presence of Chinese companies in the scenario, the company will face more problem related to maintain its market share in the power sector and also with its net profit going down and with outstanding payment of thousands of crores, they can face some serious problem in the future. Moreover the share price of the company is also coming down which shows the lack of investor confidence in the "MAHARATNA" company. From my point of view BHEL should focus on improving their profitably and effectively using the resources to move ahead of its peers and collaborating with COAL India to have an advantage over its peers. And also the Net operating cycle is increasing that means there is a need to make Improvements in receivables/Debtor's management of the company so that the dues can be paid and investor confidence can be restored. The Company should not rely on debt basically long-term funds as they increased the operating cost of the firm and decrease the profitability of the firm. The Company should try to effectively and efficiently increased volume based sale as to increase their revenue. And also the company should promote its strategy more aggressively so that the Chinese companies refrained from attaining major projects in India. The company in consultation with the government should seek a ban on Chinese companies entering into the strategic and major operations or project in the power sector.

COMPANY PROFILE

Established in 1964, BHEL is India's largest engineering and manufacturing company of its kind engaged in the design, engineering, manufacture, construction, testing, commissioning and servicing of a wide range of products, systems and services for the core sectors of the economy, viz. Power, Transmission, Industry, Transportation, Renewable Energy, Oil & Gas and Defence. The company has been earning profits continuously since 1971-72 and paying dividends uninterruptedly since 1976-77. In recognition of its consistent high performance, BHEL has been conferred with the 'Maharatna' status by the Government of India on 1st February 2013. It is now one among seven Maharatna PSEs. The company has added Power Plant Piping Unit, Thirumayam, and Tamil Nadu as its 16th Manufacturing Unit on 2nd August 2013. BHPV, the 100 percent subsidiary of BHEL located at Vishakhapatnam in Andhra Pradesh, has been merged with BHEL and renamed 'Heavy Plates & Vessels Plant (HPVP)' - the 17th manufacturing unit of the company. With a widespread network of 17 manufacturing units, two repair units, four regional offices, eight service centres, eight overseas offices, 15 regional centres, seven joint ventures, and infrastructure to execute more than 150 project sites across India and abroad, BHEL provides products, systems and services to customers efficiently and at competitive prices. The company has established capability to deliver 20,000 MW p.a. of power equipment to address the growing demand for power generation equipment. The company is also setting up a new Greenfield Power Equipment Fabrication Plant at Bhandara, Maharashtra, the foundation stone for which was laid on 14th May 2013. BHEL places strong emphasis on innovation and development of new technologies. Its research and development (R&D) efforts enables a strong customer orientation for responding to changes in the market.

OVERVIEW OF THE STUDY

The current ratio is a way by which a company can analyse its shot-term solvency. It is often accepted that current assets should be 2 times the current liabilities. According to the facts and figures, the ratio during the year 2009 & 2010 was fluctuating as in the year 2009 it was high then it decreased in 2009 by 0.082%. In the year 2010 - 2011, it was down by 1.38 and in the year 2012 & 2013 it increased by 0.076% (1.83 in 2013). The most acceptable norm for Current Ratio is 2:1 respectively, which means company has attained good liquidity position. BHEL have maintained sufficient amount of current assets over current liabilities which has helped them to attain the ideal current ratio and they should repeat this in the future to try to gain the ideal ratio.

Quick Ratio it is in fact the measure of the "Instant" debt paying ability of the business enterprise. According to this study, the Acid-Test Ratio from the year 2009-2012 was going downward as in the year 2009 it was high but after that it decreased from 2010-2012 and it again increased in the year 2013, which shows that the company is able to maintain its liquidity position as the ideal/basic standard norm for Quick Ratio is 1:1 which the company has achieved which indicates its short-term solvency.

The Cash Ratio of BHEL in the 2011-2012 was fluctuation in 2012-2013 it was 0.27 times and in 2008-2009 it was 0.40 times and 2010-2011 it was reduced to 0.30. The ideal norms of this ratio are 0.5:1. From the above table the firms not maintain the sufficient level of quick assets because of the day-to-day expenses. It is fluctuating between the standard norms for this ratio is 1:2.

Debtor Turnover Ratio indicates the efficiency as well as trust with the collection of book debts. It helps in cash budgeting by measuring the efficiency of cash flow from customers to total sales. In the year 2012-2013 it was 1.51 in contrast to the last year came downwards. They have maintained their Debtor Turnover Ratio as it fluctuates every year.

Inventory turnover ratio indicates that the investment in inventory is being efficiently used or not. A high stock turnover ratio indicates brisk sales. It is the way to measure the overstocking or overvaluation. Inventory turnover of BHEL for 2009-2010 was 4.09. In 2010-2011 the inventory turnover ratio was high up to 4.69 and it was high in 2012-2013 at 5.42.

Working Capital Turnover ratio in the year 2012-2013 - 1.91 times. This is more when comparing the last previous year but it is lower when comparing it with 2009, 2010, 2011. BHEL should improve its working capital requirement so that the capital can be effectively utilized in making sales.

Working Capital trend is one of the important techniques for measuring the profitability of the enterprises. As a measuring rod of efficiency or otherwise of the trend analysis of liquidity, the analysis of working capital trend is highly relevant as it presents the composite indication of the trend values of current assets and current liabilities. In this Current Assets, Current Liabilities and Working Capital is been increasing steadily in all those years.

Various components in working capital current assets shows that during 2009-2013 Sundry account hold were only maintained in stable for the period of study. BHEL must look after its cash and bank balance as it is fluctuating in the future. In the period of 2010-2012 inventory ratios are increased. BHEL should also concentrate on its loans and advances as it also depleting in the near future.

In the investigation of Gross benefit proportion BHEL, there is a ton of variances in its information. In the year 2012-13 it was 0.212 which I higher than the past year which demonstrates that the normal rate of imprint up on the products is not appropriately kept up which can result in issues in blanket working cost and to accommodate settled charges.

Net Profit Ratio demonstrates net edge earned on an offer of Rs. 100/-. According to the facts and figures of the BHEL Company the net profit goes down in the year 2011-12 and 2012-13 by 5.16% which shows that the profitability of the business is not good. So BHEL should improve on increasing the ratio in the future.

CASE FACTS

Table 14.1

Current Ratio *(Rs. in Lakhs)*

Year	*2008-2009*	*2009-2010*	*2010-2011*	*2011-2012*	*2012-2013*
Current Assets	1633078	2106400	4327786	4871494	5095864
Current Liabilities	1032002	1442000	3134657	2872293	2783246
Current Ratio	1.58	1.46	1.38	1.69	1.83

Table 14.2

Quick Ratio *(Rs. in Lakhs)*

Year	*2008-2009*	*2009-2010*	*2010-2011*	*2011-2012*	*2012-2013*
Liquid Assets	1258640	1684600	2216978	2906405	3369935
Current Liabilities	1032002	1442000	3134657	2872293	2783246
Liquid Ratio	1.22	1.17	1.07	1.03	1.05

Table 14.3

Cash Ratio *(Rs. in Lakhs)*

Year	*2008-2009*	*2009-2010*	*2010-2011*	*2011-2012*	*2012-2013*
Cash	413398	580900	963000	667100	773205
Current Liabilities	1032002	1442000	3134657	2872293	2783246
Cash Ratio	0.40	0.40	0.30	0.23	0.27

Table 14.4

Debtors Turnover Ratio *(Rs. in Lakhs)*

Year	*2008-2009*	*2009-2010*	*2010-2011*	*2011-2012*	*2012-2013*
Total Sales	1337403	1723753	2956464	3634233	4434144
Debtors	716806	969582	2735462	2633613	2923400
Debtor Turnover Ratio	1.87	1.78	1.8	1.32	1.51

Table 14.5

Inventory Turnover Ratio *(Rs. in Lakhs)*

Year	*2008-2009*	*2009-2010*	*2010-2011*	*2011-2012*	*2012-2013*
Sales	1337403	1723753	2956464	3634233	4434144
Inventory	374437	421767	629630	835490	817634
Inventory Turnover Ratio	3.57	4.09	4.69	4.34	5.42

Table 14.6

Working Capital Turnover Ratio *(Rs. in Lakhs)*

Year	*2008-2009*	*2009-2010*	*2010-2011*	*2011-2012*	*2012-2013*
Sales	1337403	1723753	2956464	3634233	4434144
Net Working Capital	601076	664286	1193129	1999201	2312618
Working Capital Turnover Ratio	2.23	2.59	2.47	1.81	1.91

Table 14.7

Working Capital For Trend Analysis *(Rs. in Lakhs)*

Year	*2008-2009*	*2009-2010*	*2010-2011*	*2011-2012*	*2012-2013*
Current Assets	1633078	2106297	4327786	4871494	5095864
Current Liabilities	1032002	1442011	3134657	2872293	2783246
Working Capital	601076	664286	1193129	1999201	2312618

Table 14.8

Various Components In Working Capital Current Assets *(Rs. in Lakhs)*

Particulars	*2008-2009*	*2009-2010*	*2010-2011*	*2011-2012*	*2012-2013*
Inventories	22.93	20.03	21.28	27.75	23.16
Sundry debtors	43.90	46.03	53.12	53.94	57.57
C& B balance	25.30	27.58	18.7	13.66	15.22
Other assets	0.52	0.95	0.6	0.30	0.39
Loans and advances	7.35	5.41	6.28	4.32	3.65
Total	100	100	100	100	100

Table 14.9

Gross Profit Ratio *(Rs. in Lakhs)*

Particulars	*2008-2009*	*2009-2010*	*2010-2011*	*2011-2012*	*2012-2013*
Gross Profit/Profit before tax	256435	373607	900600	103020	943200

Total Sales	1337403	1723753	2956464	3634233	4434144
Gross Profit ratio	0.192	0.217	0.304	0.028	0.212

Table 14.10

Net Profit Ratio *(Rs. in Lakhs)*

Particulars	*2008-2009*	*2009-2010*	*2010-2011*	*2011-2012*	*2012-2013*
Net Profit/Profit after tax	167916	241470	601100	704000	661500
Net Sales	1337403	1723753	2956464	3634233	4434144
Net Profit ratio	0.126	0.140	0.203	0.193	0.149

STATUS REPORT

1. The standard Current Ratio is 2:1 and for BHEL it is 1.83:1 which is good and satisfactory and they should maintain this performance in the future period.
2. The standard Acid test ratio is 1:1 but for BHEL it is always high from 2009-2013 but it is not very high which means they don't have excessive liquidity in their firm.

   1.Debtors of the company are fluctuating every year but in the 2013 year it was more than the last year which shows recovery is slow as most funds are blocked but the recovery has been increasing as debtor turnover ratio was more in the last year than the last year.

   1.Inventory turnover ratio is fluctuating from 2009-2013, which shows there is no consistency and also in the last year it was higher than all the previous year which shows overstocking on the company part and they should reduce the ratio in the future.
3. Working capital turnover ratio was high in 2009-2011 but it is going down which means capital is not utilized effectively in the company.
4. Production capacity is also not utilized or effectively used to the full extent.

Questions for Discussion

- As per the ratios, give a detail comment on the trends in the components of Working Capital.
- What is the impact of profitability on the trends in liquidity of the company? Explain.

References

- Nandi K.C. (2012), "Trends in Liquidity Management and their Impact on Profitability: A Case Study", Great Lakes Herald
- Bhunia, A. and Brahma, B. (2011). "Impact of Liquidity Management on Profitability", Asian Journal of Business Management, Volume (3) 2, 108-117.
- Pandey, S. and Jaiswal, V.K. (2011). "Effectiveness on Profitability: Working Capital Management", SCMS Journal of Indian Management, Volume (8) 1 , 73-80.
- Singh, J.P. and Pandey, S. (2008). "Impact of Working Capital Management in the Profitability of Hindalco Industries Limited," The ICFAI University Journal of Financial Economics, Volume (6) 4, 62-72.
- Sur, D. (2001). "Liquidity Management: An overview of four companies in Indian power sector", The Management Accountant, Institute of Cost and Works Accountants of India, Kolkata, June, 407-412.
- http://www.bhel.com
- http://www.myaccountingcourse.com/financial-ratios/working-capital-ratio
- http://academic.regis.edu/dbush/Finance/Financial%20Statement%20Analysis/Financial%20Statement%20Analysis%20Ratios/fsa_working_capital_management_ratios.htm

15

Manufacturing Sector in National Capital Region: Challenges and Opportunities

Achyut Chandra • Tavishi[15]

Abstract

Manufacturing Sector is the backbone of every economy. The very existence of it determines the actual performance of the country. Since, long India has been yearning to attain an Industrial Revolution. The advent of the IT Sector did bring the much needed Foreign Cash Flows to the Indian Economy along with the employment avenues however; the service sector cannot sustain an economy for long.

This research involves the study of all the challenges faced by the Manufacturing Sector and its industry segments, viz., Auto Ancillaries, Chemicals, Electric Equipment, Electrodes/Graphite, Fertilizers, Infrastructure - General, Oil Drilling and Exploration, Packaging, Pharmaceuticals, Power - Transmission/Equipment, Power Generation/Distribution, Sugar, Textiles-Spinning - Cotton Blended, Textiles-Spinning-Synthetic Blended in Noida. The companies targeted have a turnover greater than 100 Crores and are the leading players in their respective field.

In this qualitative research, a total of 18 companies are screened using secondary data and primary data is gathered using Focused Interview Sessions to accomplish the goal of the project.

All the factors are studied and noted which affect the Manufacturing Sector and its Sub Industry segments in general with focus to those key players that shape the face of the sector.

Keywords: Manufacturing sector, Challenges, NCR, Industrial revolution.

INTRODUCTION

Manufacturing companies are under increasingly diverse and mounting pressures due to more sophisticated markets, changing customer choice and global competition. The market for products is becoming increasingly international. In this international marketplace, companies find themselves having to adopt international standards. Community groups and environmentalists are bringing increased pressure to bear

---

[15]Achyut Chandra is a student of B. Tech + MBA programme Class of 2015 and Tavishiis Asst Prof in the Area of Economics with Amity Business School. The authors have developed the case solely for class discussion for the programmes in management.

on manufacturers to improve the reliability and safety of their products and manufacturing processes. In such a competitive scenario companies have to search for new processes, new materials, new vendors, new shop floor design, and new channels to deliver their products and services at competitive price.

COMPANY PROFILE

Mott MacDonald is a $2bn engineering, management and development consultancy delivering excellence in 140 countries, through 16,000 local experts in 180 principal offices.

The organisation works with its esteemed customers to plan, design, procure and deliver projects on any scale; provide management consultancy built on technical know-how, shape and implement development policies and programmes; and advance sustainability. The portfolio ranges from small projects worth thousands of pounds to the world's largest multidisciplinary, multi-billion pound programmes.

Mott MacDonald, being a multi-sector organisation caters to all areas of the Industry, viz. Buildings, Communications, Defence, Education, Environment, Health, International development, Industry, Mining, Oil and gas, Power, Transport, Urban development, Water and wastewater. The services offered being multidisciplinary include Planning, Studies and design, Infrastructure finance and technical advisory services, Project and programme management, Management consultancy, Strategic asset management, Forensic engineering and expert witness.

A global company with a local presence, Mott MacDonald operates through 170 principal offices in nearly 50 countries, giving it local market insight and resources on the ground to support every client.

The company has been at the forefront of Management, Engineering and Development consultancy in India for more than 42 years.

The firm was appointed as the lead technical advisor for Indira Gandhi International Airport in New Delhi. The company is proud with its phenomenal track record which can be seen with many landmark projects being executed, viz. Delhi Metro, Delhi-Mumbai International Airports, Petrochemical investment region, etc. It has been contributing across India from pharmaceuticals to hydro powers to high-ways, etc. which gives it a Multi-Sector and Multi-Disciplinary Organization. It provides services in the health sector too, and is apparent in both, the private and public sector.

PROBLEM STATEMENT

Indian companies have quite often followed an opportunistic approach to growth as opposed to a capability driven approach, and paid very little strategic attention to their shop floors in the last few decades (Chandra and Sastry, 1998). This was reflected in poor quality of products, little awareness about competitiveness, little integration of various functions such as marketing, sales, production, etc.

Between the 1950 s and the 1990 s, India's industrial development policy was characterized by excessive regulation. Initially set up to avoid over capacity in a capital scarce economy, it spawned a maze of regulations governing product, capacity, technology and foreign exchange availability.

In the late 1980 s, inflows of foreign technology and equity were permitted and manufacturing capacity constraints lifted. The gradual opening of the Indian economy resulted in the entry of foreign competitors and expanded production by domestic manufacturers. By the 1990s, the Indian economy was undergoing structural change and imports were largely unregulated (Upadhyay and Kanavi, 1999).

Since the introduction of reforms in 1991, Indian firms are facing a very different competitive scenario compared to the past. The abolition of the license regime meant the end of protection and control measures. Manufacturing in India is at a critical juncture. The Indian perspective on manufacturing is characterized as a support activity for marketing and finance and invited little top management attention. Most of firms are still very far from world class practices. Meanwhile international competitors are continuously working on improving manufacturing, bringing in new products and making manufacturing more proactive and responsive (Chandra and Sastry, 1998).

As a result of this, Indian industry is facing competition both from imports and from multinational companies in the domestic markets. The new competition is in terms of reduced cost; improved quality, products with higher performance, a wider range of products and better service, all delivered simultaneously. Mohanty (1995) has elaborated on the corporate-manufacturing relationship in the contemporary context of global competition. He has also outlined a need for improvements in corporate learning and development of effective methods for managing manufacturing function from a strategic perspective.

In this light manufacturing strategy is urgently needed for Indian firms to:

- Respond to business strategy or corporate objectives;
- Correct present weaknesses or to exploit strengths;
- Cope with anticipated environmental changes;
- Get distinctive competence which is currently not available;
- Make manufacturing function strong;
- Achieve internationally competitive performance objectives.

AUTO ANCILLARIES SEGMENT

The Indian auto component industry faced challenges during 2012-13 with the growth rate squeezing on account of economic slowdown. The demand was restrained by higher interest rates, inflation, fuel prices, volatile commodity market, industrial unrest and adverse forex fluctuations. The Indian vehicle market, after a few years of consistent good performance, witnessed a distinct slowdown in growth. While passenger vehicle segment saw witnessed an overall volume growth rate of single digit for consecutive two years i.e. 4% in 2012-13 and 5% in 2011-12, the sale of Commercial Vehicles declined by 4% after registering impressive growth in the last two years. Industrial unrest, high interest rates and slowdown in infrastructure projects contributed to lower demand for commercial vehicles. Two wheelers volume growth was subdued at 2% in comparison with 16% during 2011-12. With the

CHEMICALS SEGMENT

The chemical industry in India is poised for explosive growth in the coming years. India's population has grown nearly as large as that of China, with its consuming middle class accounting for about a third of its population. Disposable income in India is rising, potentially driving growth of chemicals consumption at exponential rates. India's GDP growth exceeded 9% for the last fiscal year, fuelling double-digit growth of its chemicals industry. India's government has set in place policies and special economic zones to promote investment in its petrochemical sector, and several key domestic companies have unveiled ambitious expansion plans for the next few years. The Indian Chemical Industry Outlook is the only chemical conference in India organized specifically to address a broad range of issues impacting the industry. The conference will take a look at different segments of the Indian chemical industry, and explore the growth opportunities and challenges in each segment.

ELECTRIC EQUIPMENT SEGMENT

The ever-evolving market scenario makes the Indian electrical industry fairly dynamic. Operating in a highly competitive environment, it is challenged by competition not only from emerging indigenous players, but also cheap imports of global producers struggling to balance the contraction of demand in the developed markets, like Europe. In contrast to matured markets in developed countries, the Indian markets are still in a growth stage. Buoyed by rising income levels, resulting from the sustained GDP growth witnessed over the last decade, as well as changing lifestyles and aspirations shaped by the higher exposure to media, print and television, consumption demand has remained fairly robust. The higher spending power has also seen consumers shifting to branded products. And, within the branded category, there is a discernible move towards affordable premium products category.

ELECTRODES/GRAPHITE SEGMENT

Graphite electrodes are energy-carrying conductors used in steel making through the Electric Arc furnace (EAF) route. While they constitute only 2-3% of the total production cost of steel, quality is critical. Quality is also essential in maintaining market share in a depressed sectorial environment. Steel represents the backbone of a country's economy; per capita steel consumption represents one of the critical indicators of socio-economic development. Steel is the foremost engineering material, environment friendly and recyclable.

FERTILIZERS SEGMENT

India meets 80 per cent of its urea requirement through indigenous production and is largely import dependent for meeting its requirements of the potassic and phosphatic fertilizer requirements. The consumption of fertilizers in nutrient terms has shown improvement.

The Government has notified the New Investment Policy 2012 (NIP-2012) in the urea sector which will encourage investments leading to increase in indigenous capacities, reduction in import dependence and savings in subsidy due to import substitution at prices below import parity price (IPP). It is expected that fresh investment will come for expansion, revival and setting up of Brownfield and Greenfield projects. Priority allocation and reasonable pricing of domestic gas would be crucial for cost competitiveness of urea plants.

GENERAL INFRASTRUCTURE SEGMENT

The real estate sector is a critical sector of our economy. It has a huge multiplier effect on the economy and therefore, is a big driver of economic growth. It is the second-largest employment-generating sector after agriculture. Growing at a rate of about 20% per annum, this sector has been contributing about 5-6% to India's GDP. Not only does it generate a high level of direct employment, but it also stimulate the demand in over to 50 ancillary industries such as cement, steel, paint, brick, building materials, consumer durables and so on.

The shortage of affordable housing space continue to be one of the biggest challenges towards ensuring equitable and inclusive economic growth. The right mix of government policies and easing of norms for land acquisition are the prerequisites to address the same. The other key challenges that the real estate industry is facing are rising manpower and material cost, shortage of labour, etc.

OIL DRILLING AND EXPLORATION SEGMENT

Rising oil consumption to meet the growing energy demand of the country is a major cause of concern for the economy. The consumption of petroleum products has risen by 4.92% in 2012-13, with total consumption of 155.417 MMT of petroleum products. The country is dependent for about 75% of its crude oil requirement on imports. Though the oil prices moderated a bit, the falling rupee posed a serious problem for the domestic oil industry in terms of rising under-recoveries of the oil marketing companies and the sustained high subsidy burden on upstream crude oil producers.

This is also expected to result in lower subsidy burden on domestic crude oil producers. The Govt. has time and again made its intention clear that to increase the domestic output of oil and gas and reduce country's dependence on oil imports; it will take all necessary steps to attract large investment in country's E&P sector.

PACKAGING SEGMENT

Flexible Packaging has gained popularity worldwide for its benefits over rigid packaging. With benefits such as functional convenience in handling & transportation, cost effectiveness and brand protection, flexible packaging industry worldwide is led by a strong growth. The global packaging industry witnessed influence of technology innovation and development, a key reason for the industry's robust growth over the last few decades. Over the years, technology development has been moving in sync with growing consumer demand for convenient and quality packaging. Eclectic packaging solutions, for instance, have evolved to offer exceptional product packaging advantages to manufacturers and consumers alike. Technology advancements have redefined the functionality of packaging from beyond the traditional need for mere product protection.

PHARMACEUTICALS SEGMENT

The pharmaceuticals industry is riding on a growth wave in line with a rapidly strengthening scientific base, growing demand for medicines due to increasing and ageing global population, longer life expectancy, higher prevalence of infectious and chronic diseases and the removal of former impediments to free trade with the objective of providing lower cost healthcare services and improved access for all sections of society. Agricultural chemicals have been proven to be highly effective in reducing crop losses caused by pests, diseases and weeds and to enable farmers to grow crops that meet growing demand and consumer expectations at reasonable prices.

POWER-TRANSMISSION/EQUIPMENT SEGMENT

The year 2012 witnessed sluggishness in the market mainly due to fuel constraint for Thermal (Coal & Gas) and statutory clearances for Hydro projects. However, Government seen taking some measures to revive the sector namely Presidential directive to Coal India to implement Fuel Supply Agreements, revision of Power tariffs, restructuring package offered to loss making Discoms. Tariff hike for imported coal based new plants is also expected. Furthermore, given the aggressive targets being set for the XIIth Five Year Plan of the Government of India, it is still expected that the demand for power equipment and services will grow in near future. Coal will still be the major power installed capacity by 2020. The country is aiming at setting up nuclear power reactors based on both domestic programme as well as international.

POWER GENERATION/DISTRIBUTION SEGMENT

The Indian Power Industry is one of the largest and most important business in India as it fulfils the energy requirements of domestic and various other industries. It is one of the most critical components of Infrastructure that affects economic growth and the wellbeing of our nation. India's GDP growth rate is related to the growth of power sector and hence, in order to sustain the growth of 8% to 9% in GDP, India needs to continuously add the power generation capacity commensurate with this pace.

SUGAR SECTOR

As per Indian Sugar Mills Association (ISMA), Sugar Production for Sugar season 2012-13, sugar mills have crushed about 244.2 million tonne of sugarcane, to produce 24.62 million tonne of sugar with 10.08% reported recoveries across states. However, this year total sugarcane crush is only about 1% lesser, but sugar production is about 3%lower as compared to same corresponding period during last year. This is due to lesser reported recoveries across country, which is about 0.17 points lesser than last year.

Maharashtra, this year again, being leading sugar producing state, produced about 7.98 million tonne of sugar by crushing 69.8 million tonne of sugarcane with 11.44% reported recovery. Till date sugar production is about 10% lesser than last year during same corresponding period. Sugar mills this year crushed 8% lesser sugarcane with about 0.21 point lesser reported recoveries than last year.

In Uttar Pradesh crushing season has come to an end and has produced 7.49 million tonne of sugar using 81.6 million tonne of sugarcane crushing with 9.19% reported recovery. Due to 0.12 points better reported recoveries than last year, till date state has produced 7% higher sugar with only 5% higher sugarcane crush than last year. Western & Central UP have reported better recoveries than last year, while Eastern UP has reported lower.

Karnataka has already closed crushing operations with 3.388 million tonne of sugar production as against 3.72 million tonne last year. This year 10.44% sugar recovery were 0.56 points lesser than last year.

Tamil Nadu is still operational with 23 mills as against 41 mills under crushing during last year. Till date state has produced 1.543 million tonne of sugar which is about 1% lesser than last year. Andhra Pradesh is almost closed and till date produced 0.986 million tonne of sugar as against 1.11 million tonne last year.

TEXTILES-SPINNING-COTTON BLENDED

The Textile industry in India traditionally, after agriculture, is the only industry that is generating huge employment for both skilled and unskilled labour and is one of the leading producer of textile products in the world. India is the second largest producer of fibre in the world and the major fibre produced is cotton. Other fibres produced in India include silk, jute, wool, and man-made fibres. 60% of the Indian textile Industry is cotton based. Indian Textile Industry is predominantly export oriented and earns about 27% of total foreign exchange earned by India. It also contributes about 14% of the total industrial production and 3% of GDP of the country. It offers direct employment to over 35 million in the country and also opens up scope for the other ancillary sectors and also supports agriculture.

TEXTILES-SPINNING-SYNTHETIC BLENDED SECTOR

The Indian textile industry enjoys an overwhelming presence in its economic existence as it contributes 4% to the gross domestic product, approximately 14% to industrial production, 12% of the country's total exports and is the second largest employment provider. India's commercial banks enjoy an exposure of about Rs. 1.60 lac crore to the country's textile sector. Performance: The Indian textiles sector rebounded after a catastrophic 2011-12. As per CMIE estimates, industry sales grew about 7.5% backed by higher volumes and improved realisations; total yarn production increased about 6.8% while fabric production grew about 7.1%.

DATA ANALYSIS AND INTERPRETATION

- **Industry Wise Distribution of Sectors**

As the basic criteria used for industry segmentation was the annual standalone turnover, it was found out that the Sugar Sector comprised 26%, Auto- Ancillaries comprised 22%, Infrastructure comprised 12%, Textiles Spinning - Cotton Blended 11%, Power Generation comprised 11%, and, others comprised 18% of the Total Manufacturing Sector worth.

Manufacturing Sector is facing from the following issues which can be seen as a hindrance to the development of the country and this challenge can be dealt with by proper channelization of the Company resources and Policy Maker Decisions.

- High Interest Rates.
- Lack of domestic demand.
- High oil/energy prices.
- Pressure for increased wages.
- Legislative or regulatory pressures.
- Decreasing profitability.
- Unavailability/high price of raw materials.
- Competition from foreign markets.
- Foreign exchange volatility.

The case involved various interactions that were all focused interviews. It was a general notion that the times to come will yearn for more impetus being given to the Manufacturing Sector. The case aimed to gather attention towards Noida, which is key to the development of Delhi, being a contributor to the Manufacturing Sector and hence strengthening the backbone of the country.

Questions for Discussions

1. Identify the main problems of the Manufacturing Sector and explain the process to overcome the problems faced.
2. Which Industry segment in the Manufacturing sector can be classified as one which is facing challenges and suggest ways to overcome the same?
3. Why is it necessary to improve the overall outlook of the Manufacturing Sector particularly in Delhi/NCR?

References

- FICCI and PWC (2013), India Manufacturing Barometer Report.
- http://www.supportbiz.com/cluster/Delhi-NCR
- http://www.mottmac.com
- http://www.adb.org/publications/series/key-indicators-for-asia-and-the-pacific

16

Risk Management – Perspective on Prevention of Frauds

Arushi Sharma • Manjula Shastri[16]

Abstract

The project "Risk management - perspective on prevention of frauds and mapping people perception on investor's protection" focuses on what is risk management and role of risk management in today's world and gives out the policy implications in prevention of frauds i.e. how can we mitigate the frauds . The project underlines the constructive work undertaken by KPMG, Reserve bank of India, SEBI in protection of investor's rights. The Project has been made with the aid of Primary as well as Secondary data. The Former part of the report is analysed on the basis of secondary data and the latter part is analysed with the help of primary data. In order to write this report various research papers, literal material, KPMG's documents and policies, Reserve Bank of India and SEBI's documents and other online databases were referred. The data so procured was tabulated and analysed with the help of the graphs and discussions with the concerned managers of the department. The study aims to check the various instruments investors invest in and the problems faced by them which led to financial loss to them and the measures suggested by them.

Keywords: Risk management, Fraud, Investor protection.

INTRODUCTION

India has been among one of fastest growing economies and is known for a good base of economic policies and has a strong investors' confidence be it international or domestic but due to increasing cases of frauds and scams, this confidence has been reducing and thus arising a need for good governance on part of government as well as companies. With 'Companies Act 2013' focusing on Investor Protection and Higher Audit Accountability, government is trying to make the environment for investors safer. Thus along with government, corporate play an integral

---

[16] Arushi Sharma is a student of MBA programme Class of 2015 and Manjula Shastri is an Asst Prof in the Area of Finance Amity Business School. The authors have developed the case solely for class discussion for the programmes in Management. The case study does not represent or endorse the views of the managements about the issues in the case.

role and 'risk management' team can help to prevent it at the very first stage by ensuring strict internal norms and controls.

COMPANY PROFILE

KPMG is a provider of one of the largest professional services and is one of the Big Four auditors. It is a Swiss cooperative and was founded in 1987 with the merger of Peat Marwick international and Klynveld main Goerdeler, hence its name out to be KPMG.

It is headquartered in Amstelveen, Netherlands and global CEO being John B Veihmeyer and KPMG India CEO is Richard Rekhy. KPMG employs 152,000 people and has three lines of services: audit, tax, and advisory. Its tax and advisory services are further divided into various service groups. it was established in India in September 1993, and has rapidly built a significant competitive presence in the country. The firm operates from its offices in Mumbai, Pune, Delhi, Kolkata, Chennai, Bangalore, Hyderabad, Kochi, Chandigarh and Ahmedabad, and offers its clients a full range of services, including financial and business advisory, tax and regulatory, and risk advisory services.

KPMG has various departments, one of them is 'risk management' and it is subdivided into 3 departments.

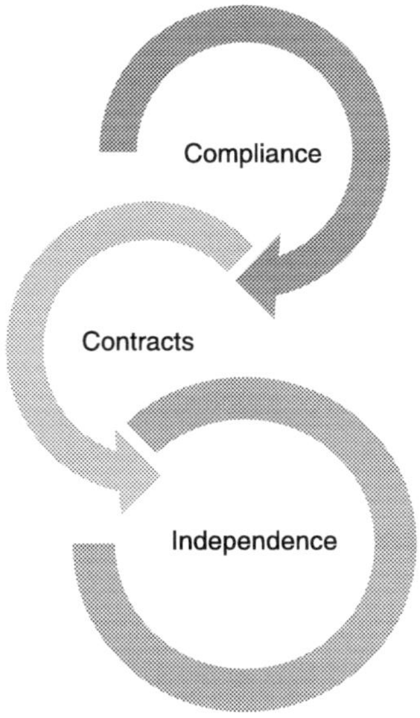

Figure 16.1 Departments of risk management.

Each department plays an integral role in mitigating risks and checking whether the procedures and process followed by employees at all level are in compliance with the rules and regulations and accordingly prevent possible risks.

Risk management is the responsibility of each partner and employee and it includes the need to understand and at the same time to be in compliance with the policies and procedures of the firm. Risk Management develops and maintains policies and procedures to help keep high standards of quality and integrity and prevent financial damage. KPMG International has an integrated monitoring and compliance program that covers all member firms to assess the relevance, adequacy, and effective operation of key quality control policies and procedures.

Each team works at different level and aims at mitigating risks.

'Independence' team works at the basic level i.e. it aims at integrating the very first customer which includes all the employees, as discussed at the beginning, there are 4 major trainings imparted to the employees, each of these trainings have a certain objective and are needed to be done in a certain stipulated time period, thus independence team aims at checking whether all the employees are in compliance with this or not.

The 4 major types of trainings are:

1. **New joiner's independence training:** To be completed within 10 days of joining.
2. **Protecting information in KPMG:** To be completed within 30 days of joining.
3. **Sentinel training:** To be completed within 30 days of joining.
4. **Acting with integrity:** To be completed within 30 days of joining.

The very first training which has to be completed within 10 days of joining is the most important as KPMG being an audit firm has to give out a fair view of its audit client and we need to ensure that the employees doesn't hold any interests in the client as it would lead to conflicts of interests and this is known as 'independence violation' and a system called KICS (KPMG Independence and Compliance Systems) is used to do the same which keeps a track of all investments of the employees and then cross check it with the 'restricted entities ' list and every employee is given a period of 14 days to sell of the investments and if he does not or sells it on the 15th day and books a profit then it goes to KPMG rather than the holder.

The second training talks about 'protecting information in 'KPMG', its related to confidentiality, each employee is expected to be in compliance with this clause.

The third training is sentinel that is you are in compliance with all the policies, we even have a sentinel team and before making any investments, you have to obtain an approval from them and renew this approval within 15 days. It is the principal tool that KPMG member firms use for conflict identification and clearance.

The fourth one is 'Acting with Integrity' about acting with ethics and always being open and honest and valuing the relationships with co-workers, customers and stakeholders. Integrity for KPMG means being consistently straightforward and honest in professional and business

Compliance team, before entering into any engagement there are various risks checks that are needed to be done like seeing that the client is not our audit client as then we cannot provide him with non-audit services and checking the financial status of the client. Thus compliance team evaluates:

- Assess the reputational and financial risks of the KPMG member firm being associated with the prospective client and identify the steps required to mitigate those risks.
- Evaluate the prospective client as being Low, Medium or High Risk.
- Obtaining various approvals in accordance to their risk levels.
- Evaluate any threats to compliance with any applicable laws, regulations and professional standards.
- Balance the risks and rewards involved.

Even when a potential client is accepted in order to mitigate further risks.

- Assess any changes to the reputational and financial risks of the KPMG member firm being associated with the existing client.
- Identify any steps required to mitigate those risks.
- Identify circumstances where the KPMG member firm may decide not to continue to be associated with the client.
- Re-assess the matters addressed in client acceptance or the last client continuance evaluation based on current information, including the integrity of the client.
- Re-evaluate the existing client as being Low, Medium or High Risk.
- Document how any new or modified risks may be mitigated.
- Obtain required approvals.

Once a potential client has been accepted it does not mean that we are going to perform business with, before the actual engagement which is done by the CONTRACTS team, we need to check certain things such as:

Independence and conflict of interest: A critical component of engagement acceptance is ensuring that there are no independence or conflict of interest issues that will prevent the KPMG member firm from undertaking the engagement or require safeguards to be introduced or identified. The main tool for this is the Sentinel system.

Engagement evaluation for each engagement: Complete an engagement evaluation for each new engagement. For significant amendments to the engagement, (e.g. add-ons, follow ups), create separate or amended engagement acceptance evaluations.

Evaluating clients and engagements at the same time: Client and engagement evaluation can be undertaken at the same time but a KPMG member firm cannot actually accept an engagement unless the client acceptance procedures have been completed and the required approvals have been obtained.

Contract for engagement's scope of work: When the decision is made to accept an engagement for a client, the client and the member firm sign a contract detailing the scope of the work the KPMG member firm is to perform. The contract forms an element of the risk management process, and professional consultation may be necessary when drafting the contract terms.

Thus the contracts team oversees the contract being made with the client is in compliance with the firm's policies and if any change in the contact is needed that is addition of clause by the clients then it has to be approved by the team, risk management team and the specified partner

OVERVIEW OF NATIONAL RISK MANAGEMENT AT KPMG

The work under the National Risk Management department at KPMG is associated with risks company faces in case of any default by its employees. One part of it includes is making all the new joiners undergo various trainings to make them aware of companies rules and regulations.

The 4 major types of trainings are:

- New joiner's independence training- to be completed within 10 days of joining.
- Protecting information in KPMG- to be completed within 30 days of joining.
- Sentinel training- to be completed within 30 days of joining.
- Acting with integrity- to be completed within 30 days of joining.

The very first training which has to be completed within 10 days of joining is the most important as KPMG being an audit firm has to give out a fair view of its audit client and we need to ensure that the employees doesn't hold any interests in the client as it would lead to conflicts of interests and this is known as 'independence violation' and a system called KICS (KPMG Independence and Compliance Systems) is used to the same which keeps a track of all investments of the employees and then cross check it with the 'restricted entities ' list and every employee is given a period of 14 days to sell of the investments and if he does not or sells it on the 15th day and books a profit then it goes to KPMG rather than the holder.

The second training talks about 'protecting information in KPMG', it's related to confidentiality, each employee is expected to be in compliance with this clause.

The third training is sentinel that is you are in compliance with all the policies, we even have a sentinel team and before making any investments, you have to take an approval from them and renew this approval within 15 days. It is the principal tool that KPMG member firms use for conflict identification and clearance.

The fourth one is about acting with ethics and always being open and honest and valuing the relationships with co-workers, customers and stakeholders. Integrity for KPMG means being consistently straightforward and honest in professional and business.

MAJOR ISSUES

Every month over 1500+ employees are recruited and as mentioned above every employee at all levels have to perform these trainings within the stipulated period of time and the role of 'National risk management department' is to keep a track of these trainings and clarify any doubts regarding and also help the employees out if they are faced with any problem.

Along with the training all the employees have to fill a 'New joiner's affidavit' which has various understanding clauses regarding firm's policies and clauses regarding the trainings. This affidavit varies across designation and their role (client or non-client facing) in the organization. The affidavits are broadly of 4 types:

- Affidavit for senior manager and senior manger.
- Affidavit for NON-PDM client service staff.
- Affidavit for partners and directors.
- Affidavit for support staff.

Now firstly, manual trackers are to be made which are then compared with the computer generated global reports and simultaneously have to update the trainings done by the employees and these trainings differ according to the employee's designation and his role, whether it is a client facing role or a non-client facing role. Moreover the trainings have deadlines and also if they aren't completed within the deadlines we have to send them reminder mails for the same which are manually generated and there are around 3 remainder mails to be send and along with segregation according to their designation and hence a follow up is needed to be done.

Moreover the new joiners affidavit submitted by the employees have various understanding clause which are usually marked wrongly by the employees for which manual remainders have to be sent again again till the problem is rectified. Also if a certain clause has been left unanswered and the affidavit is not accepted so again, the process of sending the reminder mails has to be done. All these problems lead to:

- Lack of standardization.
- Inconsistencies.
- Duplication of data.
- Time consuming.
- Unstructured processing.

Thus, we can summarize the problems faced as:

- Over 1500+ employees recruited and only one nation-wide department is there to do this job.
- New joiners affidavit is an offline form which has various clauses and they need to be checked manually.
- The affidavit also varies from employee to employee and sometimes it is filled wrongly from which manual mails are needed to be sent which is time-taking.
- Manually generated trackers about the details of each and every employee and the date of completion of the trainings.
- Manually generated and updated trackers regarding the completion of trainings and follow ups in the form of remainder mails sent if otherwise.
- Remainder mails are to be sent manually.
- Less number of employees in the department as compared to the employees recruited.
- A lot of data is there and as all the work has to be done manually so it is time consuming.

Steps taken by the organization:

- In order to increase the efficiency of the department and reduce the over lapping of activities, various steps have been taken up by the organization.
- Knowledge management department has been involved in this process and links for various training has been generated with their help.
- In order to convert the new joiner's affidavit into online form, the process for the same has been initiated so that the mandatory questions and understanding clauses shall be attempted and shall not be accepted if not filled completely as well as if filled incorrectly.

- Reminder mails which are ought to be sent on fixed time basis are planned to be automated.
- Global reports are aimed to be updated on a daily basis and moreover timely.
- Computerizing the trainings and the deadlines for the same.
- Talks of more of budget allocation to the team has been initiated to computerize the process.
- Loan staff is taken by the department to overcome the situation of lack of staff as compared to the data present.

Questions for Discussion

Discuss the instruments investors invest in and the problems faced by them presented in case. What your suggestive measures?

17

Working Capital at Narora Atomic Power Stations

Komal Agrawal • T.V. Raman[17]

Abstract

The aim of this case is to evaluate the WORKING CAPITAL formulation system, based on the standard tools and techniques. Moreover, it also gives due stress on the control and monitoring part, where the observations in the proposed Ratios are made and corrective measures are suggest forthwith.

The facts and figures expressed in financial statements are meaningful, but these facts have no meaning unless expressed in relation to other figures of same type in the statements of different periods. Analysis of financial statements *is the, "systematic numerical calculation of the relationship between the one fact with the other to measure the profitability, operational efficiency, solvency and the growth potential of the business."*

This case serves the interests of shareholders, debenture holders, investors, creditors, bankers, economists etc. The analysis of financial statement makes it simple, intelligible and meaningful for all the concerned parties. The case simplifies summaries and systematized the monotonous figures.

The comparison of the actual and the estimated budgeted figures have been included in the analysis part and the findings and conclusions arrived at, there from, are supported by suggestions and recommendation.

Keywords: *******.

INTRODUCTION

Nuclear Power Corporation Of India Limited (NPCIL) is a public sector enterprise, wholly owned by government of India, under the administrative control of the DEPARTMENT OF ATOMIC ENERGY (DAE). It was registered as a Public Limited Company under the Companies Act 1956, in September 1987, with the objective of undertaking

---

[17]Komal Agrawalis a student of MBA programme Class of 2015 and T.V. Raman is an Associate Prof in the Area of Finance Amity Business School. The authors have developed the case solely for class discussion for the programmes in management. The author does not intend to illustrate effective or ineffective handling of a managerial situation. The case study does not represent or endorse the views of the managements about the issues in the case.

the design, construction, operation & maintenance of Nuclear Power Station for generation of electricity in pursuance of schemes & programs of government of India under the provision of the Atomic Energy Act, 1962.

NPCIL was earlier known as Nuclear power Board under total control of DEPARTMENT OF ATOMIC ENERGY. In 1987-88 Government of India decided to convert it in to a Public Limited Company with a view to step towards self-reliant fund management, cost effectiveness, and professional management. The ultimate idea was to make the power sector more competitive and transparent. With its past performance in last 15 years NPCIL has justified the decision with continuous profit, safe operation, nuclear awareness, high growth rate and challenging future prospects. The mission of NPCIL is to develop Nuclear Power Technology & produce in a self-reliant manner, Nuclear Power is a safe, and Environmental Friendly & Economically viable source of Electrical needs of the country. "Generate more & more environment friendly nuclear electricity to provide energy and security to the nation" is the vision of NPCIL. The corporation has set of objectives like maximize the power generation & profitability, increase nuclear power capacity in the country consistent with available resources in a self-reliant, safe, economical, & rapid manner, continue & strengthen quality assurance activities, strengthen the environment protection measures and public awareness activities relating to nuclear power generation, share appropriate technological skills & expertise at national & international levels, bring about modernization & technological innovation, support capacity addition program in keeping with the growth of energy demand in the country.

The present total installed power capacity in the country is 124287 MWe & capacity addition on an average of about 10,000 MWe per year needs to be added in the country to make the growing demand of electricity. No single source is able to meet this demand. The Indian Power Sector comprises a State, Central & Private sector. The contribution of Central sector in all India Installed capacity is about 32% with share of 42% in generation. Nuclear power project are Central sector project & the share of Nuclear power in Central sector generation & capacity are about 57%.

Nuclear power is environment friendly, technologically proven, economically competitive & associated with the advantage of energy security & diversity. Nuclear power is, thus, an important component to complement generation from other sources in near terms.

Energy is essential for growth of civilization & for any substantial rise in the standard of living of people in a country, not having plentiful fuel resources, it is necessary to exploit all other sources including nuclear energy for the generation of electricity. Realizing the importance of nuclear energy in India, a three-stage nuclear power program was formulated by the Department of Atomic Energy (DAE).

Welfare measures taken as social responsibility are large number of direct and indirect employment, economical and infrastructural development, company organizes medical camps with free medicines and immunization of children in rural areas, lectures on first aid by trained medical trained staff, construction/renovation of schools building, providing books, and uniform to the children of weaker section of the society. These measures have helped in creating a healthy & co-operative atmosphere among the local population towards the company.

Sources of funds of NPCIL

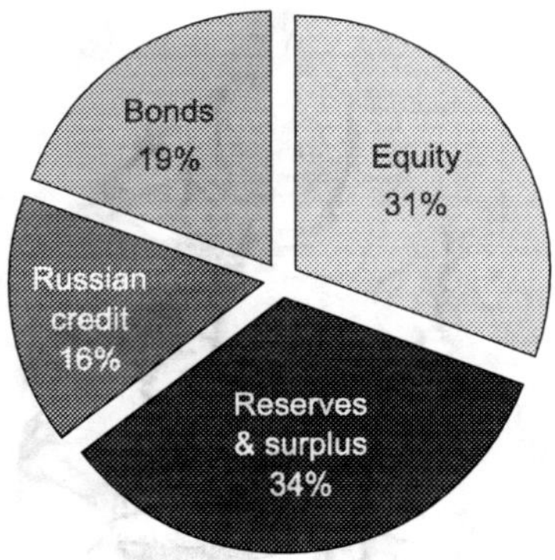

Narora Atomic Power Station (NAPS) is the first Nuclear Power Station, a unit of NPCIL (A Govt. of India Enterprise), which is indigenously designed, constructed and commissioned. The Company Overview: Narora Atomic Power Station (NAPS) is a unit of Nuclear Power Corporation of India Limited (NPCIL), founded in September1987 under the control of Department of Atomic Energy (DAE).

Two units with a capacity of 220 MW each. Both units were brought to existence in the year of 1989 and 1991 respectively. The basic designed of these units is CANDU type i.e. Heavy water Pressurized Reactor. Narora is a small ancient village, which is situated on the bank of holy river Ganga in the district of Bulandshahr in the state of Uttar Pradesh. The generated Electricity is being supplied to the Nine (09) neighboring states in which UP is the main state, through Northern Regional Electricity Grid. The Reactors use natural uranium available in India as a fuel, and heavy water produced in the country as moderator and coolant.

The Indian Engineers and Scientists have done including design, engineering, erection, commissioning and operation the execution of the project cost of Rs. 723 crores - mostly for the import of special materials and equipment.

NAPS is the Fourth Nuclear Power Station in the country after the Tarapur in Maharashtra, Rawatbhata in Rajasthan & Kalapakkam in Tamil Nadu and First indigenous Nuclear Power plant of India.

NAPS is certified for Environment Management System (ISO 14001) on 19th August 1999.The total strength of manpower at NAPS is about 1400 Employees. Atomic power stations which are operating in India are Tarapur (4 units), Rawatbhata (6 units), Kalpakkam (2 units), Narora (2 units), Kakarpara (2 units), Kaiga (4 units).

Analysis: Maintaining working capital is an important aspect of financial management and the same is with NAPS. Money is required there for both fixed and working capital. Narora Atomic Power Station fixed assets include building, plant and machinery, furniture and fitting etc. They are required to be retained in the organization for a long period and yield returns over the life of such assets. The main objective at NAPS is to determine working capital requirement. Working capital includes four major items of balance sheet like inventory, cash management, creditors, and debtors.

Gross Working Capital: According to this concept working capital means gross working capital, which is the total of all the current assets of the business.

Gross Working Capital = Total Current Assets

Net Working Capital: According to this concept, working capital means net working capital, which is the excess of current assets over current liabilities.

Net working capital = current assets - current liabilities

As said by various researchers "Working capital means total of current assets." —Mead, Mallott and Field. And "Any acquisitions of funds which increase the current assets increase working capital, for they are one and the same." —Bonneville and Dewey. "The most common definition of net working capital is the differences of firm's current assets and current liabilities."

Working capital can be negative, zero, positive. As discussed net working capital is the excess of current assets over current liabilities. If current assets are equal to current liabilities, net working capital will be zero and if current liabilities are more than current assets, net working capital will be negative.

Current assets mean those assets which are converted into cash within a short period of time not exceeding one year. Current liabilities are those liabilities which have to be paid within a short period of time in no case exceeding one year.

Along with the fixed capital NAPS require working capital though the extent of working capital requirement differs in their business. Working capital is needed for purchasing raw materials i.e. heavy water and uranium. Then raw material is then converted into finished goods by incurring some additional costs on it. Now electricity is sold. This sale does not convert into cash instantly because there are invariably some credit sales. Thus, there exists a time lag between sales of electricity and receipt of cash. During this period, expenses are to be incurred for continuing the production of electricity and for this purpose working capital is needed which shall be involved for the purchase of raw materials to the realization of cash. The time period, which is required to convert raw materials to the realization of cash and the time period, which is required to convert raw materials into electricity and then into cash is known as operating cycle or cash cycle. The time need for working capital can also be explained with the help of operating cycle.

Operating cycle of manufacturing electricity involves four phases:

- Conversion of cash into raw material.
- Conversion of raw material into electricity.
- Conversion of electricity into debtors by credit sales.
- Conversion of electricity into cash by realizing cash from them.

Since the operating cycle is a continuous process there remains a need for continuous supply of working capital. However, the amount of working capital required is not constant throughout the year but keeps fluctuating. On the basis of this concept, working capital is classified into two types.

The need for working capital or current assets fluctuates from time to time. However, to carry on day-to-day operations of the business without any obstacles, a certain minimum level of raw materials, work in progress, finished goods and cash must be maintained on a continuous basis. The amount involved as permanent working capital has to be from long term sources of finance e.g., debentures long-term loans etc. but NAPS has its own resources so they don't require any financing from outsiders. The amount over and above the permanent level of working capital is called temporary, fluctuation or variable working capital. Due to seasonal changes, level of business activities working activities is higher than normal during some months of year and therefore additional working capital will be requiring along with the permanent working capital. In case of NAPS it is not so because it is required on continuous basis.

After determining the requirement of working capital, the next important task before the financial manager of NAPS is to select the appropriate sources of working capital. There are mainly two sources include bonds, equity shares, preference shares, inter unit transaction units.

Working capital requirements of a firm are basically related to nature of business. For, instance NAPS required a large amount of working capital and have to invest in fixed assets. Their working capital requirements are much because they have credit sales only and supply services and not products.

The size of business also has an important influence on its working capital requirements. Size measure the scale of operations obliviously, larger the size greater would be the need of working capital. As NAPS is a large organization which require a large amount of working capital to meet its daily expenses.

The manufacturing cycle refers to the time involved in manufacturing of goods i.e converting raw material into electricity. Thus, the larger the time span of the manufacturing cycle, larger will be the working capital requirements of the firms and vice-versa.

Changes in the unit price of electricity also influence the requirements of working capital. Rising prices would necessitate the need of more funds for maintaining the existing level of activity.

The firm should maintain a sound working capital position. Both excessive as well as inadequate working capital positions are dangerous from organization's point of view.

The danger of excessive working capital in NAPS can be unnecessary accumulation of inventories, indication of defective credit policy, makes management complacent, which degenerates into handling of material inefficiency. While inadequate working capital is also bad like it stagnates growth, fixed assets are not efficiently utilized for the lack of the working capital funds, not able to honor short term obligations.

As a result the organization faces the tight credit terms. An enlightened management should, therefore, maintain a right amount of working capital. Only then proper functioning of business operations will be ensured. Sound financial and statistical techniques, supported by judgment should predict the quantum of working capital needed at different time periods. An organization net working capital is not only important as an index of liquidity, but it also used as the measure of the organization's risk. Lenders consider a positive working capital as a measure of safety. All other things being equal, the more the net working capital a firm has, the less risky that it will default in meeting its current financial obligations.

Cash is the important current asset for the operations of the business. Cash is the basic input needed to keep the business running on a continuous basis; it is also the ultimate output expected to be realized by selling the service or product manufactured by the firm. Currency and cheques held by the organization, and balances in its bank accounts.

Cash management is concerned with the managing of; (1) cash flows into and out of the organization, (2) cash flow within the organization, and (3) cash balances held by the organization at a point of time by financing deficit or investing surplus cash.

In order to resolve the uncertainty about cash flows prediction and lack of synchronization between cash receipts and payments, the firm should develop appropriate strategies for cash management such as cash planning, managing the cash flows, investing surplus cash, optimum cash level. The organization use to hold cash to achieve the various motives. The transactions motive mainly refers to holding cash to meet anticipated payments whose timing is not perfectly matched with cash receipts. The precautionary motive is the need to hold cash to meet contingencies in the future. It provides a cushion to buffer to withstand some unexpected emergency. The speculative motive relates to the holding of cash for investing in profit-making opportunities as and when they arise. Compensation motive is to hold cash balances is to compensate banks for providing certain services and loans. Banks provide a variety of services to business firms, such as clearance of cheques, supply of credit information, transfer of funds, etc. while for some of the services banks charge a commission or free, for others they seek indirect compensation.

In the normal course, NAPS have to make payments of cash and a continuous and regular basis to suppliers of goods, employees and so on. Cash is therefore aptly described as the "oil to lubricate the ever-turning wheels of business: without it the process grinds to a stop."

The need for maintaining cash balances arises from the non-synchronization of the inflows and outflows of cash: if the receipts and payments of cash perfectly. Coincide or balance each other, there would be no need for cash balances. Cash flows are inseparable parts of the organization. An organization needs cash to invest in inventory, receivable and fixed assets and to make payments for operating expenses in order to maintain growth in sales and earnings while the production of electricity. It is possible that organization may be making adequate profits, but may suffer from the shortage of cash as its growing needs may be consuming cash vary fast. Cash planning is a technique to plan and control the use of cash. It helps to anticipate the future cash flows and needs of the organization's profitability and cash deficits, which can cause the organization's failure.

NAPS prepared budget for the organization to plan for and control cash receipts and payments, which may vary from organisation to organisation. Monthly and yearly budgets are prepared for determining cash requirement if cash flows show extreme fluctuations. Cash budget for a longer intervals are prepared because cash flows are relatively stable.

Cash forecasts are needed to prepare cash budgets. Cash forecasts are done one on both short or long-term basis. Generally, forecasts covering periods of one year or less are considered short-term; those extending beyond one year are considered long-term. The important functions of carefully developed short-term cash forecasts are to determine cash requirements, anticipate short-term financing, and manage investment of surplus cash. Long-term cash forecasts are prepared to find an idea of the company's financial requirements in the distant future. Long term forecasts are not detailed as short term forecast.

There are many aspects of working capital management, which make it an important function of the financial manager like it require much of the financial manager's time, large portion of total investment in assets, great significance in the organization but it is very critical for small firms and directly related to firm's growth.

Credit standards are the criteria, which NAPS follow in selecting the states for the purpose of giving electricity on credit. The organization have tight credit standards that is, it may sell mostly on cash basis, and extend credit only to the most reliable and financially strong customers. Such results will result in no bad-debt losses, and less cost of credit administration. Various debtors of NAPS are CSEB (Chandigarh State Electricity) BOARD, DTCL (Delhi Transco Limited), HVPNL (Haryana Vidyut Prasarad Nigam Ltd), HPSEB (Himachal Pradesh State Electricity Board), J&K SEB (Jammu & Kashmir State Electricity Board), PSEB (Punjab State Electricity Board), AVVNL (Ajmer Vidyut Vitran Nigam Limited), JVVNL (Jaipur Vidyut Vitran Nigam Limited), JDVVNL (Jodhpur Vidyut Vitran Nigam Limited), UPPCL (Uttar Pradesh Power Corporation Ltd), UPCL (Uttaranchal Power Corporation Ltd).

Credit analysis influences the quality of the NAPS customers. There are two aspects of the quality of customers: (i) the time taken by customers to repay credit obligation and (ii) the default rate which do not exist in NAPS. The average collection period (ACP) determines the speed of payment by customers. It measures the number of days for which credit sales remain outstanding. The longer the average collection period, the longer the organization investment in account receivable. On the basis of past practice and experience, the financial or credit manager should be able to form a reasonable judgment regarding the chances of default.

Recommendations: Ratio analysis is a mean of better understanding of financial strength and weakness of any company. And hence the study is based on the data related to last years and the financial analyses are made on the basis of these ratios.

Liquidity refers to the ability of an organization to meet its current obligations as and when these become due. The short term obligations are met by realizing amount assets should either be liquid or near liquidity. These should be converted into cash for paying obligations of short-term liabilities, if current assets can pay off current liabilities, then liquidity position will be satisfactory. On the other hand, if current liabilities may not be easily met out of current assets then liquidity position will be bad. To measure the liquidity of a firm, the following ratio can be calculated:

Current ratio of NAPS states that in the year 2012-13 it is very high hence it shows idleness of funds. But also in the year 2013-14 short term financial position of the enterprise is very sound because its current assets are more than twice of current liabilities. It is a positive sign that it works on desired level.

Quick or acid test or liquid ratio of NAPS is more than 1:1. So it is satisfactory. It means that current assets are more than current liabilities, the short term financial position is very good.

Absolute liquidity ratio of 2012-13 is high. So it shows that there is adequacy of cash and short-term securities, which is satisfactory. As NAPS has large amount of idle funds so results in positive view for the organization.

Inventory turnover ratio of NAPS is satisfactory in 2013-14 as compared to 2012-13. It means funds are not blocked in inventory. So, management should take some important decision regarding inventory management. At least they should invest some funds in inventory to meet the unforeseen circumstances.

Debtor collection period of current year is more than that of the previous year, which is not satisfactory which indicates deferred payment by debtors and hence increases the chances of bad debts. But if you consider the collection period of current year i.e. 2012-13 it is satisfactory.

Working capital ratio reveals how efficiently the fixed assets are being utilized. Compared with the previous year there is a decrease in the ratio, which shows that assets have not been used efficiently as they had been used in the previous year. So they should work upon the increase in the production capacity to meet the desired criteria.

Net profit ratio indicates that NAPS is earning a good amount of profit which they can contribute to various CSR (Corporate Social responsibility) activities.

"SWOT" ANALYSIS OF NAPS

Strength	*Weaknesses*
Strong technological base. Highly skilled professionally qualified workforce. Units accredited with ISO-14001, IS-18001. Adoption of innovative fuel optimization. Outage management. Won many safety awards from GOVERNMENT OF INDIA, results in gaining the confidence of the society as a whole; acts as a great strength.	The manpower at NAPS is in excess that is a burden on a PSU. In production department some machines are too old.

Opportunities	Threats
NAPS have become a generic name in the power generation. So, company has great opportunities in such market if supply will be regular with reasonable prices. Diversification in the areas of conventional and non-conventional power generation.	If competitor is providing electricity at more reasonable prices than NAPS, then the customers of the company may be lost. Expansion of thermal power plants and hydro power plants.

Questions for Discussion

- Discuss the impact of profitability on the trends in liquidity of the company? Explain.
- Further analyze the SWOT and give your inputs.

References

- Pandey, S. and Jaiswal, V.K. (2011). "Effectiveness on Profitability: Working Capital Management", SCMS Journal of Indian Management, Volume (8) 1 , 73–80.
- Singh, J.P. and Pandey, S. (2008). "Impact of Working Capital Management in the Profitability of Hindalco Industries Limited," The ICFAI University Journal of Financial Economics, Volume (6) 4, 62–72.

18

A Case on Hypothetical Merger Between Molson Coors and Sab Miller Plc

Chirag Bhushan • Anita Veniak[18]

Abstract

Beer is a popular alcoholic beverage that is produced by fermenting and brewing starch from malted barley. The global market for beer was estimated to be worth USD 104,978.3 million in 2010, and is projected to be valued at USD 137,458.9 million by 2015 registering a CAGR of 6.3% between 2010 and 2015. The beer market faces challenges in the form of competing alcoholic drinks such as spirits and wine among others. The brewing industry is has started to see industry consolidation in past few years, the present report assumes Molson Coors, a brewing company to be a potential target which is planning to merge with another brewing company, SABMiller. It aims to see the practicality of a merger at an enterprise value of $15.4bn. Various multiples & ratios have been used in this report to analyze long term growth of companies and to calculate the true value of the company. Geographic footprint of the merger aims to develop an understanding about the future of the combined entity (Molson Coors merged with SABMiller). Pro forma of this merger and a synergized impact helps us see the increase in the EBITDA margin.

Along with all this, the report includes analysis of the precedents over the last 15 years which aids in defining the premium that any company seeking merger and acquisition opportunities in this sector should pay.

Finally it is concluded by stating that any such merger may prove to be beneficial for both the companies, Molson Coors and SABMiller.

Keywords: Brewing sector, Molson coors, SABMiller, Deleveraging profile, S&P 500 Index.

INTRODUCTION

Beer is a popular alcoholic beverage that is produced by fermenting and brewing starch from malted barley. The global market for beer was

[18]Chirag Bhushan is a student of MBA programme Class of 2015 and Anita Veniak is an Asst Prof in the Area of Information Technology with Amity Business School. The authors have developed the case solely for class discussion for the programmes in management. The author does not intend to illustrate effective or ineffective handling of a managerial situation. The case study does not represent or endorse the views of the managements about the issues in the case.

estimated to be worth USD 104,978.3 million in 2010, and is projected to be valued at USD 137,458.9 million by 2015 registering a CAGR of 6.3% between 2010 and 2015. The beer market has demonstrated moderate to mature growth in markets such as the United States and Europe. On the other hand, growth remains average in countries such as India, Thailand, China, and Nigeria. There has been an increasing realisation that not all developing markets are equally attractive.

The beer market faces challenges in the form of competing alcoholic drinks such as spirits and wine among others. As well as trading up into beer, consumers are trading up within the beer category. Local premium brands increased their share in developing markets with international premium brands often growing just as strongly, albeit from a lower base. The brewing industry is has started to see industry consolidation in past few years. And this industry consolidation has left many companies with fragmented IT and back-office systems, presenting opportunities to improve global efficiency without losing local flexibility.

Continuing the industry consolidation trend, the present case assumes Molson Coors, a brewing company to be a potential target which is planning to merge with another brewing company, SABMiller. This case aims to see the practicality of a merger between Molson Coors Brewing Company and SABMiller Plc. At an enterprise value of $15.4 bn, Molson Coors brews and distributes licensed products under various brand names in countries like Europe, Canada, United States and Puerto Rico.

An in-depth analysis of Molson Coors provides us with a better insight of the financials of the company and its long term growth prospects. A comparison of Molson Coors with its peer group gives us an actual view of which company is performing in better in current market conditions and which one has the potential for future growth. To analyze any possible merger prospect between any two companies, an investment banker cannot rely on one multiple or one ratio. Hence various multiples & ratios have been used in this report to analyze long term growth of companies and to calculate the true value of the company. Some multiples that are often used to determine a company's valuation in the case of a potential acquisition or a merger are EV/Revenue, EV/EBITDA, P/E and PEG Ratio. Various valuation and operational benchmarking graphs have helped assess this study.

To further access our study, current market conditions in the global brewing sector have been analyzed by valuing a few other major players in this sector.

Companies often take on excessive amounts of debt to initiate their growth. However, using leverage substantially increases the riskiness of the firm. Hence, a deleveraging profile of SABMiller has been included which helps us calculate the implied firepower of the company.

Geographic footprint of the merger aims to develop an understanding about the future of the combined entity (Molson Coors merged with SABMiller). Pro forma of this merger and a synergized impact helps us see the increase in the EBITDA margin of the combined entity.

Along with all this, the report includes analysis of the precedents over the last 15 years which aids in defining the premium that any company seeking merger and acquisition opportunities in this sector should pay.

Finally it is concluded by stating that any such merger may prove to be beneficial for both the companies, Molson Coors and SABMiller.

CASE PROBLEM

Molson Coors with poor compound annual growth rate, both in the case of revenue and EBITDA and also with less EBITDA margin, seems to be in a need of a merger. On one hand MCBC is more debt worthy and is more likely to handle its debt burden; also the company's stock is undervalued given its earnings performance, so the company has more long term growth than any of its competitors. And on the other hand, SABMiller has the least Capex as of sales and quite decent CAGR and margin ratios, stating that the company is utilizing its fixed assets efficiently.

With Molson Coors having a strong foothold in the developed markets and SABMiller wanting expand its business to the developed markets; SABMiller can enter such markets with a possible future merger.

MOLSON COORS - COMPANY OVERVIEW

Molson Coors Brewing Company manufactures and sells beer and other beverage products. The company brews and distributes licensed products under various brand names in countries like Europe, Canada, United States and Puerto Rico. It creates extraordinary, premium beer at breweries from the Rocky Mountains of Colorado in the US to the storied Burton-on-Trent brewery in the UK, to Prague's celebrated brewing heritage in the Czech Republic, and the oldest brewery in Montreal, Canada. It also sells brands through a joint venture, Cobra Beer Partnership Ltd.

The company was formerly known as Adolph Coors Company changed its state of incorporation to the state of Delaware in August 2003. And in February 2005 the company changed its name to Molson Coors Brewing Company. Molson Coors Brewing Company was founded in 1786 and is headquartered in Denver, Colorado. It today has a portfolio of more than 100 beer brands.

In April 2012, the company acquired StarBev of Amsterdam, Netherlands for $3.54 billion and today provides employment to about 17,650 people.

Miller Coors is a joint venture that combined the US businesses of Molson Coors and SABMiller and employs around 9,000 people.

(Molson Coors Brewing Co.-B)(About Us: Our Company)

BRAND PORTFOLIO

The company has a diverse brand portfolio which it distributes and sells across the globe. Mainly it categorize its brands into two broad categorize i.e. signature and partner brands but it also have a global portfolio of about 100 brands selling under its companies name.

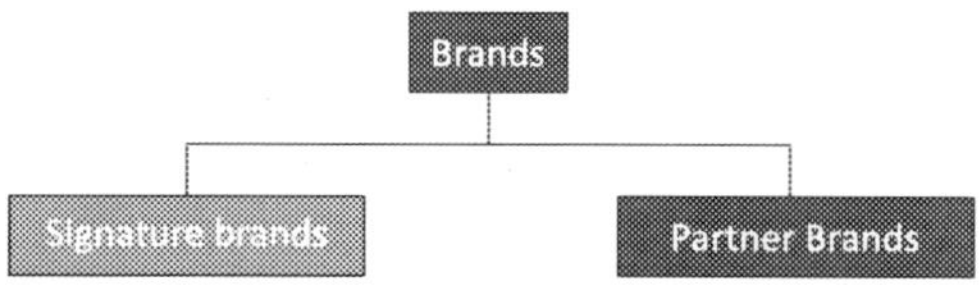

The geographical presence of its various brands can be stated as:

The company sells its products in Canada under the Coors Light, Molson Canadian, Molson Export, Molson Canadian 67, Molson Dry, Molson Canadian Cider, the Rickard's family, Carling, Carling Black Label, Pilsner, Keystone Light, Creemore Springs, the Granville Island, and Coors Banquet brands.

It also brews or distributes licensed products under the Heineken, Amstel Light, Murphy's, Newcastle Brown Ale, Strongbow cider, Miller Lite, Miller Genuine Draft, Miller Chill, Milwaukee's Best, and Milwaukee's Best Dry brands. In addition, the company distributes the Corona, Coronita, Negra Modelo, and Pacifico brands, as well as Singha brand.

Further, the company sells various brands in the United States and Puerto Rico comprising Coors Light, Miller Lite, Miller High Life, Keystone Light, Blue Moon, Leinenkugel's, Coors Banquet, Miller Genuine Draft, Icehouse, Mickey's, Milwaukee's Best, Hamm's, Old English 800, Blue Moon, Henry Weinhard's, Molson and Foster's, George Killian's Irish Red, Redd's, Peroni Nastro Azzurro, Pilsner Urquell, Grolsch, Batch 19, Worthington's, St. Stefanus, Third Shift, cider, Coors Non-Alcoholic, and Sharp's.

Additionally, it sells various brands in Europe that include Carling, Ozujsko, Jelen, Staropramen, Coors Light, Kamenitza, Niksicko, Bergenbier, Branik, Worthington's, Sharp's Doom Bar, Borsodi, Ostravar, Noroc, Astika, Apatinsko, and Blue Moon; and various regional ale brands, as well as factored brands. The company also sells brands through a joint venture, Cobra Beer Partnership Ltd. In addition, it sells Zima, Iceberg 9000, King Cobra, Coors Gold, and Coors Extra brands.

FINANCIAL ANALYSIS

Stock Price (22-May-14)	$64.55
52 Week High-Low	$65.46-$46.94
Market Cap	$11.9bn
Enterprise Value	$15.4bn
Total Debt	$3.8bn

FYE 31/12	2012A	2013A	2014E	2015E
Revenue (in $ mn)	7176.2	7482.4	7521.9	7617.1
% Growth	7.32%	4.27%	0.53%	1.27%
EBITDA (in $ mn)	1397.9	1468.5	1400.7	1473.4
% Margin	19.48%	19.63%	18.62%	19.34%
EBIT (in $ mn)	1005.3	1025.6	1052.8	1112.2
% Margin	14.01%	13.71%	14.00%	14.60%
Gross Profit (in $ mn)	2863.7	2956.9	3050.1	3077.3
% Margin	39.91%	39.52%	40.55%	40.40%

Multiples	2012A	2013A	2014E	2015E
EV/Revenue	2.15x	2.1x	2.0x	2.0x
EV/EBITDA	11.02x	10.5x	11.0x	10.5x
P/E	19.80x	15.7x	15.0x	14.9x

ANNOTATED STOCK PRICE PERFORMANCE

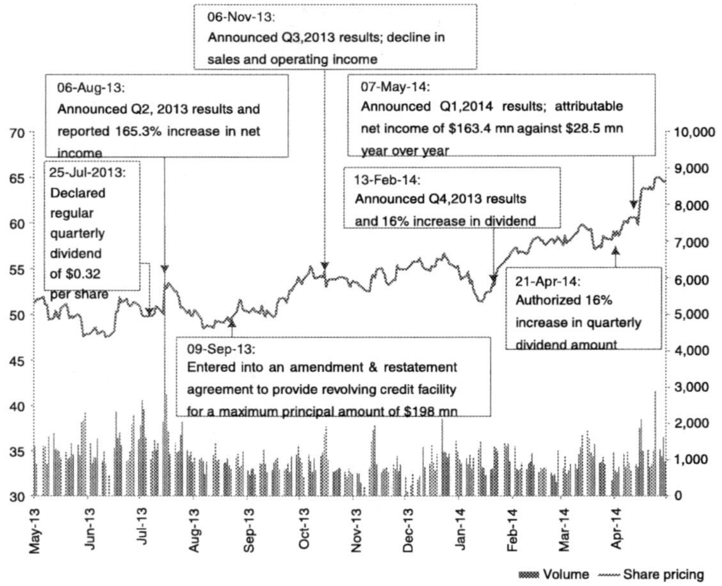

Source: *Company Press Releases and Capital IQ.*

COMPANY OVERVIEW

SABMiller, through its subsidiaries, engages in the manufacture, distribution, and sale of beverages. It offers beer, soft drinks, and fruit juices. The company is also involved in brewing and hop farming activities. In addition, it bottles soft drinks for The Coca-Cola Company in El Salvador and Honduras; and for PepsiCo International in Panama. The company offers its products primarily under the Pilsner Urquell, Peroni Nastro Azzurro, Miller Genuine Draft, Grolsch, Águila, Castle, Miller Lite, Snow, Tyskie, and Victoria Bitter brands. SABMiller plc has a portfolio of approximately 200 beer brands.

The company serves various customers in the United Kingdom, Australia, Colombia, South Africa, the United States, and internationally. SABMiller plc was founded in 1895 and is headquartered in London, the United Kingdom.

The Company employs about 70,000 people globally. Company's past & present investors include Allan Gray Limited, Altria Group Inc. (NYSE:MO), BevCo Limited, Kulczyk Investments S.A., Vontobel Asset Management AG.

It trades on the London Stock Exchange with a market capitalization of $91.3bn and has a EV/LTM revenue multiple of 4.0x.

SNAPSHOT OF MOLSON COORS

Molson Coors Stock Price Performance

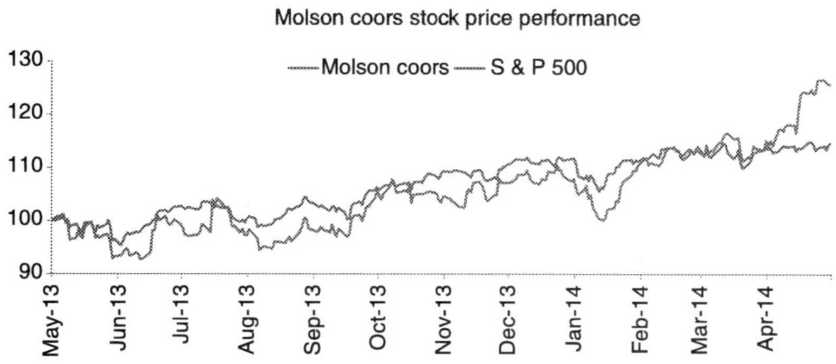

Source: *Capital IQ as of 22-May-2014.*

Inference

The above figure shows the stock price performance of Molson Coors Brewing Company compared with the S&P500 index. Here we can easily notice that the stock price of Molson Coors is in complete sync with the movement in S&P500. However the stock price of the company has increased drastically in the past two months, thereby surpassing the index.

This increase in the stock price is majorly because of the strategic decision taken by the management to declare an increased regular quarterly dividend of USD 0.37 per share, payable on March 17, 2014, to Class A and Class B shareholders of record on February 28, 2014. This dividend represents a 16% increase from the previous quarterly rate of USD 0.32 per share and raises the annual dividend rate to USD 1.48 per share.

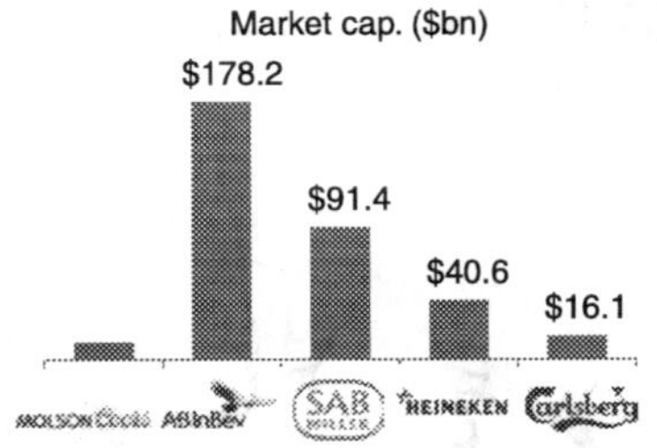

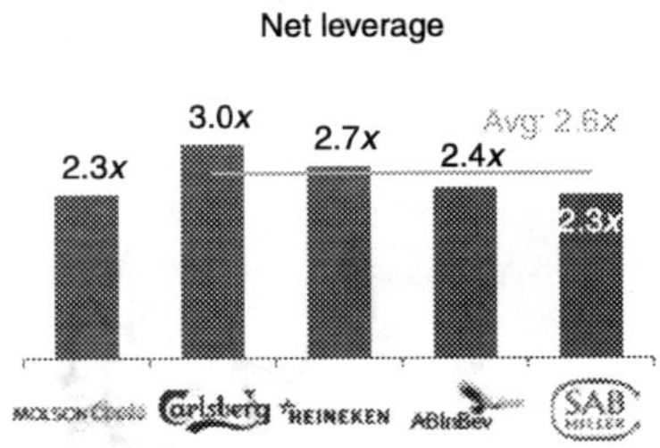

Notes: Our peer index includes companies like ABI, SABMiller, Carlsberg and Heineken.

ABI data also includes new debt and EBITDA for Oriental Brewery acquisition.

Source: *Capital IQ as of 22-May-2014*

Inference

In the above figures we can see that even though the equity value of the company, Molson Coors; is less than that of its peers, the net leverage is better than the average of its peer group. This means that the company is giving more EBITDA in lesser amount of Debt as compared to its peers.

For most industries ratios higher than 4 or 5 of net leverage typically set off alarm bells, indicating that a company is less likely to be able to handle its debt burden. But in case of Molson Coors, the company is more likely to be able to handle its debt burden and also is more worthy to fetch more debt from the investors to grow its business or even be ready fora merger in the near future.

VALUATION BENCHMARKING

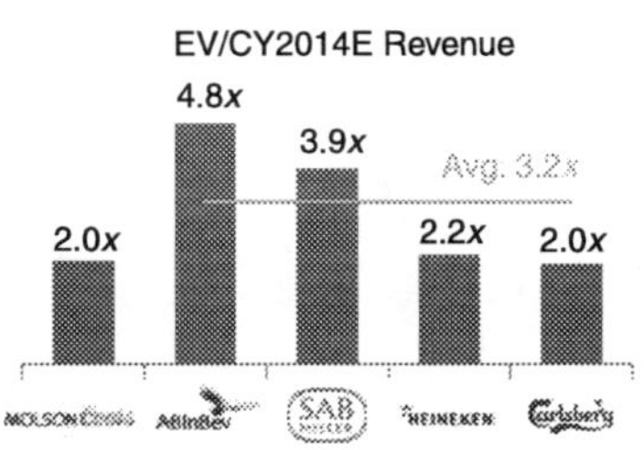

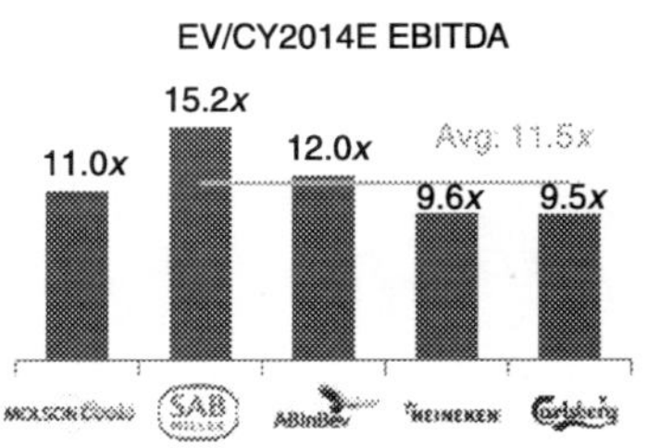

CY2014E P/E[b]

CY2014E PEG Ratio

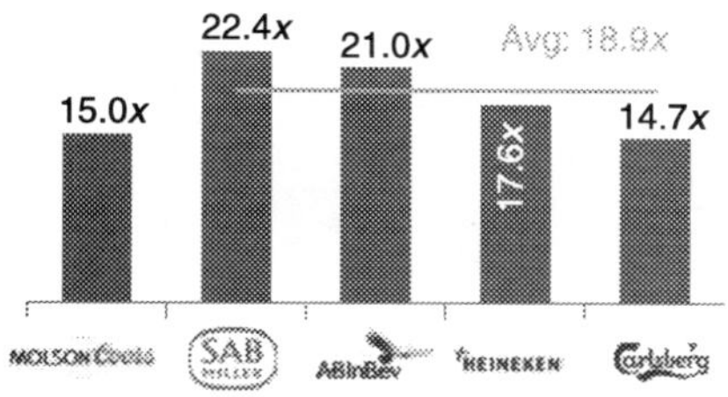

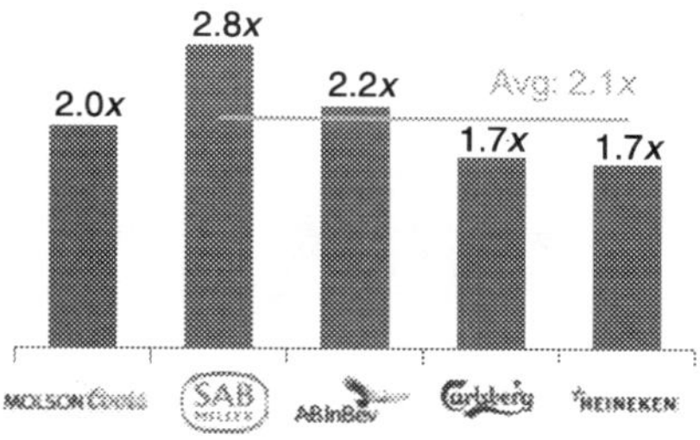

Note: Multiples that are negative or above 70x are considered not meaningful.

Multiples that are negative or above 100x are considered not meaningful.
Source: *Capital IQ as of 22-May-2014*

Inference

The above figures help us to get an idea of the company's relative financial health. On comparing Molson Coors' multiples with that of other public companies in the peer group we see that Molson Coors has lower EV/Revenue and EV/EBITDA multiples than its peers, this means that Molson Coors is undervalued as compared to its peers. Basically at same enterprise value Molson Coors would generate more revenue and EBITDA. This also indicates that our company has more returns, ultimately strengthening the company for any future merger possibilities.

We also see that the P/E ratio of Molson Coors is less than that of its peers, which suggests that investors are expecting lower earnings growth in the future compared to companies with a higher P/E. But as well already know that PEG Ratio is a better measure to judge a company's long term growth, so we can see that with lower PEG ratio, the stock of Molson Coors is undervalued given its earnings performance. Hence it is clear that the company has more long term growth than any of its competitors.

Also we can see that SABMiller has almost come to a maturity state with higher multiples than any other company in the peer group and with Molson Coors showing such potential, making it a more likely prospect for any future possible merger.

VALUATION OVERTIME

Note: Total Shareholders Return includes both share appreciation and dividend paid.

Source: Capital IQ as of 22-May-2014

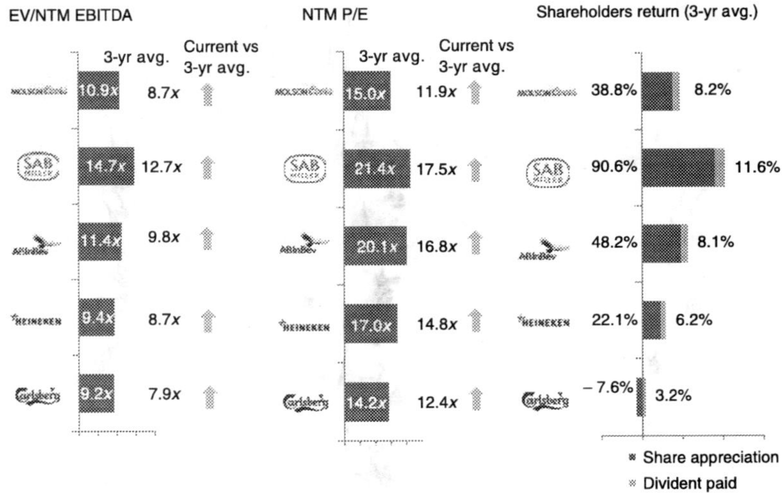

Inference

From the above figures we again see that the EV/NTM EBITDA of Molson Coors is less than that of its peers, which basically means that even when we see the EBITDA of the next twelve months of the companies. We again see that Molson Coors is undervalued as compared to its peers.

Next when we see the NTM P/E multiple, Molson Coors again has lesser P/E than its peers. And in the case of total return, Molson Coors has given comparatively more dividends than the peer group average and also when we see the past three years average, Molson Coors has had decent share appreciation as well. All this shows us that MCBC has better long term growth prospects than its peers.

TOTAL SHAREHOLDERS RETURN

Note: Total Shareholders Return includes both share appreciation and dividend paid.

Source: Capital IQ as of 22-May-2014

Inference

In the above graphs we can see that in the beginning our company's shareholders return was quite less as compared to that of our peers. This was majorly because Molson Coors implemented a different set of strategies in which instead of paying dividends in the early course of business, they started accumulating the profits in the form of reserves; with their plans to acquire a profitable company; a step towards achieving long term growth for the company.

We can also see that after the acquisition of StarBev on 03-Apr-2012, Molson Coors started giving more dividends than any other company in its peer group and hence thereby impressing its investors.

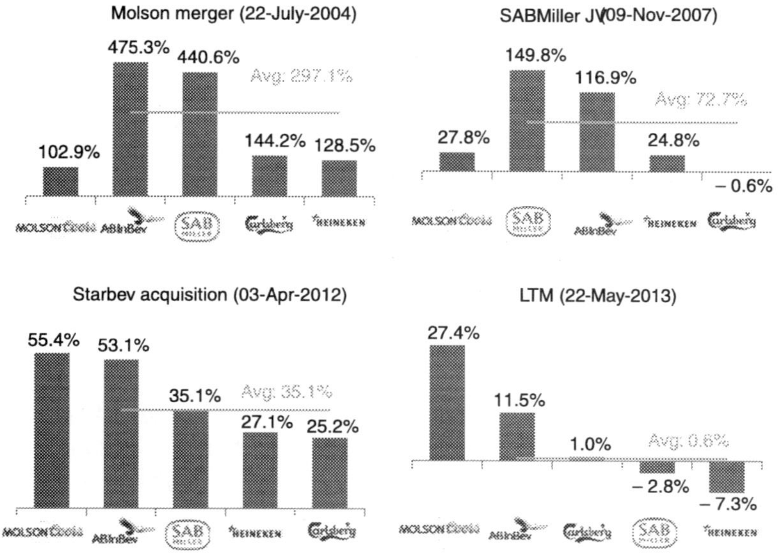

Also in last twelve months when some companies even had negative shareholders return, Molson Coors had a 27.4% shareholders return, thereby surpassing all other companies in its peer group. We can see this trend continuing till 2014.

OPERATIONAL BENCHMARKING

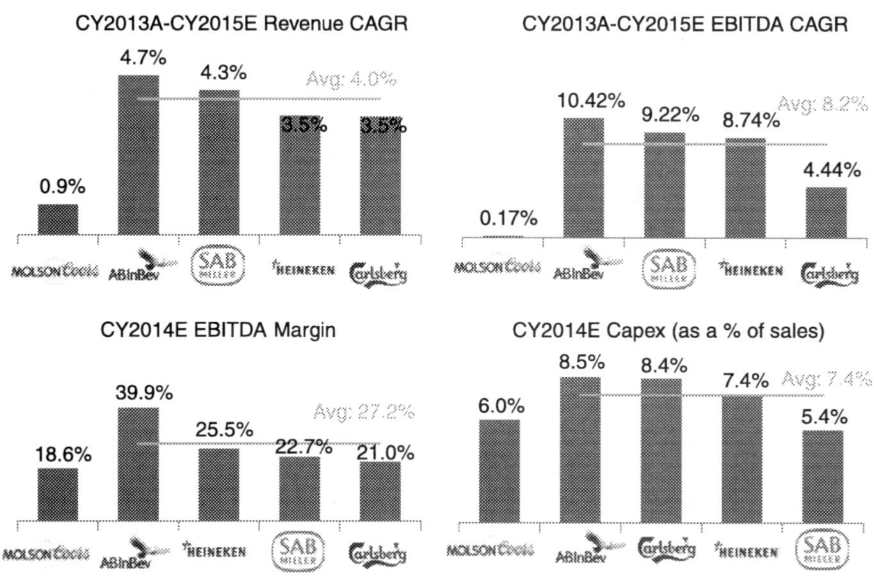

Source: *Capital IQ as of 22-May-2014*

Inference

As we already know that our company has very sound financials in its books of account and also the company has less net leverage and is worthy of taking more debt from the market but from the above graphs we can see that the company shows poor compound annual growth rate, both in the case of revenue and EBITDA. Also the EBITDA margin of the company is lesser than that of the peer groups' average. This basically is one of the few reasons that why Molson Coors should merge with some another company in the near future. Though the company is under-performing as of now but it will most likely improve on such aspects after the merger.

We can also see that even though Molson Coors has less CAGR and margin but the company also has less Capex, which means that the company is using its existing fixed assets efficiently. Same is true in the case of SABMiller, the company has the least Capex as of sales and quite decent CAGR and margin ratios; hence the company is utilizing its fixed assets most efficiently than those in its peer group.

SABMILLER/MOLSON COORS | OVERVIEW

Pro Forma Geographic Footprint (CY2013 Revenues)[(a)]
Global Market Position (Beer Volume in mhl)[(b)]

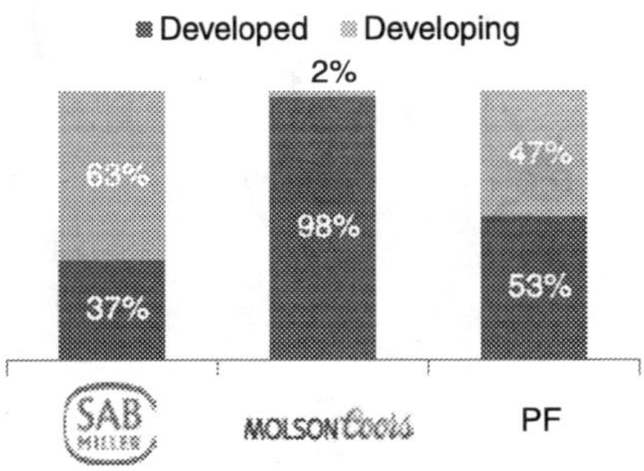

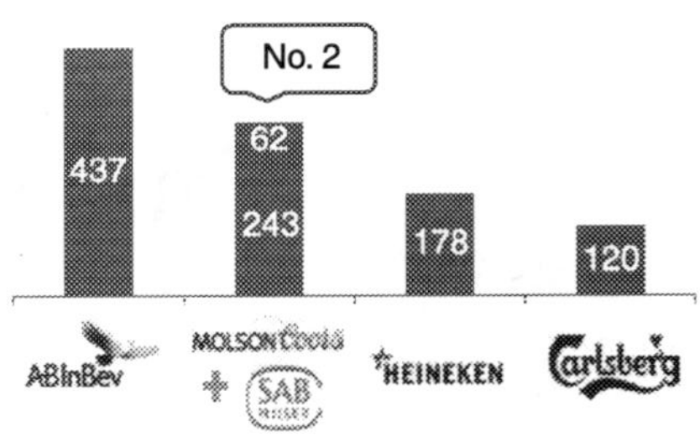

Source: Company Filings and Capital IQ

Notes: Sales split by developed (America and Europe) and developing (Latin America, Asia and Africa); SABMiller data is LTM as of Sep 13; data includes MillerCoors proportionate share.

ABI data includes Oriental Brewery volumes.

Inference

The figure no. 23 shows us the sales split between developing and developed markets of both SABMiller and Molson Coors. Here we can see that SABMiller has its portfolio of brands spread across both developing and developed markets but we can see that company's major geographical presence is in developing markets, while about only 37% in developed markets. On the other hand we see that our company, Molson Coors is majorly dealing with developed markets like America, Europe and Canada. But if we calculate the pro forma of the two companies, we see that the share of the new combined entity has a 53% share in developed markets than the earlier share of 37% of SABMiller. This ultimately means that SABMiller will prefer to merge with Molson Coors because of MCBC's hold and reach in the developed market.

The next figure shows us that the combined entity of the new merger will become number two player in the industry in terms of beer volume. Not just that but with Molson Coors having brighter future prospects and a good long term growth, the combined may surpass ABInBev in the long term.

Key Considerations:

- Rationale: Cements SAB's position/influence in some key profit pools (e.g., US, Canada, UK).

  Already close partnerships in the US(MillerCoors)
- Potential Issues: Complicated- Molson/Coors families.

  Does not really move the needle for SABMiller and limited benefits geographically/for brand portfolio.
- Potential US issue: Some potential overlap issues post StarBev deal (Czech Republic and Romania)
- Growth/margin dilutive to SABMiller: Synergistic potential likely to be more limited (already realized in the US via JV, limited overlap elsewhere).

MILLER/MOLSON COORS | FINANCIAL CONSIDERATIONS

Key Financials[(a)]Volume Growth Impact (5 yr.) [(a)]

Notes: Based on financials calendarized to December year end except SABMiller which is LTM as of Sep 13.

Includes respective portion in MillerCoors but except cash contributions from associates and joint ventures other than MillerCoors.

Based on synergies of 7% Molson Coors last FY net sales.

Sources: Broker Notes and Capital IQ

Inference

From the above graphs we can see that the beer volume growth of the Molson Coors and MillerCoors of the last five years is negative, which means that the beer sales have been decreasing of both these companies.

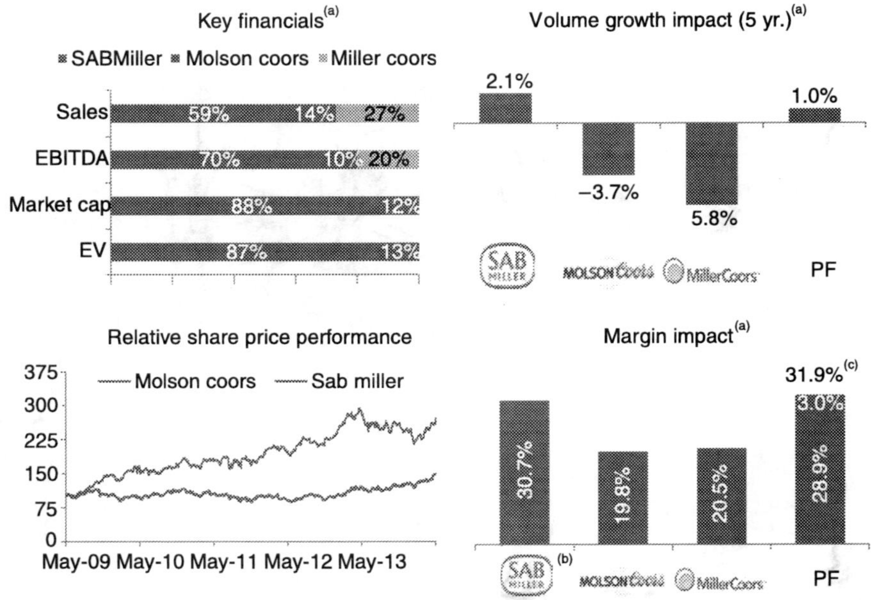

We see that the new combined entity of SABMiller, Molson Coors and their joint venture in US will still have a 1% positive beer volume growth.

Also from the relative share price performance graph we can see that SABMiller has outperformed Molson Coors in the share price performance in the last 5 years. But if we take into considerations only the past one year performance of the two companies, we can see that the share price of SABMiller has fallen while the share price of Molson Coors has risen and has outperformed SABMiller with a quite a margin. This basically means that while SABMiller is almost reaching maturity, Molson Coors has better future prospects because of its better long term growth.

In the final graph we take into account the EBITDA margin of the both the companies and their joint venture and then work upon to calculate the synergized impact of any future merger. Here we can see that SABMiller has a EBITDA margin of 30.7% and that of Molson Coors is just 19.8%. But when take into consideration the synergies of 7% of Molson Coors last financial year net sales, we see that the EBITDA margin of the combined entity will be 31.9%, showing a synergized impact and a margin increase of 3%. This is majorly because of the cost reduction of the combined entity which could be because of factors like economies of scale or any other efficiency.

TRANSACTION COMPARABLES

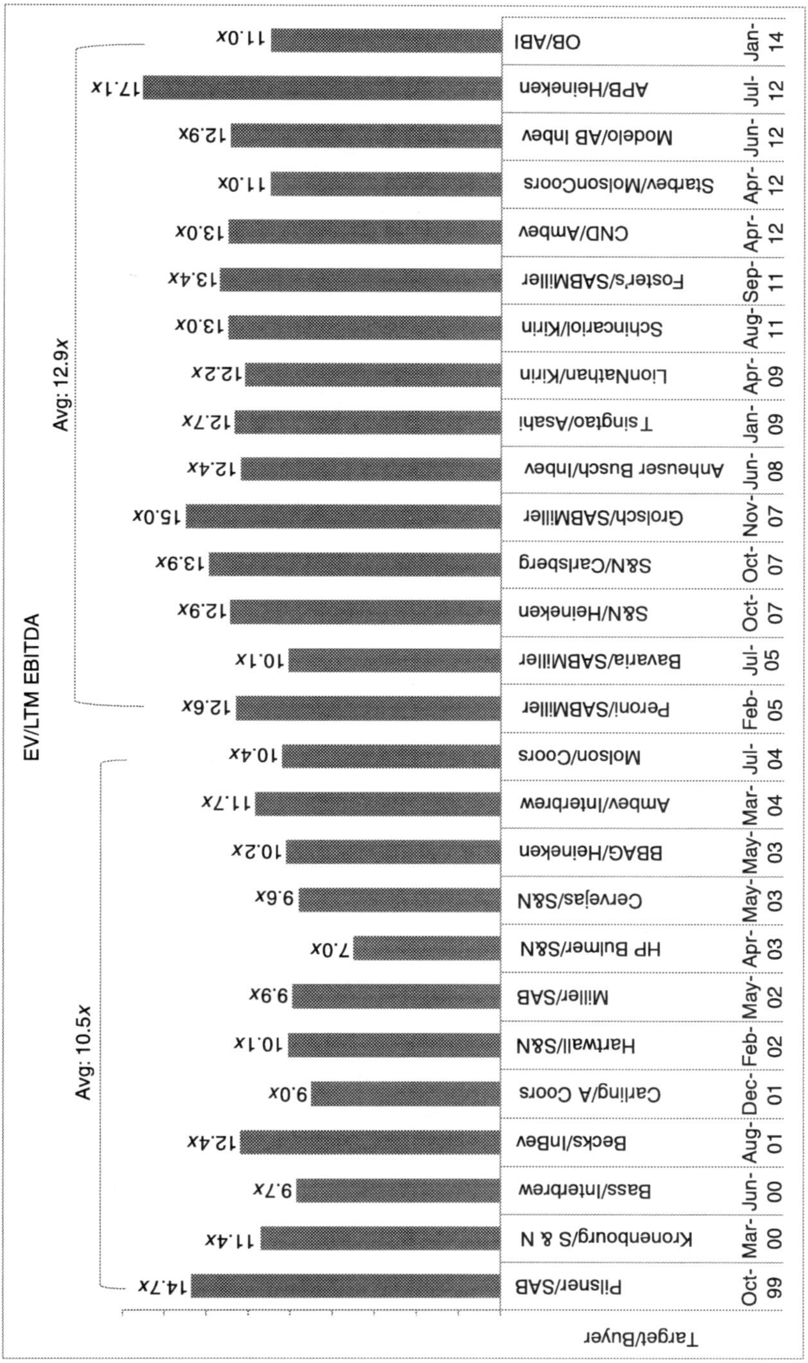

Source: Company Filings, Press Releases and ThompsonOne

Inference

In this particular case we have taken the value at which the company was acquired by the acquirer which we take as the Enterprise Value and then we take the EBITDA of that company one day prior to the date of announcement to calculate the EV/LTM EBITDA multiple.

Now from the above comps we can see that the multiple at which the companies were being acquired has risen from 10.5x to 12.9x with the course of time. This gives us the understanding that if today Molson Coors plans a merger or offers itself for an acquisition, we can multiply this multiple with its EBITDA to calculate the value at which the company should be bought at. This basically would help us define the premium that any company has paid in any merger or acquisition situation.

Say if according to Transaction Comps any company is valued at $30bn and that company is sold at $33bn, then the premium paid by the acquirer would be $3bn.

Part III

"People Management Processes: Art as Well as Science"

19

Recruitment and Selection at Fedders Lloyd Corporation Limited

Aneesha Razdan[19]

Abstract

Recruitment and selection policies have changed from the past time that is it has transformed from traditional sourcing of recruitment to modern sourcing that involves the use of social media that is various websites like Linkedin, twitter, facebook etc. Every organization has its own recruitment and selection policies. In case of Fedders Lloyd Corporation Ltd. The process starts with searching on portal that is (naukri.com) that is based upon the budget prepared by the top management, followed by the years of experience, CTC etc. After these things are clear then searching start on the portal and list down the candidates who are apart for the required position after listing them, telephonic round is conducted so as to get clarity in terms our requirement and the candidate's knowledge, skill and ability to perform that particular task. Then after telephonic round the candidates are short-listed and called for an interview round. Now here the round of interview varies for different positions. In case of top management there are 2 rounds of interview are conducted in case of middle and lower level management there are 3 rounds of interview which are conducted. Before the interview round for fresher's a technical test is conducted. After the interview and test, if the candidate is selected then offer letter is being issued. Employee referral is also being used to recruit candidates. As environment is dynamic there are different ways of selecting candidates.

Keywords: Recruitment, Selection, Traditional methods, Employee referral, Portal (naukri.com).

INTRODUCTION

The Lloyd group (Brij Raj Punj Group) is US$ 500 million group in India. The group is recognized as the pioneer and well established name acknowledged in the field of Air Conditioning in India. The group consists of many companies with diversified portfolios with active involvement in business ventures consisting of manufacturing in:

---

[19]Aneesha Razdan is a student of MBA(HR) programme Class of 2015 in Amity Business School. The authors have developed the case solely for class discussion for the programmes in management. The author does not intend to illustrate effective or ineffective handling of a managerial situation. The case study does not represent or endorse the views of the managements about the issues in the case.

- Air conditioning industry.
- Chillers.
- Scaffolding formwork.
- Sheet metal fabrication.
- Structural steel fabrication.
- Cable and storage management.
- Manufacturing of heat exchange radiators.

The group consists of Fedders Lloyd Corporation Limited and Lloyd Electric and Engineering as its flagship companies. Lloyd group consists of Fedders Lloyd corporation limited ,Lloyd electric and engineering limited, PSL Pvt. Ltd, Airserco Pvt. Ltd, Regal.

Lloyd Electric and Engineering Ltd. has plants in Pant Nagar, Bhivadi Rajasthan, Tauru Haryana, Kalamb, Motor division. PSL Jabalpur division is into steel ducting. Airserco division is into overhead electrification.

Corporate Objective:

Fedders Lloyd Corporation Ltd. has maintained highest standards of practices, principles and corporate Governance Policies. The company ensures that they maintain highest standards for all its internal and external interactions complying with all applicable laws, rules and regulations, leading to effective management.

The policies, procedures are reviewed and assessed periodically to ensure their effectiveness and efficiency is maintained with respect to all the stakeholders of the company.

Its management consists of:

Name	*Designation*
Mr. Brij Raj Punj	Executive Chairman and Managing Director
Mr. S.S. Dhawan	Whole Time Director
Mr. S.S. Kumar	Director
Mr. T.V.P. Punj	Director
Mr. K Lall	Director
Mr. S.K. Sharma	Director
Mr. Ajay Dogra	Director
Mr. Bharat Punj	Director

The company is into manufacturing of LED TV, Air conditioning window, split, tower, portable Ac, commercial type electrical chest freezer, washing machine fully and semi automatic both, water dispensers, room heaters, induction cookers. Recruitment policy of FLCL group provides equal opportunity to all applicants. The purpose is to employ the most suitable candidate for the job, taking into consideration the job fit and the cultural fit.

The recruitment process begins with manpower approval is taken from the department head, then the HR head decides the sources of recruitment that is external or internal, they hire through two sources one is naukri. com(portal) or second through referral hiring and in case of hiring B.Tech fresher's they go for campus recruitment. Neha, one of the recruiter who takes care of the recruitment, shortlists the CV's of prospective candidates by searching it on the portal as per the job description, then telephonic interview is conducted to check their background as well as communication skills after this a list of suitable candidates are chosen according the job description. Taking an example of position that is account for this 1st of all job description is prepared that is:

	LLOYD ELECTRIC & ENGINEERING LIMITED
	Job description
Job title	Accountant
Department:	Finance and Accounts
Reporting to	Director
Job description	Employees in this job should be able to prepare process and reconcile a wide variety of accounting documents such as invoices, department billings, employee reimbursements, cash receipts, vendor statements, preparation of journal vouchers, make deposits and prepare reports, complete and review the information.

Roles and Responsibilities:

- Accounting: Preparation of journal, ledger and trail balance, balance sheets, bank reconciliation statements.
- Posting of financial data to appropriate accounts in an automated accounting system.
- Verifies items billed against items ordered, received and reconciles difference through follow-up with the vendor or with other employees.
- Should be able to design prepare and maintain spread sheets.
- Develop, maintain and analyze budgets, prepare periodic reports that compare budgeted cost to actual cost.
- Candidate should be able to analyze revenues, commission and expenses to ensure that they are recorded on monthly basis.
- Candidate should be able to properly monitor the internal controls.
- Candidate should be able to manage cash transactions.
- Contacting clients and vendors to resolve the issue.
- Maintaining and monitoring of stocks and tallying of physical and books of accounts.

- Preparation of MIS reports (Sundry Debtors and Sundry creditors).
- Preparation of income tax returns and tax deductions.
- Generation of Tax audit reports and filing with authorities.
- Preparation and maintaining of cash book.
- Candidate should be able to record transactions on day to day basis.

Job Skills

- Should be a good team player
- Should be good in mathematical calculations.
- Analytical thinking
- Should have knowledge of Ms.word/excel ,spreadsheets etc.

As per the job description a suitable candidates are searched on naukri. com.

For instance, after this telephonic round of interview is conducted in which Neha call around 20 people after seeing their CV's out of which 8 people are selected for the 1st round of interview. The day and the time were finalized with consultation of Mr. Seth. Candidates where informed through mail the time, venue and the day of interview. Neha gave them a call for conformation as well but out of 8 only 4 turned up. After this on the day of interview the 1st round was taken by Neha followed and for 2nd and 3rd round of interview the candidates were called on some other day as per the availability of hire-ups this reduced their moral because they had to wait for week or maybe 15 days sometimes. The 2nd round taken by the Mr. Seth who is VP-HR and the 3rd is taken by the Head Finance under whom the candidate will work. After 3 rounds of the interview process the discussion happens between Neha, Mr. Seth and Head Finance, the outcome was that out of 4 they found only 1 candidate who was suitable for the position that is Mr. Mishra. After this Neha issued an offer to Mr. Mishra in which she includes his date of joining, salary etc. Once the letter was received by Mr. Mishra he had a problem with the salary, then he was again called by Neha and she made him understand and gave him a raise of Rs. 2000/- more initially he was issues Rs. 28000/- in his offer letter but after negotiating they finally reached to Rs. 30,000/-. Then Mr. Mishra was satisfied and his joining date was 19th June.

On 19th morning Mr. Mishra joined the day started with an induction programme which is of 7 days and at end of it the candidate has to submit the report to their immediate boss.

According to the survey the ratio between the turn-up and line-up of candidates is 3-4 on the scale of 10, this implies on the day of interview the candidates don't turn up.

On the other hand, the company uses various tests like for B.Tech fresher's 1st a technical test is conducted followed by interview in case of other positions aptitude, personality and intelligence test is conducted. In case of recruiting a top management candidate for example DGM,VP etc 2 rounds of interviews are conducted and in case of middle and lower level of candidates 3 rounds of interview are conducted. The major issue in this organization is that the candidate does not join even after being selected this because here the recruitment process is slow, they get another opportunity.

The average attrition rate in a year of the company is 30%.

The organization consists of 1500 employees wherein they have different departments of HR, finance, International marketing, import and export etc. It consists of 76% of males and 24% of females. They contribute to CSR as well where they have schools for small children. In spite of so many drawbacks Neha does her job in a very systematic manner.

Key learning's:

- The company considers portal (naukri.com), employee referral as the medium of hiring candidates. The most important feature we need to take into consideration that is the ratio between turn-up and line up candidates. After the survey it was found out that the ratio is 3-4% which implies out of 10 candidates 3, 4 turn up for the interview, now this purely depends upon the position for which we are lining up the interview. In Regal department of Fedders Lloyd Corporation Ltd.they take technical tests for fresher's and junior level candidates which is followed by an interview with the concerned head of that particular department. The recruitment of the prospective candidate for a particular post is based on experience, age, qualification and percentage in the academic year. The selection process is totally based on skills, communication, personality and technical qualities. There are 2, 3 rounds of face to face interview. Personality, aptitude, technical, intelligence tests are being conducted in Fedders Lloyd.

Questions for Discussions

- As an HR manger how would you improve the recruitment and selection process at Fedders Lloyd Corporation limited?
- Suppose you are in place of Neha how would you recruit Mr.Mishra? Suggest some effective ways which should be both economical and time saving. Give suggestions on how the company should reduce their attrition rate?

References

- Gilmore, S. and Williams, S. (2009). Human Resource Management. Oxford: Oxford University Press. Chapter 5 takes a themed approach to the topic of employee selection.
- Thompson, P. and McHugh, D. (2009). Work Organisations: A critical approach, 4th ed. Basingstoke: Palgrave Macmillan.
- Arnold, J. et al (2005). Work Psychology: Understanding human behaviour in the workplace4th ed. Harlow: FT Prentice Hall.
- http://www.hrwale.com/recruitment/88-2/
- https://www.nd.gov/hrms/managers/guide/selproc.html
- http://www.eohrecruitmentsolutions.co.za/live/content.php?Item_ID=2101

20

Organization's Culture: A Critical Element for Success!

Ashutosh Agrawal • R. Sujatha[20]

Abstract

An organizational culture encompasses all that is valued in the system, leadership styles, jargons and symbols, routines, traditions and vision of the organizations involved. In start up organization, such as UAS International, culture hotspots appear across teams, functions, product groups, each with a different style of work culture. That sometimes makes it very difficult to organize and coordinate efforts of all organizations. For example, is a very common problem among marketing, human resources and R&D departments of not being supportive of each other and blame the other department for their own shortcomings. Mainly because each unit has developed its own work ethic, methods and unique culture. It is also very important to understand that these subunits outside their own culture also bear the imprint of the culture of all organizations. A closer look at the most typical elements of organizational culture can be found in their work styles. In assessing the culture of an organization is important to focus on the entire organization for analysis or other means to evaluate the different cultures of the subunit, and then add them to get results. It is a good way to implement organizational change. The Problem now lies as to how the change drivers of the organization can identify the ways in which the culture of their organizations can be diagnosed and changed. There are usually two ways of doing so. Either implement change at the organizational level or the level of cultural analysis must occur in the subunits that can be started and added cultural change across the organization. The ultimate goal is to improve the overall performance of organizations.

Keywords: Organization culture, Competing values framework, Types of culture.

INTRODUCTION

Many studies and scientific papers have emphasized that successful companies, those with above-normal profits and sustainable advantage,

---

[20]Ashutosh Agrawal is a student of MBA (HR) programme Class of 2015 and R. Sujathais an Associate Prof in the Area of OB & HR with Amity Business School. The authors have developed the case solely for class discussion for the programmes in management. The author does not intend to illustrate effective or ineffective handling of a managerial situation. The case study does not represent or endorse the views of the managements about the issues in the case.

are characterized by six key elements. The first is the existence of barriers to entry. Fewer competitors always mean higher profits and market share for your business. The second element is the non-replaceable. Whenever other organizations can not duplicate the product you make or its unique characteristics, the organization does not mean losing the market loses ongoing revenue streams. The third element is a large market that would allow the company to capitalize on economies of scale and efficiency. The largest player in the market can have a say in the price, Drive the competition, and also go for acquisitions that lead to more and better resources sharing. The fourth element is the low level of bargaining power with buyers. If the organization is a key product of daily consumption of customers, who have a higher than consumers will buy whatever currency exchange rates. Fifth element that has the biggest impact is that suppliers have little bargaining power. When providers become so dependent on prices of raw materials companies for swimming. Prices of major raw materials lead to reduced profit margins higher costs in this way. The sixth element stands out as the rivalry between firms in the same market share. Competition raises the standards of society. These features are perceived and widely accepted as a prerequisite for any successful business. Despite the remarkable result on the basis of a study of the most successful companies in the United States during the last twenty years have not had one of those elements that work for them. The top five countries without these preconditions are "Southwest Airlines (21,775% return), Wal-Mart (yield 19 807%), Tyson Foods (18,118% yield), Circuit City (16,410% yield) and Plenum Publishing (15,689 % return) (Compustat services 2005 data)". All these companies had no apparent advantages over the six points mentioned above, but the main feature that proved to be his most important, the most powerful competitive advantage of all the elements of the organizational culture. The next obvious step in this evolution is how to accurately diagnose and change the organization's culture. Herein, Competing Values Framework comes into being. The reason for using the competing values framework to diagnose and to a change in the culture of the organization, was given by Cameron and Quinn. It is a framework that is derived empirically and was found to have both empirical validity and face and creates an integrated framework that takes into account the different dimensions as proposed by several authors.

Competing Values Framework has been designed to have a high degree of congruence with categorical schemes known and widely accepted that aim to organize the process of how people think about their values and assumptions. The first dimension relates to differentiate performance criteria that focuses on flexibility, dynamism and discretion of the criteria that focuses on control, order and stability. This implies that some organizations are considered effective when they are adaptable, changing and organic, while other organizations are considered effective if they are stable, predictable and mechanistic. This continuum ranges from the flexibility and versatility of the organization at one end of the sustainability of the organization and strength of the other end.

The other dimension refers to the efficiency criteria of differentiation that focuses on a unit, integration and orientation of focusing on external orientation, competition and internal differentiation. Implying that some organizations are considered effective when they have harmonious internal characteristics as how HP "While others are considered effective if they focus more on their external environment and care to focus on the outside. Here is the continuum of the cohesion of the organization and sounding on one hand, and organizational independence and separation from each other. Together, the two dimensions form four quadrants with each quadrant representing a very different set of indicators of organizational effectiveness.

Figure 20.1 illustrates the relationships that exist between these two dimensions. These indicators illustrate what people like the performance of the organization in terms of the four quadrants containing fundamental values on which an organization is evaluated. The point to note is that the four core values are opposite or competitive nature. Each quadrant shows a value that is completely opposite to the other end, such as stability and internal vs external vs flexibility also. These dimensions are finally compete in the organization values. This leads to under the name of knowledge. The value framework in which competition tool for assessing organizational culture is based. Each quadrant of the figure is marked to distinguish the most notable features i.e. Clan, adhocracy, hierarchy and market.

It is important to realize that the names quadrants were not selected randomly, but in reality, have been drawn from various academic publications explaining how over time the different organizational values

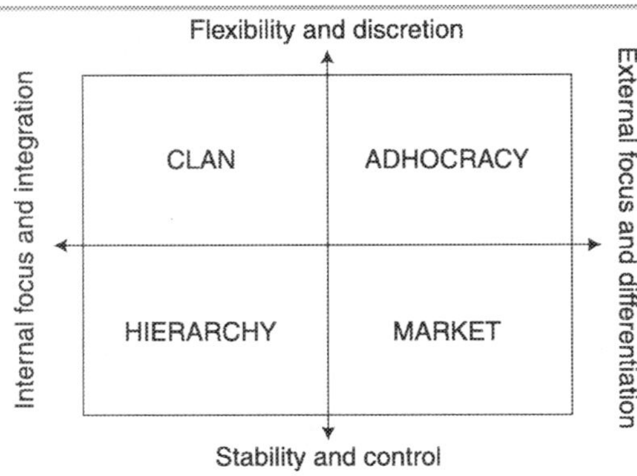

Figure 20.1 Competing values framework from the model of cameron & quinn's work.

have become common in various forms of organizations. Cameron and Quinn found that the four quadrants that stood in their studies accurately reflect the main forms of organizational culture that have developed in the course of the science of organization. These quadrants resonate with theories of management in successful organizations, the quality-oriented approach, strong leadership roles and management skills.

UAS International: An Analysis of Organizational Culture with Competing Values Framework

From the analysis of the organization using the OCAI Tool to assess the organizational culture of UAS International, the following conclusion can be drawn: UAS Dominant Organizational Characteristics is clan Culture. It means that the organization is having a dominant culture which lays emphasis on team work, mentoring and employee development. Management of Employees in the organization is having a need for an HR Manager. The HR managers do play the role of employee's champion. In such clan culture it depicts a Organizational Glue Characteristics. UAS emphasis on family at work place or work family. Criteria of success is clan Culture. Which means that the organization is having a dominant culture which lays emphasis on team goals, incentives and rewards.

ORGANIZATION CULTURE AS PREFERRED IN FUTURE

Clan culture preferred to be more dominant than at present and with a want of market culture or competitiveness to reduce. The preferred culture by UAS is more or less same with the HIERARCHY culture preferred to be more dominant than at present and with a want of market culture or competitiveness to reduce and clan culture to increase.

Table 20.1 Summary of Findings

Parameters	*Now*	*Preferred*	*Action (Increase {I} or Decrease {D})*
Overall Interns	clan	clan	{D} Market Culture
Overall Management	HIERARCHY	HIERARCHY	{D} Market Culture
Dominant Characteristics	clan	clan	{I} Clan Culture
Organization Leadership	clan	clan	{I} Adhocracy
Management of Employees	clan	clan	{I} Clan Culture
Organization Glue	clan	clan	{I} Hierarchy {D} Market Culture
Strategic Emphasis	clan	clan	{I} Clan Culture {I} Adhocracy
Criteria of Success	clan	clan	{I} Clan Culture

Takeaways

The company was established just over a year ago and the analysis derived through OCAI assessment holds true on the trend followed by new companies i.e., the company starts with the adhocratic style with the vision and direction of the founder and then as time progresses it becomes a close knit group of employees which start deriving satisfaction from working with their new organizational family then the need for rules and regulations is felt as the organization grows and finally to be able to actively compete the organization moves towards market style to generate profits. During maturity organization finds an optimum balance suited for them between the four quadrants. Major studies have shown during validation of competing values framework that the most successful organizations have once core element common, they have an impeccable organization culture which caters to the need of its human resources and aligns their personal objectives and working ideologies with the organizational strategies creating an in house competitive advantage which no other organization can replicate and take away from. An organization which is in in its early stages of conception is known to go through all the four quadrants of the competing values framework but ultimately as per the organizational environment settles into the quadrant most suitable for its functioning. UAS International is going through its nascent stages and this evaluation of its organization culture can be a plus point at this early stage. Once the culture has set in its very difficult for the organization to manage change. An accurate assessment will give them an early possibility for corrective measure. Thus, enhancing their competitive advantage.

Questions for Discussion

- Explain what you understand by 'An optimum organization culture can be the difference between Sustained Competitive advantage and sustained competitive dis-advantage.?'
- Discuss the role of HR Managers in diagnosing and change implementation of the organization's culture?

References

- Jaques, E. (1951). The changing culture of a factors. London: Tavistock.
- Hellriegel, D., & Slocum, J.W., Jr. (1974). Organizational climate: Measures, research, and contingencies. Academy of Management Journal, 17, 255-280.
- Louis, M.R. (1981). A cultural perspective on organizations. Human Systems Management, 2, 246-258.

- Louis, M.R. (1983). Organizations as culture bearing milieux. In L.R. Pondy, P.J. Frost, G. Morgan, & T.C. Daudridge (Eds.), Organizational symbolism (pp. 39-54). Greenwich, CT: JAI Press.
- http://artsfwd.org/4-types-org-culture/
- http://managementhelp.org/organizations/culture.htm
- https://www.boundless.com/management/textbooks/boundless-management-textbook/organizational-culture-and-innovation-4/culture-33/types-of-organizational-culture-187-3936/
- http://www.ocai-online.com/about-the-Organizational-Culture-Assessment-Instrument-OCAI/Organizational-Culture-Types

21

Attrition Due To Crossfire Politics in Indian Organizations

Sanjeev Bansal[21]

Abstract

The IT industry in India is considered as the 'New Age Economy' industry and represents a microcosm of the Indian society. The tendency of the seniors to favour the junior employees with similar inclinations is very common especially in Indian organizations. When an employee's performance is considered secondary to personal beliefs, backgrounds or decisions made may not always be the organization's interest. When these practices prevail in an organization, they cause favouritism, loss of leadership's credibility in the eyes of the employees and also high performing individuals.

Creation of such situations in the organizations is not healthy because the employees can be dissatisfied and they can eventually leave the organization. This is also one of the most common reasons of high Attrition rate in Indian organizations specially the IT industry.

The Human Resources Department has a key role to play in eradicating or minimizing this problem. On a strategic level, HR must implement well-framed policies and practices in employee selection and promotions. They must keep an eye on all such activities to ensure compliance and a fair play.

Keywords: Performance, Attrition rate, Organizational politics.

INTRODUCTION

This case deals with a problem which is common in most of the Indian organizations. Most of the organizations tend to hold language, cultural or regional biases, in spite of having matured employees in a culturally diverse environment. This case has some typical characteristics. It's a typical example of the organizations which have dual reporting structures. And as a result, it is very natural that individual biases come into play in

---

[21]Sanjeev Bansalis Director & Prof in the Area of Decision Science with Amity Business School. The author have developed the case solely for class discussion for the programmes in Management. The author does not intend to illustrate effective or ineffective handling of a managerial situation. The case study does not represent or endorse the views of the managements about the issues in the case.

these organizations. It is unique from the viewpoint of a typical political issue which highly provoked strong sentiments in two key people in this case who are, Arunav and Arputharaj at SH Technologies. From Saurabh's perspective, he felt that he got stuck or became a victim of the politics going around between these two senior management people.

From an individual perspective, these practices encourage individuals not to focus on enhancing their skills and knowledge to become more competent but they rather encourage them to focus on getting positions based on affiliations. Because of this, some people 'win' for short term, get good roles, assignments and promotions. However, the organization loses both in the short and the long run. The person appointed for the assignment may not be having the best skill sets for the job at hand and that is the reason, the organization may loose its customers, several business opportunities, its effectiveness as well as its competitiveness.

From the perspective of the organization, this case can be viewed from three positions, from the viewpoint of HR, the senior management and the above mentioned managers to whom Saurabh reported.

Saurabh Kumar, sitting in his high rise California apartment is thinking about the last few years which he had spent at his native town, which is located in Karnataka. Thoughts of his parents and many other childhood memories are flashing to his mind. As he recollects his memories and the time spent in India with his family, he is filled with nostalgia. Then, suddenly he remembers an ugly episode which took place at his earlier workplace.

Saurabh Kumar, aged about 38 years, comes from a very small town of Bellandur district, 180 km from Bangalore. He has more than 16 years of work experience in the Information Technology (IT) sector. He has worked on several projects both in India as well as abroad. He has always been a very sincere, studious student and he has always topped his class though he comes from a very modest background. In his final year engineering examinations, because of his hard work and dedication, he won the Gold medal. As a result of this, he got placed in one of the most respected companies in the IT sector. He remembered the day when he was selected from his campus for his first job in India. He remembered the exact feeling of getting the first job and how happy he was that day. Since then, he moved forward in his career and life and never looked back. He worked in India for a couple of years and then moved to US and there he joined a very large and popular consulting organization in the IT sector. He worked for around 12 years in that same organization and he was regarded as a very efficient and productive employee. For about a decade, he worked successfully in a multi-cultural environment and he maintained a good and healthy relationship with all his seniors, clients and colleagues. He had a very peaceful personal and professional life and he was never discriminated at any point while working in the US.

However, sometimes he missed his parents who were in India and felt increasingly homesick.

Fortunately, he got a job offer from a mid-sized IT company named SH Technologies which was based in Bangalore. He got excited about the offer and he finally decided to come back to India. After getting to know the fact that Saurabh was now moving to a relatively smaller company, his friends got surprised as the company was offering comparatively lower compensation package. His wife also had some doubts about his decision of moving back to India and she was not happy with his decision. His close friends also warned him about the prevailing work culture in India and they all advised him to be careful of the politics, lobbing and several other management problems that goes around in most of the companies in India.

In 1980, SH Technologies, a mid-sized IT company was founded by six engineers with just US$ 200. It registered its first office in Delhi and then relocated its corporate headquarters to Bangalore. The company has branches in all the major cities in India as well as abroad. It has several offices and development centers in some countries like US, UK, Australia and Europe. It has more than 30,000 employees and it enables its clients to exceed the competition and stay ahead of the innovation curve by focusing on building future enterprise.

From the very start, the company was founded on the principle of generating and implementing innovative ideas to enhance lives and to generate solutions for clients. For about three decades, the company worked on the same principle.

It provides various services like database management, software development, integration, maintenance, data validation, Business process outsourcing (BPO), 24*7 technical support, strategic outsourcing, portfolio management, data warehousing, business intelligence according to the requirement of its clients. It also creates and develops its own tools which simplify the work and helps in providing quick solutions to the clients. One of its most known tools is 'Pinnacle' which provides banking solutions.

Saurabh Kumar had a switch from a very big organization to a relatively smaller one and he joined SH Technologies with a rich global experience. Being a committed employee, he started off with his new assignment by investing his time and utilizing his wide experience. He was hard working, dedicated and sociable person. His skill sets and expertise in the area made him one of the most liked employees in the company. He implemented several innovative ideas which helped the company to improve its overall performance. He also helped his team to develop and implement new concepts. He was handling multiple projects with limited number of resources which proved his competency. Earlier, the group used to deliver two projects in a year on an average but now because of Saurabh's involvement and supervision, the group was able to deliver around four to five projects a year. In a very short period of time, he became the star performer and the top management was also very happy with his performance. He was regular with all the tasks given to him and he was never late for important meetings. He was rewarded for his excellent performance and was promoted to the next level with a very good hike in his compensation in a short span of time.

His next level supervisor, Arunav, also supported him in every possible way. Arunav, coming from the same region as Saurabh had a soft corner for him. Arunav was always in favor of the people belonging to his region.

Soon there was an opening for a position in Florida. Arunav and another senior employee, Arputharaj, were both interested for the same position. Arputharaj was senior to Arunav though both of them worked in different modules. Arputharaj belonged to some other region of the state. Arputharaj and Arunav both knew each other as both were from the same engineering college, though Arputharaj was two years senior to Arunav. However, they both were having different political views and often had several disagreements on defending their own particular region. Both of them were considered to be the bright future of SH Technologies as they both had contributed a lot towards different major processes in the organization. They were always the first choice of the top management to take up new challenging responsibilities.

Soon, Arunav proved himself successful for the opening in Florida and he was offered an assignment there for the next three years. Arputharaj considered himself more deserving than Arunav and because of this, he was unhappy with the results. Arputharaj tried to blame the HR leader, Gopi Reddy for the same. He strongly believed that all of this happened because Gopi and Arunav belonged to the same region.

Arunav soon left for Florida to complete his assignment but there was no change in the reporting structure. Saurabh was still handling the things as smoothly as earlier and the distance hardly mattered. Everything was going as usual until all of a sudden the top management decided to re-structure certain businesses and because of this re-structuring happening in the organization, Arputharaj was given the position of the BU Center Head in Bangalore. As the reporting structure changed now so Saurabh now started reporting to Arputharaj locally. Arputharaj became the second line manager for Saurabh now. He soon began to keep a close check on Saurabh and his team members. There were other three team members who worked with Saurabh and they were Pratibha, Vishal and Devi Prasad. They were also well-versed with the technology and they were also the skilled and competent performers of the organization. All of them also reported to Arputharaj as their front line manager after the re-structuring happened in the organization. All of these three team members had come from different parts of the country and they were also not happy with Arputharaj as their front line manager and had different reasons for the same. But when Saurabh joined the team, they all were very happy and they all shared a good relationship with him. Whether it was a lunch break or a tea break, they always had this common topic of discussion that why did Saurabh come back to India from US and joined this organization. They considered Saurabh as an efficient performer and also respected him for the same. They always looked up to him if they had any problem regarding the tasks assigned to them. They wanted to learn and gain as much knowledge as they could from his experience.

Arputharaj continued to keep a close check on all of them but Saurabh had no idea at all about the motives of Arputharaj. He regularly shared all the updates about the team and the projects with him because he considered it as his duty and also he needed support from Arputharaj for his work. He was also unaware about the fact that Arputharaj and Arunav did not share a healthy working relationship. Although in sometime he got to know about the whole situation knowing the fact that Arunav was not happy with the change in reporting structure. Arunav also asked Saurabh to be careful of Arputharaj as he was biased against the people who did not belong to his own region. Saurabh was already perplexed that despite having Arunav still as his first-line of manager but as he was in USA so he had to report to Arputharaj locally who actually was his second line manager. Now Arputharaj starting interfering in all the activities and tasks related to Saurabh and did not allow him to work in his own way and started imposing his own way of doing things on Saurabh. There were certain project related tasks which were being approved by Arunav but Arputharaj started blocking them. Saurabh eventually began to realize that his performance was being affected because of the cold relationship between Arputharaj and Arunav. Because of Arputharaj's behavior and due to late decisions taken the overall productivity started falling down. Saurabh even requested Arunav to talk to Arputharaj and sort out things with him but he was unable to do the same. From the past one year, Saurabh had the same kind of working relationship. He was giving his best efforts but still he was facing the heat as Arputharaj always perceived him more close to Arunav than him. At times, Saurabh tried to address certain matters which sometimes worked out for both Arunav and Arputharaj. But as Arputharaj's intentions were only to oppose Arunav, he used his authority to influence the decisions which were not in favor of the company and had a negative impact on the performance.

After a few days, SH Technologies got a very important project which could help the company to generate more revenue. But as the project had a very strict deadline, Saurabh started looking for people with certain skill sets and expertise. So he asked for two more resources to carry on the project within the prescribed timeline. He started searching for people with good amount of experience in handling challenging projects of similar type. Arunav also tried to help Saurabh and Arputharaj by forwarding them a few profiles. After short listing, Saurabh called some of the eligible candidates for the interview. It also included names which were given by Arunav as the profile were quite impressive. Arputharaj intervened in this matter and he asked Saurabh to include the names of few more candidates as referred by him. He did so because the company had a money making referral scheme. Saurabh was now not left with any choice that is why he had to call the candidates referred by Arputharaj. After the interviews got over, Saurabh was extremely happy and satisfied to find the right talent for the right job that would fit all the requirements. He selected one person which was referred by Arunav and another one who appliead through normal process. Saurabh discussed with both Arunav and Arputharaj the reason for the selection of the candidates. He found out that Arputharaj was not at all happy with the selections. Saurabh soon realized that Arputharaj was not at all concerned about the non selection of the candidates which he suggested but he was more worried about the candidates who get selected through Arunav's referral. Arputharaj took this matter personally and he started arguing with Saurabh on the selection criteria. He wanted Saurabh to drop those candidates which were referred by Arunav. But as Saurabh was aware of the criticality of the project and the need of the hour, he intentionally gave importance to the merits of the candidates. Arputharaj wanted to have a meeting with both the candidates before the formal appointment was communicated to them. Saurabh had already this thing in his mind that Arputharaj would not sit quietly about this matter and as he expected, Arputharaj sent a critical mail suggesting the rejection of the candidate which was referred by Arunav.

Saurabh decided to discuss the situation with the HR location head, Gopi Reddy as he was very sure about the suitability of the candidate. He even made a point to Gopi that the project would greatly suffer, if the candidate was not included in the team. However, Gopi tried to stay out of this matter and asked him to sort out his issues with Arputharaj himself. When Arputharaj came to know that Saurabh met the HR location head regarding this issue, he was furious and he even gave a warning to Saurabh not to repeat the same thing in future.

Because of all this, Saurabh had to find a replacement but unfortunately, he failed to do so in the next one month. He was quite concerned about the successful completion of the project in the given time. He also found that his quarterly appraisal ratings for the last quarter were very low and he didn't except the same. Furthermore, he was also not nominated to attend an advance-level project management training for a week long in abroad. He then discussed these developments with Arunav, who in turn suggested him to escalate the issue to the senior level management person of SH Technologies at their corporate office. He even told Saurabh that he would talk to the senior management himself beforehand at the corporate office.

Saurabh finally decided to go to the corporate office. He then met the senior management person and tried to explain him the whole situation. He also expressed his desire to get him released from that project or to change his second line manager that was Arputharaj. He got an assurance from that person that necessary actions would definitely be taken to resolve this conflict. Then, he discussed this scenario with Arunav again and Arunav asked him to wait for a few days.

He then waited for quite some time as told by Arunav and tried to follow-up with the senior management person but did not get any positive response from his side. Later on, after a few days, Saurabh somehow came to know that the person whom he met at the corporate office belonged to the same region as Arputharaj. He came to know that both of them were good friends as well. The matter did not go to the top management as the person from the corporate office manipulated the whole situation. In fact, in the end, the whole situation turned up against Saurabh only.

Saurabh was finally fed up and he then decided not to take up this matter further anymore. He started thinking about his old company where he never faced such kind of management issues. He started blaming himself for the decision he took to leave the job in the US and returning back to India. He now realized that it was a costly mistake. He found out that his wife and his friends were right about the difference in the work culture between India and US. All this politics and management issues had completely shattered him and had a negative impact on his performance and productivity in the organization.

He really felt that he was victimized in the conflicts between his seniors without any fault of his own. As everything was going against him in this organization, he finally decided to give his resignation and return back to his earlier company in the US. With all this, it also ended his comeback dream.

Saurabh left abruptly in a short period of time without even completely serving his notice period and the management was also unable to find his replacement, so, as a result, there was a lot of work pressure on the other team members. Due to this immense amount of work pressure and other conflicts with the management including Arputharaj, they also started handing over their resignations one after the other.

Questions for Discussion

- The top management of the company got worried about the whole situation but the matter had gone out of their hands now and they could not stop them from leaving the organization.

- How could have the entire issue be tackled? Can you propose any suggestive model to functional use of organizational politics within organizations?

References

- Porter, L.W., Allen, R.W., & Angle, H.L., (1983). The politics of upward influence in organizations'. Organizational influence processes. 408–422.
- Richard, O.C., & Johnson, N. B., (2001). Strategic human resource management.
- Effectiveness and firm performance. International Journal of Human Resource Management. 12(2), 299–310.
- Valle, M., & Witt, L.A. (2001). The moderating effect of teamwork perceptions on the organizational politics – job satisfaction relationship. The Journal of Social Psychology. 141(3). 379–388.
- Zanzi, A. (2001). Sanctioned versus non-sanctioned political tactics. Journal of Managerial Issues. 13(2). 245–262.
- Drory, A., & Romm, T., (1988). Politics in organization and its perception within the organization. Organization Studies. 9(2). 165–179.

22

Talent Acquisition at RJIL

Shubhi Bajpai • Taranjeet Duggal[22]

Abstract

Talent acquisition deals with recruitment, selection and retention primarily. Earlier organizations did not give much importance to talent acquisitions but now they realized the importance of it in competitive market. One of the reasons behind growth of talent acquisitions is competitive market and all the organizations strategy is to acquire best possible talent. Talented employees are having more ability of pay back to the organization in less time. The pay back of investment in right people is not key objective of HR only but for other departments also like Marketing and finance. Talent pool and talent bank is also included in talent acquisitions. Now it is the time differentiate between talent acquisitions and recruitment. The present case aims to capture HR learnings on Talent Acquisition Group (TAG) in Reliance Jio helps business gain a competitive talent advantage through proactive talent acquisition capabilities and services.

Keywords: Talent acquisition, Investment, Capabilities.

INTRODUCTION

Recruitment is different from talent acquisitions in many ways. Recruitment is limited to filling vacant position when he leaves or is promotion is done in the organization. Recruitment is limited to screening of candidates whereas talent acquisitions are complex and proactive process, it requires good networking skills also. Social media plays important role in talent acquisitions as it uses modern recruitment methods like Facebook and linked in. These networking sites have also been constantly innovating themselves to fit into the recruitment space. Hence, dynamics of talent acquisitions are re- defining the role of solution providers too, who needs to constantly innovate to meet theses changing requirements. Talent acquisition is the targeted recruitment/acquisition of high performing teams for example; in sales management or financial

[22]Shubhi Bajpaiis a student of MBA (HR) programme Class of 2015 and Taranjeet Duggal is Prof in the Area of Behavioural Science & Psychology with Amity Business School. The authors have developed the case solely for class discussion for the programmes in management. The case study does not represent or endorse the views of the managements about the issues in the case.

traders into a company from a competitor or similar type of organization. Organizations requiring external recruitment or head-hunting firms are now employing "talent acquisition" specialists whose job it is to identify approach and recruit top performing teams from competitors. This role is a highly specialized role akin to that of a traditional recruiter/head-hunter specialist but carrying greater visibility and strategic importance to a business. In many cases the talent acquisition person is linked directly to a company's executive management, given the potential positive impact a company can benefit from by getting high-performance sales people into the business, whilst removing the same performing sales people from competitors.

Development in countries like India has traditionally been viewed as the responsibility of the governments because of the massive scale of its operations and the limited or no capacity of its beneficiaries to pay for the services. While the need for social development in developing countries like India is enormous, the resources available even with the governments are limited. Besides, the government machinery and the bureaucracy are less equipped to monitor the implementation of social development projects at the grass-root level. Demand for top talented people is at an all-time high, because of the recent market trends, working employees have more option than never before and companies are trying to keep up with the fact that there are not enough talented professionals to go around. China and India have strengthened their incentive programs to lure recent graduates, as well as older professionals, back to their home countries. This has further boost the need for U.S. companies to address their own strategy for retaining talent after internships, post-graduate fellowships and other special programs expire. While the need for innovation and farther-reaching human resources strategies is just recently widespread across the workforce, the most common responses to the problem have mainly been ignored. This approach has tended to follow a general sales model where employers might allocate resources to advertise positions in specific market sectors and then target the prospect talent as a sales agent would approach a prospective client. The barrier with a sales approach in today's scenario is that it can fail as a vehicle to reel in the best candidates in a way that builds long-lasting relationships with company.

In today's market condition all employees are not looking for the same thing. Supple benefits are a key component of successful talent acquisition, there is a strategy that company makes a candidate feel that they are being treated like an individual throughout the entire process. Human resources managers building their corporate leadership skills today have many provocations. One of the greatest challenges is putting together a variety of choices and presenting them appropriately. For instance, tuition benefits may mean little to a recent graduate, but to a student who wants to stay in the workforce and update skills, the tuition benefit may be attractive. New parents may like flexible work start times, while old employees may appreciate a longer lunch hour.

Many current companies need to renovate their current system of interviewing and communicating skills in addition to the details of benefits. The adaptive communicative strategy use to induce potential hires should be fresh, engaging and relevant. In today's market scenario one employee-fits-all sales pitch approach is not effective. Manager of human resources need to have the strong interpersonal skills and communication ability to differentiate the interview process to reflect the motivators and needs of eligible employee. Putting the time in to prepare the interview process carefully is more important than it was a generation ago. The best of the best today have the world at their doorsteps, and the employees know it. For a manager of human resources understanding and effectively addressing the complex dynamics of a modern workforce takes in-depth preparation, problem solving with creativeness and an ability to develop programs and resources that will be flexible enough to address a wide range of employee needs for human resources managers, understanding and effectively addressing the complicated dynamics of a modern workforce takes in-depth preparation, creative-problem solving and an ability to develop programs and resources that will be flexible enough to address a wide range of employee needs.

BACKGROUND

Reliance Jio Infocomm Limited (RJIL), a subsidiary of Reliance Industries Limited (RIL), India's largest private sector company, is the only pan India operator with Broadband Wireless Access ('BWA') spectrum across 22 circles capable of offering fourth generation (4G) wireless services. Indian telecom sector is more than 165 years old. Telecommunications was first introduced in India in 1851 when the first operational land lines were laid by the government near Kolkata (then Calcutta), although telephone services were formally introduced in India much later in 1881.Reliance industries entered into telecom sector in 2005 with their subsidiary company reliance communication then in 2013 January 22nd reliance 4G was introduced. Though the product has not been launched yet and expected launching is in September 2014 there should not be any further delay in the launchingJio is born from the Reliance ethos – Achieve impossible ambitions by empowering ordinary people to do extraordinary things. Jio is here to empower every Indian and encourage them to lead better lives with the help of reimagined technology. Jio will drive a data movement by allowing every Indian to access not only data, but Opportunities that can sculpt their futures. Jio is currently testing its launch services, including connectivity, enhanced communications and video entertainment.

In Reliance Jio Infocomm Ltd talent acquisitions is the primordial asset that enables the success of any organization. Without extraordinary talent, Reliance can't exploit market opportunity, raise capital, create iconic products, recruit extraordinary talent, and deliver great customer service. Talent acquisitions are the vital part of the company because it concentrates primarily basic functions of Human resources which are recruitment, selection and retention. Today's dearth of extraordinary talent is painfully obvious to all businesses regardless of industry, size, geography, or financial position. In today's environment, businesses need to recruit, develop, and retain extraordinary talent to remain competitive. Talent Acquisition Group (TAG) in Reliance Jio helps business gain a competitive talent advantage through proactive talent acquisition capabilities and services. In the organisation talent bank is the very important feature which talent acquisitions have, talent bank saves the CV's and resumes of the candidates who applied for the company and there competencies also match the companies requirement but they didn't get selected because of the other better employees so for future references company save there CV's in talent bank. Reliance Jio Infocomm has merged with Himachal futuristic corporation limited (HFCL) when the company was established in 2012, Reliance conduct Aptitude test i.e. RPAT and psychometric test i.e. PI index for reliance employees only not for HFCL employees but they work under the same roof. PI and RPAT test is conducted for the middle level of management not for lower level employees in the company. Another problem for candidates who want to apply in the company do not have any other source apart from referrals and job portals, Reliance Jio Infocomm should work on creating their official website where employees can apply in the company directly.

As the company was established in year 2012 and its products and services are not introduced yet to the public, so it's all focus is on the product and as a telecom company they are engaged in constructing masts for the network availability, company can't focus on employee engagement activities. For human assets experts looking to create administration aptitudes to relieve these current difficulties, the method is two-fold. On one hand, human assets executives need to secure the best preparing from projects that are profoundly dedicated to get ready pioneers decently outfitted with "best-polish" hypothesis and sound functional aptitudes to assemble the projects that will help a solid workforce crosswise over industry. In the meantime, best human assets chiefs need to be knowledgeable in systems to help accelerate the corporate model in spots where some top executives are as of now holding quickly to an old fashioned deals model methodology to representative recruitment and maintenance.

Main source of recruitment in reliance industries is through references that is the internal source of talent acquisitions process. It has certain merits and demerits, merits are as followed:

- Economical
- Suitable
- Reliable
- Satisfying

Some of the demerits which affect the organisation recruitment and talent acquisitions process as well are:

- Limited choices
- Inbreeding
- Inefficiency
- Bone of contention

It is the regular practise for the organisation that for higher positions they hire through internal sources like transfers, promotions and upgrading of employees and for lower positions they higher through external sources like job portals, press advertisements, educational institutes, unsolicited applicants, recruitment at factory gate etc. Company should recruit from both the sources that are internal and external both. So, that it can benefit society and should not go on the path of favouritism or nepotism. Being a newly established organisation talented employees are not in bulk in the organisation. Organisation in its official site somewhat lack behind, company should have its own official site so that the candidates can directly apply in the company through carrier option, stake holders can also get information about they want.

Companies product is expect to launch in September end, HR's primarily focus is to higher more and more talented employees in the organisation because of it there is no employee engagement activity in the organisation since it was established because of it employee in the office very less interact with each other so employee engagement activities are very important in the company.

Reliance Jio Infocomm head quarter is in Navi Mumbai at Reliance corporate park, Mumbai circle was the only circle whose office was not in the in its own city but in Navi Mumbai head quarter April 2014 reliance Jio office Mumbai circle shifted to Bandra kurla complex, Mumbai, employees were not happy with this office shifting because 80% employees residence was in Navi Mumbai and after it they need to travel for 1 and a half hour and sometimes 2 hrs. During traffic jam to reach their office, because of this issue 4-5 employees left the organisation because of the travelling issue.

Organisation decides to conduct a survey on recruitment to make their recruitment process more effective; Survey topic name was 'employee experience during recruitment processes. Questionnaire method was used for the survey. This is method of survey which aims to collect the information and experience of the employee that can be analysed, evaluated and subsequently used by the organisation for improvising the recruitment process if required in the company because the recruitment process of an employee is the first interaction with company. Analysis was done on SPSS and Excel both. in the questionnaire sampling was done on 38 employees from around 10 different functions and they were divided into 4 categories on the basis of their tenure in the company, which is as follows:- (i)1 month - 6 months (ii) 6 months - 1 year (iii) 1 year - 2 years (iv) More than 2 yrs. Analysis was done on the basis of functions also and respondents who perform specific functions in the company are ISP (inside plan), Construction, FC & A (Finance), O&M (Operation and management), QSD, HSE, and Mast. Common source of recruitment, information provided to the candidates during recruitment process, proper position and responsibility communicated or not, results of interview in timely manner, technical interview experience, Average interview rounds,

Support from HR, Comfort level while negotiating with HR, Percentage of PI and RPAT test, Comfort level during overall recruitment process, joining time after receiving offer letter, induction and on boarding process experience were the findings which organisation got through the questionnaire. Key observation of the survey was that In the analysis it is found that references (referred candidates) are the main source of recruitment in the organization and the second most opted method is in house HR through , Positions and responsibility are thoroughly informed and communicated at the beginning of recruitment process, Results of interview are given on time but few of the joining between 6 months - 1 year feel that there results were not given on time, Being a telecom industry technicality is the essence of the company so, technical interview is very much emphasised and majority of employees had good technical interview, But 13% employees feel so that they do not have good technical round and those 13% employees lies between 6 months - 1 year, HR team of the company found to be very supportive as all the employees marked yes, PI and RPAT test is conducted on the employees after the interviews and before HR interview. The above test is not a part of HFCL recruitment process, In the analysis it has been found that 72% results are given before 15 days whereas 22% result took more than a month and Employees who joined between 6 months - 1 year is the category who answered no mostly as compare to any other category.

Some of the suggestions which came out are as per survey it is found that employees who joined between 6 months to 1 year need to be communicate well because in the questionnaire mostly employees who marked no are from this category, Reliance Jio Infocomm has no official website so, for the website company should emphasise, In the company references are the key source of Recruitment Company should more emphasis on other sources also like social media and consultancies, PI and RPAT test should be done on HFCL employees also, Results of the interview should be given within 15 days as candidate might opt for some other job meanwhile and we might lose a good resource, and Employee engagement activities should be there in the company.

The results of this research provide some evidences on the way an organisation thinks and implements talent acquisitions with the help of recruitment, selection and retention. With the help of analysis gathered from the employees and also the data of the company, it is proven that the companies are looking for better employees. They are keen in following right employees at the right place with less recruitment cost. From the analysis done on tenure wise, among the employees it is found that employee's referrals are the main source of recruitment in the company next opted method is in house HR.

In the nutshell, talent acquisitions increase the success rate of selection process by decreasing number of visibly under qualified or overqualified job applicants, it also reduce the probability that job applicants once recruited and selected will leave the organization only after a short period of time. Talent acquisitions meet the organizations legal and social obligations regarding the composition of its workforce and Begin identifying and preparing potential job applicants who will be appropriate candidates but last not the least talent acquisitions also Increase organization and individual effectiveness of various recruiting techniques and sources for all types of job applicants.

Questions for Discussions

- Reliance Jio Infocomm is newly established company, whose primary focus is to introduce their new products and services as soon as possible because of it recruitment and selection in the company is at high rate company cannot focus on employee engagement activities. What are the low cost employee engagement activities which an HR should conduct?
- If you were HR head of the company what are the decisions you would make for improvisation of talent acquisitions process of the company?

References

- Mathew J. Manimala, (2011), "Talent Acquisition and Retention in Social Enterprises: Innovations in HR Strategies." Indian Institute of Management Bangalore.

- Bhatnagar, J. (2007). Talent management strategy of employee engagement of Indian ITESemployees: key to retention, Employee Relations, Vol. 29 No. 6, pp. 640–63.
- Ronn, K. (2007). ''Rethinking talent acquisition'', Business Week Online, 3 June.
- Saurabh Rai Bhatnagar (2010). "Talent retention will be key this year".
- Taylor, M.S. and Collins, C.J. (2000). ''Organizational recruitment: enhancing theintersection of theory and practice'', in Cooper, C.L. and Locke, E.A. (Eds), Industrial and Organizational Psychology: Linking Theory and Practice, Basil Blackwell, Oxford.
- http://www.recruitingtrends.com/thought-leadership/80-effective-talent-acquisition-is-the-key-to-a-competitive-future
- https://www.insideindianabusiness.com/contributors.asp?id=1942
- https://www.recruiter.com/talent-acquisition.html
- http://humanresources.ku.edu/process-guides-recruitment

23

Implementation of Business Performance Management

Akanksha Kaushik[23]

Abstract

Business Performance Management is a business management approach which looks at the business as a whole instead on a division level. Business performance management entails reviewing the overall business performance and determining how the business can better reach its goals. This requires the alignment of strategic and operational objectives and the business' set of activities in order to manage performance. Because BPM seeks to aggregate available information, managers are more informed about the company's position and are able to make better decisions. It is also called corporate performance management. BPM is an integral part of the organization. It is very important to regulate its framework and keep updating all the BPM's perspectives. Effective implementation of BPM is although a major concern, for simple reason because it is a very tedious job. It requires regulation of the activities on intervals. Different organizations have their different BPM framework, process and technology, data architecture, business review framework and Planning and reporting content and templates. There is a common problem being faced by every company which is the forecasting largely being done manually. It turns out to be complex and is time consuming as well. Therefore the automation of forecasting should be done which requires a huge investment to be made. This now depends primarily on the businesses of the organization. As different companies have varied businesses which if not is inter related then the huge investment made would be a wastage. In such a case a different automation technique should be deployed for them. The gap between the actual vs. forecast should not be large. It should be significantly correct. All the external factors and internal factors which can impact the business should be considered. The business performance management should be reviewed in short intervals as it assures the working of BPM with the objectives of the company. Also if it goes wrong at some point, it becomes easy to correct it at that point else it gets difficult to notice the fault later on. The right Key Performance Indicator should be known by each company. As each industry has a different KPI which drives it performance. The right KPI is the key to well implemented BPM. It has been observed that most of the

---

[23]Akanksha Kaushikis a student of MBA (HR) programme Class of 2015 in Amity Business School. The authors have developed the case solely for class discussion for the programmes in management. The author does not intend to illustrate effective or ineffective handling of a managerial situation. The case study does not represent or endorse the views of the managements about the issues in the case.

companies invest in Business Intelligence or online tool so that their management report formats are supported by visualization enablers such as a dashboard, drill-down with navigation features, intuitive graphs and charts to identify business trends, historical performance comparison, sensitivity analysis, etc.

Keywords: ****

INTRODUCTION

The implementation and the continuation of a Business Performance Management (or BPM) system within an organization is not an easy task. It implies a large amount of effort, the contribution of all members of the organization, well established and understood methodologies and a collaboration across all entities of the organization. In many cases, implementing Business Process Management within an organization will lead to a complete change of culture.

One of the most important roles for the success of implementing Business Performance Management within an organization lies with management. Success will depend on the attitudes, beliefs and actions of managers within the organization and on the actual impact, they can have on the organization.

Most of us have heard a little edition of the average presentation measurement clichés: "what gets measured gets done," "if you don't compute aftermath, you can't notify accomplishment from wreck and therefore you can't claim or recompense accomplishment or circumvent unintentionally recompensing failure," "if you can't understand accomplishment, you can't discover from it; if you can't understand wreck, you can't correct it," "if you can't compute it, you can neither grasp it nor enhance it," but what eludes countless of us is the facile trail to recognizing honestly crucial measurements lacking plummeting back on things that are easier to compute such as input, undertaking or operational procedure measurements.

Performance measurement is the procedure of recognizing key worth drivers that delineate metrics to prop decision making and foster affirmative deeds and actions. Presentation measures allow us understand how well we are doing, if we are encounter our goals, if our clients are gratified, if our procedures are in statistical manipulation and whereas improvements are necessary.

This case study gives a non-exhaustive list of elements that managers need to consider in order to implement a Business Performance Management System. Each element is explained in some detail to show its importance for the Business Management System and what should be done to make it work.

INTRODUCTION TO BUSINESS PERFORMANCE MANAGEMENT

Business Performance Management can be explained as a way of managing an organization through its processes. Processes will be the translation of the organization's strategy into the way in which it wants to achieve its objectives.

Business Performance Management therefore becomes an all- in system that must consider all possible aspects of the organization. Since processes are the backbone of an organization, their management includes managing materials, resources, planning, roles and responsibilities, knowledge and training, customers, products and services, risks, supporting systems and infrastructures.

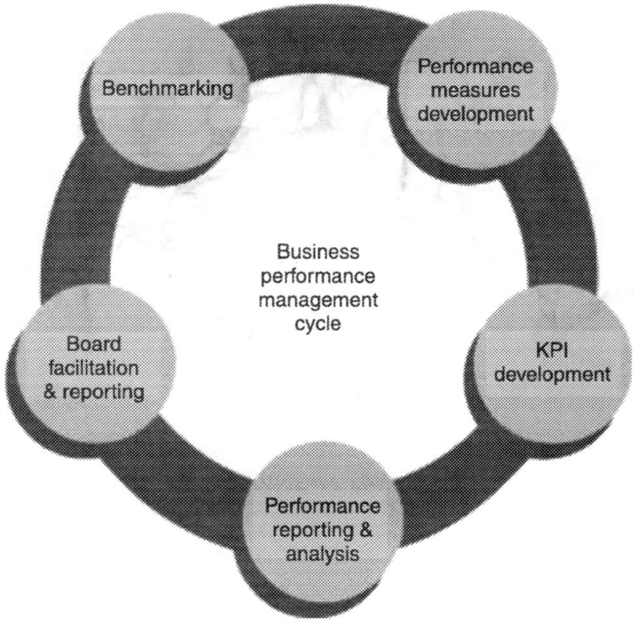

Figure 23.1 Business performance management cycle.

Why is it important?

- It focuses on reasons or drivers of success.
- It considers clients, stakeholders, stockholders, competitors and regulators.
- When requested properly, it enables association to make key decisions instead of merely recognizing problems.
- It facilitates accountability – chiefly after utilized for incentives.

In order for the Business Management System to accommodate all these aspects a number of requirements need to be fulfilled. In the following paragraphs several of the most important requirements are discussed.

BUSINESS PERFORMANCE MANAGEMENT REQUIRES VISION

Any organization requires vision, whether it is for steering the organization, providing sound financial leadership, leading its employees, etc. In order to do the right things, providing the right resources and creating the right products, an organization needs to know where it wants to go. The same is true for Business Performance Management. Managers need to establish a vision for Business Performance Management. Where they want to go in the next five to ten years with their processes? What will the processes be used for? Does the organization seek to standardize, automate or improve its processes? Who will be in charge of setting the standards of the Business Performance Management system?

Without a vision of how the processes will be used, the purpose and approach of Business Performance Management remains unclear. The people in charge of the implementation and/or ongoing process improvement within the organization are left with no choice but to improvise and follow the road they feel appropriate. Lacking the assignment of leadership and responsibility to one person, the organization will find itself at sea. Each entity within the organization could conceivably develop its own, independent and uncoordinated system of process management.

So after having chosen Business Performance Management as a means of managing the organization, managers must establish a clear vision of where they want to go with this system. They must define the purpose and objectives of the system. They must designate a person or group of persons as the custodian and overseer of the Business Performance Management system, and must delegate the power to make decisions to that person or group.

BUSINESS PERFORMANCE MANAGEMENT REQUIRES COMMITMENT

Opting for a Business Performance Management system, requires not simply a top-down decision from the top managers. To make it happen requires a commitment from the top executives to actively show the way. They must lead the organization by example and provide the means and the time required to achieve the goals of the organization. Without this formal commitment, Business Performance Management will become yet another failed initiative driven by individuals without backing and support and the empowerment to achieve the organization's goals. Despite their efforts, this initiative will die a silent death, leaving the organization disappointed.

The bottom line here is that managers must commit to a proactive leadership role in the implementation of a BPM system. They need to be aware that successful implementation will require their time and effort and will not occur overnight. They need to engage in changing the organization's culture, in making the right decisions and to training and convincing all stakeholders of the value of Business Performance Management.

BUSINESS PERFORMANCE MANAGEMENT REQUIRES APPROPRIATE TOOLS

Within the literature and the BPM community a myriad of methods for managing processes have emerged. Each can boast of a number of success stories, but not every application of a method is a guaranteed success. Although it is not my purpose to suggest the best methods in this Article, I do believe that it is important for organizations to do a critical analysis of the various methods and select the ones most appropriate for their processes. It is best to avoid selecting a single method for implementing the BPM. For example, 6 sigma methods in a low volume organization is not always appropriate. Or using Business Process Reengineering in its original format makes no sense in a mature organization where processes can only be improved incrementally.

That does not mean that existing methods should be ignored. Each has useful concepts and tools that may be adaptable to the organization's processes. In short, methods should be assessed on their value to the organization.

BUSINESS PERFORMANCE MANAGEMENT REQUIRES PRACTICAL PROCESSES

Processes are really about coordinating and standardizing activities and making their results repeatable. In order to make the results repeatable, one might think that processes should be described as highly regulated and overly detailed documents leaving absolutely no room for creativity, intervention or reasoning. This may be appropriate for parts of certain automated high-volume processes. However for processes with human interactivity, this is not an effective way of documenting processes.

When illustrating human interaction processes, it is important to show the principle steps involved in the creation of the product or service, and the interactions between the different roles as well as the flow of information and material between the entities within that process.

Trying to achieve a detailed description of the tiniest tasks within an organization from the start with the introduction of Business Performance Management is impossible and can result in uncoordinated islands of processes within the organization. So avoid attacking the Business Performance Management from the bottom. Or at least make sure that the overall picture is clear before tackling the details.

Processes should first and foremost document their interrelation with other processes and the way entities within the organization collaborate. When researcher was explaining processes and their use, one of the people attending said simply that "processes are all about coordinating the activities".

BUSINESS PERFORMANCE MANAGEMENT REQUIRES COLLABORATION THROUGHOUT THE ORGANIZATION

An important first step managers have to undertake, is to show the employees what Business Performance Management is all about. To do so, they must establish an overview of the organization's key processes. This overview, sometimes called the process map or macro process, shows in a simple manner the organization's processes that involve the customer and the processes that support them. The process map also shows the relationship between processes and entities and maps the fundamental collaboration within the organization.

There is in fact only one thing more important for an organization than its internal collaboration: the customer. When the collaboration and coordination between processes of different entities is missing, the risk of offering bad products to the customer increases. The risk of creating unnecessary costs and wastes will also increase. Activities of one entity might jeopardize those of another entity. Products of one entity might not fulfill the requirements of the next entity and require rework or create waste. Making sure that what one entity is doing works with what others are doing helps to avoid passing poor products or services to customers.

The overview of the key processes must therefore include the interfaces that exist between the different entities. Very few entities create a product without support of other entities. Key processes therefore need to include a detailed network of sub processes representing this collaboration. It is up to the managers to set up this collaboration and to define how they will work together for the customer.

Despite the mandate for collaboration within an organization, entity managers remain responsible and accountable for the proper functioning of their own entities. Collaboration creates a common goal that will further the organization's success.

In short, if the organization and its entities have a set of common objectives, the organization will benefit in the long run.

BUSINESS PERFORMANCE MANAGEMENT REQUIRES EMPLOYEE INVOLVEMENT

For a successful introduction and continuous improvement of Business Performance Management, the involvement of all employees is, of course. also required. If managers alone are engaged with the Business Performance Management system, the system remains theoretical and successful implementation is put in jeopardy. If the whole organization is involved, however, Business Performance Management will be fully deployed.

When implementing Business Performance Management into the organization, a participative approach should be used. Although managers will lead the way and define the strategy and objectives, they need to empower their direct reports to contribute to the implementation process. Managers should use the knowledge and experience of seasoned employees in order to incorporate agility in the processes, to detect deficiencies and improve the way things are done. A strict description of activities isn't adequate to the task of maximizing employee involvement in the process.

BUSINESS PERFORMANCE MANAGEMENT REQUIRES MANAGERS TO SET AN EXAMPLE

One of the surest ways to get the employees involved in an organization is management by example. If managers show what is supposed to be done by actually doing it, by stressing the importance of the processes, by showing that the results of everyone's job performance effect the whole, then people know their jobs have value. Failing to create this feeling within the organization, alienates people from the work they do. All the organization will obtain are employees who lack pride in doing the things well, in going that extra mile to satisfy the customer.

When managers themselves adhere to the processes and use Business Performance Management to manage their execution, employees will feel valuable to the organization, and individually pursue its vision and the processes that will help to attain it.

BUSINESS PERFORMANCE MANAGEMENT IS AN "ALL-IN PACKAGE"

Business Performance Management as a management system is an "all-in package". One must consider and incorporate every aspect of the system into the organization's processes. Processes must contribute to customer satisfaction and to the organization's strategy. Process improvement must be an ongoing process. Systems and the organization must be considered as well. Quality, environment, safety and risk mitigation need to be integrated in the whole system.

The point here is not to try to cherry pick. For example, don't look only at the financial implications of process improvement, since this can have a negative impact on quality, customer and employee satisfaction or safety. Do not restrict oneself to the introduction of a limited set of specific tools and methodologies within your organization. A few tools and methodologies alone can resolve some short term issues but will not lead to a systematic and integrated approach to managing the organization. If Business Performance Management is introduced only for a specific part of the organization, managers might miss out on optimal collaboration, the exchange of best practices and scale effects of similar processes.

Business Performance Management is a multidimensional and organization wide method. This doesn't mean it has to be complex and complicated. Business Performance Management should take into consideration all of the dimensions of the organization. It is important to know that Business Performance Management comprises many aspects that impact the entire organization and should not be deployed piecem.

BUSINESS PERFORMANCE MANAGEMENT IS TAKING CONTROL OVER PROCESSES

A Business Performance Management System helps an organization manage its operations. It includes methods for monitoring the organization's activities and improving them. Monitoring activities such as measurements, audits and inspections indicates where the processes go wrong.

Indicators alert when activities or product quality slip out of control. Business Performance Management Systems are there to make sure the organization has control over its activities and its resources. Not the other way around.

It should be emphasized that it is the process that is monitored. The monitoring activities aren't there to control the employees. It is a mistake to think that a negative result from monitoring activities is the fault of the people executing the tasks. Poor process results can have many causes, but the people executing the tasks within the process, as research shows, are in most cases not to blame. The process, the resources, the inputs and even the monitoring itself are more often the culprit. Using these results to evaluate employees has an extremely counterproductive effect on the implementation and maintenance of the Business Performance Management System. If the most important interaction employees have with the BPM is a repression, they will not embrace it which may ultimately undermine it.

Takeaways...

The implementation and continuous improvement of a Business Performance Management System isn't accomplished overnight. It requires time and effort, collaboration, commitment from both management and employees and the right set of tools. To get there it also requires a certain set of attitudes, beliefs and actions by the managers within organizations.

This Article enumerates places in the process where managers can influence a successful outcome in the implementation of a Business Performance Management System. The list of managerial responsibilities is not intended to be exhaustive but rather to suggest places throughout the process where their leadership can be most effective.

Questions for Discussion

- Why is Business Performance Management so important to the organization?
- How do the Chief Financial Officer engage the data that the organization produces in such a way that it creates value for the business?
- How can you ensure that the Key Performance Indicators are well-defined?

References

- Devis, B., & Brabander, E. (2009). ARIS Design Platform – Getting Started With BPM. Berlin: Springer.
- Harmon, P. (2003). Business process Change, A Manager`s Guide to Improving, Redesigning, and Automating Processe. San Francisco: Morgan.
- Kaufman Publishers. Heß, H. (2005). From Corporate Strategy to Process Performance – What Comes after Business Intelligence? In A. W. Scheer, H. Jost, H. Heß, & A.
- Kronz (Eds.), Corporate Performance Management (pp. 7-29). Berlin:Springer.
- Kiraka, R., & Manning, K. (2005). Managing Organizatios Through a Process-Based Perspective: Its Challenges and Benefits. Knowledge and Process Management, 12 (4), 288-298.
- Kruppke, H., & Bauer, T. (2005). No Business Intelligence Without Process Intelligence. In A. W. Scheer, W. Jost, H. Heß, & A. Kronz (Eds.), Corporate Performance Management. Berlin: Springer.

Website:

- http://www.som.cranfield.ac.uk/som/p16927/Knowledge-Interchange/Management-Themes/Business-Performance-Management
- http://www.capterra.com/business-performance-management-software/
- http://businessfinancemag.com/business-performance-management-1
- http://www.businessdictionary.com/definition/business-performance-management-BPM.html
- http://www.techopedia.com/definition/28075/business-performance-management-bpm

24

Rapidly Increasing Dropout Rate of Manpower: Reasons Behind

Shikha Pahwa • R. Sujatha[24]

Abstract

Recruiting & selecting being the most crucial activity, can decide on the most important outcome from any organization which is Maximum Profit making. For acquiring the desired profits and expected growth, the most important part is being played by the employees of the organization. The whole responsibility of achieving the desired goals of the organization are into the hands of every single employee working for them whether he is a clerk or he is the vice president.But if this manpower is not done properly then comes in the problem and the issue is raised. Sometimes the ones who are appointed are not to the mark and sometimes the ones who are appointing lack behind in some parameters. The recruitment and selection process is a very important process which takes much of the cost and time of the employers of the organization. So it is obviously needed to be done properly. But there comes some issues when there comes different situations which are to be handled very cautiously & they require intellectual minds of the organization. So this case study explores the reasons behind increasing dropout rate in manpower and identifies possible solutions to it.

Keywords: Recruitment, Selection, Manpower, Dropout rate.

INTRODUCTION

Overview - Relaxo Footwear Limited

In the year 1976, Relaxo Footwear Limited began as a small business, trying to make an identity in this fashion footwear industry. It got officially incorporated in 1984, & got listed later in 1995. It has been declared as the second largest footwear producer in India. The success is because of its efficient operation structure and value chain. Relaxo broke its own records last year with sales of more than Rs.8700 Million. The company

---

[24]Shikha Pahwa is a student of MBA (HR) programme Class of 2015 and R. Sujathais Associate Prof in the Area of OB & HR with Amity Business School. The authors have developed the case solely for class discussion for the programmes in management. The author does not intend to illustrate effective or ineffective handling of a managerial situation. The case study does not represent or endorse the views of the managements about the issues in the case.

aims to provide personal attention to each single footwear being produced under them. The amazingly skilled and determined employees put their maximum best effort in every footwear.

It initially started manufacturing or producing their first product that was '*Slippers*' (Hawaii). Relaxo is a brand which is providing every basic footwear suiting the needs to the every Indian Citizen. The product line of Relaxo includes Hawaii, Joggers, Canvas. Dip, Leatherite and Flite.

Having this much to handle, the issue which comes in is the man power which is there to handle this big Industry. Recruitment is the only thing which is to be done properly so that further actions could be done properly. While working in Relaxo footwear, a problem discovered was the dropout rate.

Relaxo footwear limited faces increased employees demand, and hence, a greater number of recruitment activities takes place. This case focuses on the dropout rate being noticed in the organizations these days due to some loops in the recruitment and selection process of the company directly or indirectly. The case starts with the issues being faced with the spam of time and ends on the conclusion part by stating the cause of these issues being faced.

For the so many years till now, Relaxo for the recruitment is following a particular way of recruiting which includes various sources by which the applicants are invited for the selection process. By posting the vacancies on the various online sites, posting advertisements in various ways they are bringing more and more applicants to the organizations and therefore selecting the best out of them, who fit to the organizations mould.

The Recruitment Process

The basic strategy of the organization these days are the manpower planning. So for this all the organizations are working really hard by looking out for the OUT OF THE BOX material.

As for Relaxo, the applicants are required to go through a particular process which starts from:

- Applying for a position through some force.
- Getting the details about the job in the company.
- Filling the application forms.
- Going through the selection process.

The process which is followed there is:

Realizing the vacant profiles.
Maintaining job description and specification.
Opening the posts for applicants.

Looking after the applied entries.
Selecting the eligible entries
Preparing interviews.
Arranging interviews
Finalizing the decision

Relaxo follows a well-structured process of recruiting and selecting so they before asking the applicants to join, clear all the doubts to them. But in the recent times an issue is arising in the company and that is the dropout rate. People come to join the organization clearing all their doubts and getting all the knowledge about the job including salary, extra add on, and various things which are needed to be cleared but even then they don't join the organization.

MANPOWER PLANNING

Manpower planning is the process of focusing on the organizations likely future needs of people including their numbers, talents, and the location over where they will be working. It allows the organization to think over the strategy which would help them to meet those needs with the help of recruitment and how to overcome the challenges which come in. For the companies which are growing very fast, it is very important to look over these things so that they are always ready with the solutions to all types of problems which come in. It is vital for a company like Relaxo to plan ahead, because the company is growing and it needs to recruit people who are reliable and can be trusted over their stay in the company. As these factors add on to the cost of the companies.

The manpower planning process is always done every year at the end of the January month. As the reviews of staff is being done thrice in the organization so it can be managed if it's being checked in January to adjust and recruit whenever it becomes very necessary. It allows Relaxo more time and options to meet the needs for staff and work upon the strategic objectives of the company to attain the desired profits, for example, to start new stores and maintain proper customer standards.

Relaxo tries to fulfil the positions from within the company and mainly through e-recruitment. In a way it reduces the number of dropout and in other way it motivates the presently working employees to maintain and carry on their careers in this company itself. Relaxo has a policy and a practice named as "employee planning" which focus on encouraging employees to work in the most effective way for themselves and the company both. By doing this, the talent available with the organization can improve themselves and the can make the organization attain the best possible profits. So that people can know their own worth as well and can apply for better openings in the organization itself so that it can help the organization reduce somewhat on searching for the new employees. The employees get clear about their interest and therefore proceed forward to take off in their careers with their particular interests by giving profits to Relaxo itself. The managers bring out the different skill sets, competency and desired behaviors so that the employees can look forward keeping all these things in their mind. This helps the organization achieve their goals and the employees groom their personal skills and knowledge.

The question which arises here is: "whether the employers should be cautious enough that the employees recruited does not add on to the cost of the company or it's out of their hand?"

Basically it depends on the type of source through which the company hires the employee. The different sources which are being adopted in Relaxo are:

SOURCES OF RECRUITMENT	
Internal	*External*
• Transfers • Promotions • Upgrading • Demotion • Retired employees • Retrenched employees • Dependents and relatives of deceased employees	• Press advertisements • Educational institutes • Placement agencies/outsourcing • Employment exchanges • Labour contractors • Unsolicitedapplicants • Employee referrals • Recruitment at factory gate.

CASE PROBLEM – ARE THERE ANY PROCESS SETBACKS?

The applicants came for the interview, they cleared it, they got the joining letters but when the time came for joining, the employees anyhow got disappeared and never answered back.

The recruiters called them again and again but no answer from their side. Now the thing which is to be noticed is those applicants applied after knowing all the details, they got their every doubt cleared then "why is this happening that the dropout rate is constantly increasing"?

They are usually given time between the selection date and the joining date to clear the formalities in their present organization. And this is the only time when the applicants disappear.

There could any one of the following reasons:

- They might have got some better offer from any of the competitors of Relaxo.

- Probably there was something in the organizations process which disappointed the applicant and he dropped his plan of joining there.
- May be he got some better compensation in the present organization he was working at that time.
- May be the recruiter was annoying to him by showing some type of biasness or preference of his choice and giving some nonverbal signs of dislike to him because of his nepotism.

Following are the Parameters which an employee keeps into consideration while coming for an interview:

- The current CTC.
- Educational and professional qualification.
- Relocation.
- Promotion required.
- Compensation.
- Experience.
- Work environment.

As this is obvious that they come for an interview when they find these parameters getting fulfilled. What stops them from joining the organization?

Some thoughts..

It's being noticed that in the last few months the dropout rate was increasing in Relaxo so what should be declared as the cause of this?

- Is it the wrong source?
- Is it the wrong person being considered?
- Is it the recruitment system which is lacking?
- Is it the weakness of the recruiter?
- Or something else?

A case retold...

There happened a case in Relaxo, few months ago. There were some openings for some different positions in the head office where some of the interns were also working under the recruitment team. The person who was responsible for the positions closing was the deputy HR manager. He had the responsibility of closing some positions of the office situated in Ernakulum and Coimbatore. So he started searching for various applicants through different sources of recruitment he used to follow earlier also. He involved the interns also in that project. The position to be closed was of general manager for marketing department in the office situated in Ernakulum and Coimbatore.

The interns worked on shortlisting the candidates from the various applications which came for the particular position. There were near about 10 people who were being shortlisted and were called for the interview round after taking the telephonic round. Those people came all the way from Ernakulum and Coimbatore to Delhi. They were being provided with the transportation cost of coming to Delhi and staying up there.

4 were shortlisted & they were being called for further round. 2 got selected further and they were being told about all the doubts they have or they might have. They both were selected and were being offered to join the positions in their respective places. The one who was called from Ernakulum, joined later after clearing all his records in his present organization but the one who came from the Coimbatore, he accepted the offer letter but never did the joining. He didn't even reply to any kind of calls, messages, and e-mails for a particular span of time.

Questions for Discussions

- Why is that "The dropout rate is increasing so rapidly in the organizations?" What are the possible loops on the part of the recruiter or the organization?
- Why that is the employees after accepting the offer letter deny to join the organization?
- Is the "manpower planning" process being followed in Relaxo really helpful in decreasing the dropout rate? What according to you could be the reasons behind the dropouts in the organization? Suggest some solutions to this problem.

References

- Davenport T.H., and Prusak L.," Working knowledge: How organisations manage what they know", Boston, Mass.: Harvard Business School Press.
- Flamholtz E.C., "Human Resource Accounting", Dickenson Publishing Company, California.
- Garg Dessler, "Human Resource Management", Seventh edition, Prentice Hall of India P. Ltd., Pearson | 5. VSP Rao, "Human Resource Management: Text and cases", First edition, Excel Books, New Delhi.
- http://www.managementstudyguide.com/manpower-planning.htm
- http://smallbusiness.chron.com/manage-manpower-48604.html
- http://officeneeds.sulekha.com/effective-management-of-manpower-when-planning-a-large-scale-event_599919_blog
- http://www.simprocess.net/solutions/hr_total_force_manpower.html

25

Introducing New Rating Scale in The "Punj Lloyd Limited"

Diksha Dhar • Chandranshu Sinha[25]

Abstract

The following case study is a brief discussion over the issue of the introduction of five point rating scale in the company. The case mentions the reasons for such change to take place in the organisation. Also the case describes some of the initiatives that the management has undertaken in order to implement the change. The case study will help develop a better understanding of how the management should introduce changes in the performance management system for the next year. During the process of internship, the research was conducted to understand the benefits the company will get by introducing a five point rating scale for appraising the performance of the employees. Researcher was also involved in making presentations for the discussion over the same issue. The employee involved with the PMS of the company has left the organisation because of which the Compensation & Benefits specialist is made to work on it. This has created additional workload for the manager as he was made to work on two of the key functions of HR.

The organisation should ensure that the work is carried out properly by supervising the work with a manager who has been associated with the PMS of the company and is currently deployed in some other work. This will help the manager develop confidence on the work he is doing.

Keywords: *****.

INTRODUCTION

PUNJ LLYOD LIMITED is a leading construction, procurement and engineering group of India which serves the infrastructure and energy sector of the economy with an experience of over 23 years in the industry. The C.E.O of the company is Mr. Atul Punj. It operates in almost 21 countries including Middle East, Africa, UK, China, Europe etc.

---

[25]Diksha Dhar is a student of MBA (HR) programme Class of 2015 and Chandranshu Sinhais an Associate Prof in the Area of Psychology with Amity Business School. The authors have developed the case solely for class discussion for the programmes in management. The author does not intend to illustrate effective or ineffective handling of a managerial situation. The case study does not represent or endorse the views of the managements about the issues in the case.

Its *VISION* is to be, the company of our clients in the global markets with entrepreneurial excellence and spirit.

Its *MISSION* is to, deliver reliable, high quality solutions for the infrastructure, energy and procurement sectors ensuring that the safety and integrity are at the heart of what we do.

An effective performance management process enables managers to evaluate and measure individual performance and optimize productivity by:

- Aligning individual employee's day-to-day actions with strategic business objectives.
- Providing visibility and clarifying accountability related to performance expectations.
- Documenting individual performance to support compensation and career planning decisions.
- Establishing focus for skill development and learning activity choices
- Creating documentation for legal purposes, to support decisions and reduce disputes.

CASE PROBLEMS

It will be interesting to see how will the management implement the change in the next financial year and what will be the reaction of employees to a five point rating scale. The management must prepare a report to understand the relative importance of a five point rating scale over a three point rating scale. Researcher understood the entire process of the performance management system in the company "PUNJ LLYOD LIMITED". Researcher also came to know that the company is trying to revamp its entire performance appraisal system i.e. it is planning to shift to a five point rating scale from the next financial year. The employees of the company are satisfied with the performance appraisal system that is carried out in the company. However, it was observed that most of the employees feel that they do not get enough time to clear doubts regarding their office work. Therefore, the management should try to involve supervisors with their managers for the effective completion of their tasks.

PERFORMANCE MANAGEMENT SYSTEM IN PUNJ LLOYD LIMITED

- The performance review system is applicable to regular employees only.
- Employees on time bound contracts, trainees and probations are not covered under this annual review system.

The period of review is 1st April to 30th March of the year and minimum eligibility criteria is one year of completion of service within the organisation.

The Performance Development Review works on three tier process:

- Goal setting- this process starts off on April 1st of the assessment year.
- Mid-Year Assessment – this process concludes by mid September.
- Year-End Assessment- this process concludes by March (the effective year).

The employees are given promotions, increments in their salary etc. based on their performance every year.

(A) Annual Operating Plan

During February, the annual operating plan is made by the heads of the business unit (Oil and Gas being the oldest business unit). KEY PERFORMANCE INDICATORS which is the evaluation of the success of engagement and making progress towards achieving the strategic goals.

(B) Cascading the Key Performance Indicators

After the chairman finalises the KPI'S, he cascades the same to the group CEO. It then, gets forwarded to the business unit head. After a lot of team meetings the key performance indicators are shared to the team. The basic reason to share the KPI'S is to obtain consent from the employees regarding the targets they are supposed to achieve during the year. There are around 5-7 goals that are mentioned for the team in the key performance indicators. The base targets are set for the employees. This activity usually takes place from April to mid May.

(C) Mid Year Review

During the month of October, the employees are retraced to check whether they are following the KPI'S or not. Although the employees are not given any grading at this stage of performance appraisal but the basic purpose is to know that there is alignment towards the organisational goals.

(D) Self Appraisal

In the month of March, a self appraisal process is conducted in the organisation i.e. the employees are themselves asked to see whether they have achieved the targets that they were supposed to achieve. In case the employees feel that they have not been successful, they can definitely improve their performance by discussing the problems with their supervisor.

(D) Performance Dialogue

The manager discusses the performance of the employees with them. They are given advises on how to improve their performance within the company. This ultimately helps them in their betterment of career.

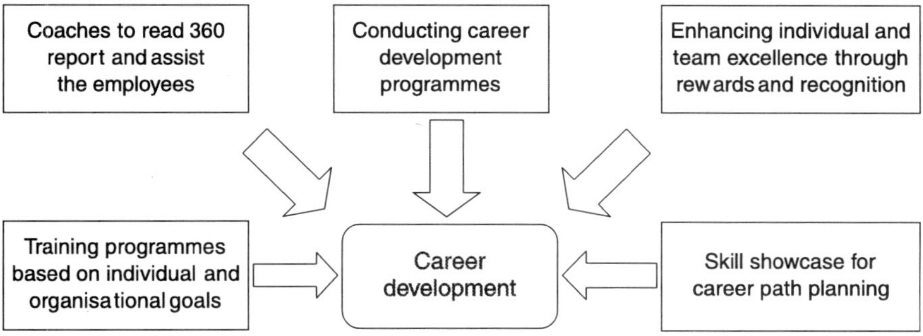

Figure 25.1 Depicting the relevance of career development.

(F) Manager's Rating

The employees are appraised on the basis of the targets they have achieved within the company. The base targets and stretch targets that are achieved by the employees are analysed by the H.R. Department.

(G) Head of the Department/Business Unit Review

After the H.R. Department analyse all the targets that the employees has achieved they head of the department reviews their rating and makes a record of it.

(H) Normalization

It is the process of categorising the employees into a set of ratios i.e. 20:10:10 in which 20 stands for good performance whereas the other 10 stands for average and bad performances respectively.

(I) Group Normalization

The vertical business units discuss the rating that are given to the employees and forwards it to the compensation committee for deciding the increments to be given to the employees.

(J) Compensation Committee

After analysing the achievements of the employees, the H.R. department analyses the market data i.e. the salary benchmarks, industry trends etc. and shares it with the compensation committee which in turn decides on the increments, salary corrections and promotions that are given to the employees. This usually ends up in the first week of July.

(K) Announcement of Bonuses

The employees who have performed exceptionally well are given bonuses. The announcement is usually done on the 1st of July.

(L) H.R. Business Partners

The company shares the information regarding the performance appraisal process of the employees with its business partners.

PUNJ LLOYD LIMITED uses a three point rating scale (likert scale) to measure the performance of its employees. The company is currently working on the revamping of this rating scale wherein it is trying to introduce a five point rating scale for the appraisal of the employee's performance. The company is facing the following issues with a three point rating scale:

- Central tendency error: The employees of the company are usually rated as average employees. For e.g.,

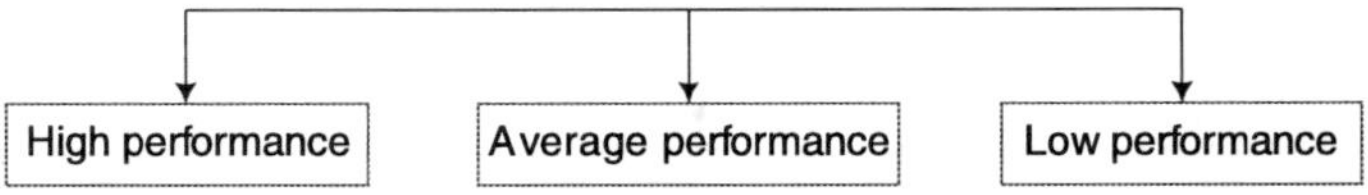

- The employees are usually ranked as average in the above scale.
- To measure the individual behaviour of the employee's , the company needs a better rating scale.
- The data analysis of this scale is not reliable and the company is not able to decide the employee who actually needs to be promoted.
- The company is not able to decide the increments that should be given to the employees since all the top performers are usually ranked the same.
- There is no flexibility in the present performance management system followed by the company.

The following are the limitations of the situation:

- The management needs a good PMS manager to understand the new method of appraising the performance.
- At present, the C&B specialist is handling the tasks of the performance management system as the person who was doing the job left the company. The employee is feeling it as a burden as he is made to do more work than before.

OVERVIEW

We have seen that the company is not satisfied with the present rating scale (three point rating scale) they use for appraising the employees so, the company is planning to introduce five point rating scale for the coming year. During the process of internship, the research was conducted to understand the benefits the company will get by introducing a five point rating scale for appraising the performance of the employees. Researcher was also involved in making presentations for the discussion over the same issue.

The following benefits were highlighted in the presentations:

- The company will be able to justify the better performers than the other good performers in the organisation.

- It will give clarity in the minds of the existing employees where their performance is lacking.
- The employee's performance can be understood better in a five point likert scale wherein there is also a partial difference between a good and an excellent performer.

As pointed out earlier, the person involved with the PMS of the company has left the organisation because of which the Compensation & Benefits specialist is made to work on it. This has created additional workload for the manager as he is made to work on two of the key functions of H.R.

The organisation should ensure that the work is carried out properly by supervising the work with a manager who has been associated with the PMS of the company and is currently deployed in some other work. This will help the manager develop confidence on the work he is doing.

Also, it is important for the management to explain it to all the employees of the company the change in the performance management system that is going to take place in the next financial year and to make them understand the reason for the change in the system. This will also help the mediocre performers to outshine themselves for the next performance evaluation that is going to take place in the company next year.

The major issues highlighted above i.e.:

- The introduction of new rating scale for the coming year and
- The vacancy for the PMS manager are the two big challenges for the human resource department in the company. The management is trying to address the above mentioned issues by carefully understanding the relative importance of the introduction of a three point rating scale over a five point rating scale. Also, the managers of the company are trying to understand the opinion of all the employees by conducting a survey (using a questionnaire method) so that the company is able to know whether the decision they are planning to implement will be readily acceptable by the other employees or not and what in their (employee's) opinion is better for the appraisal of their performance.

Firstly, it is important to understand the basic advantage of a rating scale. It is convenient to use and easy to code. Also, the data can be subject to mathematical analysis easily. The employees can easily answer the respondent by giving the response in an agreement than a concrete 'yes' or 'no'. Moreover, to know individual behaviour of employees and to extract meaningful data, it is advised to use a five point rating scale in the company.

On the hand it is important to know the various disadvantages that the presently used rating scale (i.e., three point rating scale) suffers. The basic disadvantage of a three point rating scale is that it is difficult to compare the performance of the employees in an absolute sense. For eg. A manager maybe rated as a good performer in a three point rating scale whereas the same employee maybe rated as an excellent performer in a five point rating scale.

The management is also conducting seminars to make the employees understand the difference between an appraisal system and a good performance management system. The employees should know that it is not directly linked to pay and the results that are obtained by the continuous review of performance are basically focused on enhancing the skills of the employees.

Through human development the management is trying to inculcate good managerial skills among the employees through which they will be able to develop and sharpen their skills for future potential.

The second major issue that the company has to deal with is that of hiring a PMS manager in place of the previous one. The C&B specialist who has been told to look into the work of performance management is not able to do it properly as the workload on him is too much. Therefore, the H.R. head is planning to supervise the work as he has been associated with the performance management earlier also and by supervising the work he will be able to develop confidence and motivate the other employee to perform all tasks efficiently.

The standard work expectation according to the roles and responsibilities is minimised at present because the management knows that it is difficult for a single employee to carry on both the H.R. functions i.e. performance management as well as compensation together. Moreover, the person who is being handed over the tasks is not a management graduate so the company is looking for a personnel who has the required skill sets to handle a very technical job like PMS.

Also, the earlier documents are kept to a minimum so the company is again trying to analyse the job by making the job description of a PMS specialist clearly. Research was conducted for this purpose also.

Questions for Discussions

Resistance to change is certain among employees. Do you think employees will accept the new rating scale? How will you implement the same? Hiring of a PMS manager by the reference of the previous employee working on the PMS will solve the organization issue. Comment.

References

- Anshel, M. and Webb, P. (1989). "Model for Determining Competencies in Sport: Implications for sporting organisation." A paper presented to the 1st National Management and Sport Conference, December 1989, pp. 49–60.

- Anshel, M.H. et. al., (1987). "Defining Competence for Effective Coaching of High School Football." J.O.A.R. I.C.A, Vol. 2, No. 2, April 1987, pp. 79–85.
- Campbell, J.P., Dunnette, M.D., Arvey, R.D. and Hellervick, L.V. (1973). "The Development and Evaluation of Behaviourally Based Rating Scales." Journal of Applied Psychology, Vol. 57, No. 1, pp. 15–22.
- Erffmeyer, E.S. and Martray, C.R. (1988). "A Goalsetting Process for Evaluating Teacher Professional Growth and Development and Professional Leadership." A paper presented at the Annual Meeting of the American Educational Research Association. New Orleans, Louisianna, April 8th, 1988.
- Gay, L.R. (1981). "Educational Research: Competencies for Analysis & Application." Charles E. Merril, Columbus, Ohio.
- Harrai, O. and Zedeck, S. (1973). "The Development of Behaviourally Anchored Scales for the Evaluation of Faculty Teaching." Journal of Applied Psychology, Vol. 57, pp. 261–265.

Website:

- http://performance-management.hr.toolbox.com/groups/strategy-administration/performance-appraisal/performance-rating-scale-3188781
- http://hr.anu.edu.au/employment-at-anu/recruitment-toolkit/templates/rating-scales
- http://www.hr-survey.com/PfRatingScales.htm